## Critical acclaim for Joe Booth's and Greg Lief's
### *Network Programming in CA Clipper 5.2*

"…an excellent book that is, in my opinion, an absolute must for any Clipper programmer who is required to program on a network. The information provided in the book is concise, easy to read and comes ready with many well documented working examples. **You MUST have this book!**"

**—Stephen Rowe, CompuServe**

# NETWORK PROGRAMMING IN FOXPRO

# NETWORK
# PROGRAMMING IN
# FOXPRO

**Ziff-Davis Press**
**Emeryville, California**

**Joseph D. Booth**
**and Greg Lief**

| | |
|---|---|
| Editor | Carol Henry |
| Technical Reviewer | Richard Ozer |
| Project Coordinator | A. Knox |
| Proofreaders | Cort Day and Carol Burbo |
| Cover Illustration | Carrie English |
| Cover Design | Megan Gandt |
| Book Design | Gary Suen |
| Technical Illustration | Cherie Plumlee Computer Graphics & Illustration |
| Word Processing | Howard Blechman, Cat Haglund, and Allison Levin |
| Page Layout | Bruce Lundquist and Anna L. Marks |
| Indexer | Pat Williams |

Ziff-Davis Press books are produced on a Macintosh computer system with the following applications: FrameMaker®, Microsoft® Word, QuarkXPress®, Adobe Illustrator®, Adobe Photoshop®, Adobe Streamline™, MacLink®Plus, Aldus® FreeHand™, Collage Plus™.

Ziff-Davis Press
5903 Christie Avenue
Emeryville, CA 94608

ISBN 1-56276-167-6

Manufactured in the United States of America
10 9 8 7 6 5 4 3 2 1

*To Cooke, Gizmo, Elvira,*
*and their families.*

# CONTENTS AT A GLANCE

# TABLE OF CONTENTS

## Chapter 8    Bindery: NetWare's Database    127

## Chapter 12  EMAIL Program User Reference                223

## Chapter 13  EMAIL Program Source Code                  235

# INTRODUCTION

Welcome to *Network Programming in FoxPro*. This book provides guidance to those souls who wish to write robust multiuser FoxPro applications under Novell NetWare. If you are content to merely place the required locks at the proper spots in your program, then this book may not be for you. If, however, you wish to take advantage of all that the network has to offer, then read on.

## WHO THIS BOOK IS FOR

This is not an introduction to FoxPro nor is it a networking primer. The reader is assumed to be comfortable with FoxPro programming and to know basic networking concepts. What this book offers is advice on programming on the network, and a variety of functions to access the network resources.

We begin with a discussion of network theory and how FoxPro communicates with the network operating system. We also explain the basic FoxPro commands for networks and how to design normalized databases in FoxPro. We discuss problems that you may encounter in a network environment that do not occur when only one person is using an application. Along the way, we present some usable code to handle file opening and offer suggestions on how to address some of the problems that can arise.

After the theory is explained, we provide code in the book and on the accompanying disk that permits you to communicate directly with the NetWare operating system from within your FoxPro program. Do you need to print on a network printer? Access NetWare's semaphores or its bindery files? Or how about send messages between stations? All the code needed is right here in the book and on disk!

The code in this book was written for FoxPro version 2.5. The code will work under both the Windows version and the DOS versions of FoxPro. You should find this book filled with enough material to build a solid relationship between your FoxPro application and the Novell network on which it runs.

So fire up your PC, load the network shell, and dig in. Before you know it, you will have your application running as smoothly on the network as it does on your single-user PC.

# How This Book Is Organized

Chapter 1 covers the basics of what a network is and how a personal computer can communicate with it. We also discuss some basic rules to keep in mind when you are writing a network application. These guidelines show how to reduce some of the network programming problems that can occur when more than one program wants to share data.

In Chapter 2 we explain the basic FoxPro commands and functions that are used on a network. We also provide guidance for developing a locking strategy. Finally, we discuss how to optimize your FoxPro environment for running on a network.

In Chapter 3 we talk about designing database files and normalization. We also provide code for handling file opening and indexing while detecting common errors.

Chapter 4 introduces the concept of concurrency and how FoxPro deals with it. FoxPro offers two very powerful commands, BROWSE and EDIT, for viewing files. It is important to understand how these commands and their options operate when running on a network.

In Chapter 5 we talk about messaging between workstations and programs. We include some FoxPro code to handle communications through a common DBF file, and we also discuss how Dynamic Data Exchange (DDE) works when using FoxPro for Windows.

Chapter 6 discusses transaction processing and handling of multiple file/record updates as a single unit. We talk about rollback and dealing with potential problems. We also cover the FoxPro functions that allow your program to access NetWare's transaction tracking system.

Chapter 7 covers how to communicate directly with NetWare through its API. It briefly describes the API and then provides FoxPro code and libraries to access NetWare services. We also cover how to convert data to and from the FoxPro format and how NetWare stores it.

Chapter 8 discusses NetWare's bindery, a database that contains information about all network objects, including users, groups, printers, servers, and so on. You can use the functions in this chapter to extract data from the bindery and update the bindery files.

Chapter 9 covers how to print on the network printers. We discuss the CAPTURE process that permits any application to print on a network, and we provide functions that allow you to control the CAPTURE from within your FoxPro program. We also cover the DOS print queue and how to access it. We wrap up the chapter with a general-purpose printing routine that selects where to print, and then starts and finishes the print job. This routine transparently handles printing sent to the screen, a file, any local printer, or any network printer.

Chapter 10 discusses how to send messages between workstations and the file console. All three methods for communicating between two running programs or workstations—broadcast messages, Message Handling Services (MHS), and NetWare semaphores—are covered in this chapter.

Chapter 11 covers how to connect to a file server and access the information available from it. You'll learn, for example, how to determine the server's name when you want to restrict your program to running on a single network.

Chapter 12 presents a complete e-mail application as an example of network programming. It includes many of the functions discussed in the book, illustrating how they can be used in your applications. The chapter describes a basic, functioning e-mail application you can add to your FoxPro programs.

Chapter 13 is the actual source code for the e-mail application described in Chapter 12. The source code is explained to make sure each network aspect is clearly understood.

Appendix A provides a reference for related software products and information on FoxPro and NetWare.

Appendix B discusses the routines provided on the disk that accompanies this book.

# Introduction to Networks

WHAT IS A NETWORK?

HOW DOES THE NETWORK WORK?

NETWORK HARDWARE

NETWORK SOFTWARE

NETWORK MEMORY OPTIMIZATION

NETWORK PROGRAMMING CONCEPTS

NETWORK PROGRAMMING GUIDELINES

Networks are quickly becoming the conventional method of operations for personal computers (PCs). Many applications that in the past could run only on large-scale mainframe computers have been converted and are now running successfully on networked PCs. In this chapter, we will introduce basic network concepts and discuss how a PC communicates with a network. We will also discuss hardware and software components of the network, as well as some fundamental programming concepts.

## What is a network?

A network can be simply defined as a group of computers that share resources. Most often, these shared resources are disk drives, the data they contain, and printers. In this book, we will consider two kinds of networks, the peer-to-peer network and the centralized server network.

A *peer-to-peer network* comprises any number of computers that are used not only individually, but also communally, sharing their files and/or their printers. No single computer holds a centralized set of files; rather, each computer can designate which files and printers will be shared and which ones will remain local to that particular computer.

When a peer-to-peer network is created, each computer can act as a *server*, a *client*, or both. A server computer shares its resources, usually by name, with other computers in the network. Client computers access resources from the server computers, but do not provide any shared resources themselves.

A *centralized server network* may have any of a wide variety of network configurations, but the distinguishing factor is that one or more computers in the network act as the central repository for shared files. The centralized computer is called the *file server*. Its files are made available to the other computers, which are called *workstations*. In addition, the file server's serial and parallel ports are made available to the workstations. This allows the workstations to share the network printer(s).

A centralized server network usually has a separate program running on the file server, which handles data requests and controls access to the printers and other resources. Although this arrangement is more expensive and more difficult to administer, performance is generally very good. If fast hardware is used, this configuration can actually run faster than a single PC accessing the local hard disk. Novell's NetWare product currently owns 70 percent of this market; both Banyan Vines and the LAN Manager are solid network offerings, as well.

Peer-to-peer networks are generally less expensive and easier to administer than centralized server networks. The trade-off is that peer-to-peer networks do not perform as well as centralized server networks. Netware Lite, Workgroups for Windows, and Lantastic are just a few of the peer-to-peer networks available. For a small group of computers, these options represent a fairly easy way for the computers to communicate.

In either network configuration, the server computer has resources to share, and the client computers (or workstations) can access these resources.

## How does the network work?

When the first PC appeared on the scene back in 1981, it was designed for expandability. Its hardware featured expansion slots to add functionality, and the DOS software was table driven to accommodate enhancement. The hardware and software have come a long way in the past twelve years, but the concept of expandability has always been a mainstay of these personal computers.

How can a computer designed for a single person share its data? After all, PCs were not designed to be linked together. Yet, somehow, through a magic combination of hardware and software, they can indeed be linked together to great advantage. To understand some of the principles involved in linking PCs, we will need to review first the PC's hardware, and then its operating system (DOS). The hardware and software together allow the PC to act as an integrated component in a network of computers.

## PC HARDWARE

If you open up a personal computer and look inside, you will find a large circuit board, the *motherboard*. This board contains the CPU (*central processing unit*) and may also house an optional chip known as a *math coprocessor*. The motherboard does not contain any capabilities for input and output; however, it does contain any number of slots where other circuit boards or "cards" may be added. These *expansion slots* are used to enhance the capability of the PC. A basic PC will usually have two slots occupied, with one card to control the video display and another to control the disk drives. The other empty slots are available for other peripheral devices. Figure 1.1 shows a typical personal computer configuration.

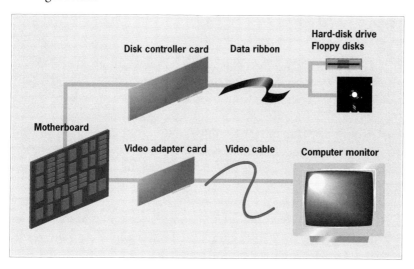

Figure 1.1: A typical personal computer configuration

## DISK OPERATING SYSTEM (DOS)

The DOS operating system software coordinates the operations of all the hardware components of your computer system (see Figure 1.2). As you enter commands through the keyboard, DOS interprets these commands and issues the appropriate instructions to the hardware. For example, when you enter a DOS command to print a file, DOS sends an instruction to the hard disk to read the file and then sends other instructions to the printer port to print the file. These services are designed into the operating system and made available to PC users.

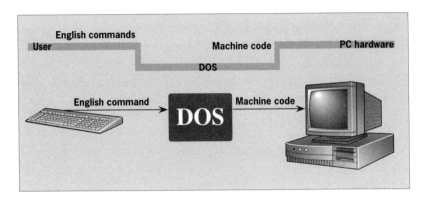

**Figure 1.2: The role of DOS in a PC**

DOS also makes these services available to application programs through a series of software *interrupts*. An interrupt is a piece of code that performs any of the DOS services. These functions have a specific syntax and are available to almost every DOS-compatible product, including FoxPro.

The DOS designers built a very flexible system. They made every available DOS service totally replaceable. Each function has a number of parameters and returns a specific value. Programs that use the DOS functions pass the required parameters and expect certain results; they do not know anything about the code that actually gets executed. (Such logic is known as a "black box routine.") As long as the routine follows the rules that DOS specifies, it has the flexibility to do anything it needs to do, including directing file input/output away from a local disk to a network interface card. It is precisely this flexibility that allows a computer designed for a single person to become a network workstation.

**DOS interrupts**  In order to get DOS to perform a task for you, you must set up some *registers* and perform an interrupt. In FoxPro terms, this is similar to calling a FoxPro *built-in function*. Following is a simple FoxPro program that calls the FV() (Future Value) function:

```
PRIVATE    payment
PRIVATE    monthly
PRIVATE    periods
PRIVATE    rate

rate    = .08
payment = 250
monthly = rate / 12
```

```
periods = 60

future  = FV( payment, monthly, periods )

? "The future amount of this annuity is "
?? str( future,11,2)
RETURN
```

When the foregoing code is executed, the computer performs the steps sequentially. Once it reaches the FV() function call, the program jumps to the address where the future value code is stored, executes the function, and then returns a value to be placed into the entity named FUTURE. The program then continues.

As an example of a DOS interrupt, let's look at how we ask DOS to open a file. First, we load registers with the parameters describing the file we want to open. Then we issue DOS interrupt 33 (or 21H in hexadecimal), which is the DOS service interrupt, and tell the computer to perform function 61 (Open File). Somewhere in DOS memory is a segment of machine code that tells the computer how to open a file; by requesting the interrupt, we are asking DOS to find that piece of code and execute it. We give DOS the parameters, and it executes the code and returns a value.

In DOS programming, interrupts do not have names, but rather numbers. To determine which piece of code to execute, DOS looks up the number in an *interrupt table*. This fixed-size table is stored in the first memory locations in RAM. It is exactly 4,096 bytes long, and consists of memory addresses for each of the interrupts. When an interrupt is requested, the computer determines the interrupt address, saves the current location, jumps to the code location pointed to by the interrupt table, executes the code for that interrupt, and returns control to the original location.

**DOS flexibility**    To provide maximum flexibility, the DOS design allows a programmer to change the interrupt table. Most of the DOS interrupts, including the very important interrupt 33, can have their table entries changed.

By changing an entry in the table, a programmer can cause the computer to execute a specific piece code instead of the assigned DOS routine. This means that a program can change the functionality of DOS with relative ease. As long as the new routine accepts the parameters and returns the proper value, the calling program has no way of knowing whether DOS or some other program performed the requested service. By way of comparison, if you wrote a new version of the FV() function that accepted the same parameters as the original version, a program would not know whether your FV() function or FoxPro's version was called.

With this level of control available, a program can easily redirect all DOS file requests (60 through 66, for example) to its own routines. Just as the standard DOS services translate file requests into the action of accessing the hard disk, a modified set might redirect all file access elsewhere. Thus, by changing these DOS addresses, a piece of software can change a single-user computer into a network workstation. To access a network, a piece of software is run on the computer we wish to use as a workstation. This software changes some of the DOS interrupts to its own routines so that the network can communicate with programs running on the workstation. (We will talk more about this software later in this chapter.)

We have seen how, in theory, a personal computer can act as a network workstation. Keep in mind, however, that every computer we intend to use as a workstation will need some additional hardware and software components in order to access the network. Let's explore these components in detail.

## NETWORK HARDWARE

Unfortunately for us software people, networks need just as much hardware as they do software, so we must become more familiar with some hardware components. (But look at the bright side—now you can blame the hardware if a problem occurs. Since hardware people always blame the software, turnabout is fair play!) Figure 1.3 illustrates the hardware setup needed to access a network through a personal computer.

### NETWORK CARDS

If you look at the back of the average PC, you will not find a place to hook up a network cable. For this function, you will need a *network card*, which serves as an interface between the PC and the cable. The network card is an add-in board that occupies one expansion slot. On the back of the card is an outlet where you connect the cable. This card contains the necessary hardware to translate disk requests from a computer to packets of information that are sent along the cabling. Additionally, each network card has a physical address that will have been burned in by the manufacturer (as with Ethernet), or can be established by setting switches (as in ARCnet). This is important because it allows the server to uniquely identify each workstation. A network card is also present in the server for the same purpose: converting disk activity into cable traffic.

The network card is also called a *network interface card* (NIC). The type of card will vary dependent upon the type of cabling. Every computer in the network will need a network card to access the cabling that connects to the file server.

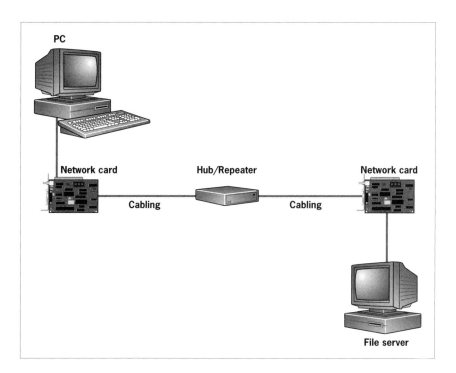

**Figure 1.3: Network hardware setup**

**Note:**  In some peer-to-peer network systems, data is transmitted through existing serial or parallel ports. Although this is helpful in reducing the overall cost of the network, these ports are not fast enough for any serious networking applications.

## CABLING

The cable is the thread that connects all the network components together. It serves as the conduit for data passed between the workstations and the file server. Many kinds of cabling can be used, depending upon the environment at the network site.

**Note:**  When installing a network, be sure that the cable and connectors are of high quality. Cheap connectors or cabling can cause all sorts of problems that are hard to detect and isolate.

**Twisted-pair cable**    *Twisted-pair cable* is one of the least expensive cabling alternatives. It consists of two wires (ARCnet) or four wires (Ethernet) twisted together and wrapped in shielding. Most commercial telephone wiring is twisted-pair. Twisted-pair cabling for data communications must meet more stringent specifications than telephone wire, however, and may also have additional external shielding.

Twisted-pair wiring (see Figure 1.4) offers good throughput, but is somewhat susceptible to electromagnetic interference. If the network uses twisted-pair wiring, cables should be no more than 100 yards long, and should be installed to avoid any potential sources of electronic noise (such as fluorescent lights and elevator motors).

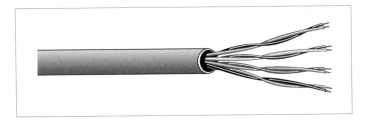

**Figure 1.4: Twisted-pair cable**

**Coaxial cable**    A *coaxial cable* (see Figure 1.5) usually consists of a shielded copper cable surrounded by a plastic casing. A second wire casing is wrapped around the interior plastic casing, and the entire cable is then wrapped in insulation. The cable is terminated at each end by a terminator (50 ohm resistor). This type of cable is most frequently used with ARCnet or Ethernet, and offers good transmission speed and data protection. The type of coaxial cable used by ARCnet is called RG-62, and that used by Ethernet is called RG-58-Au.

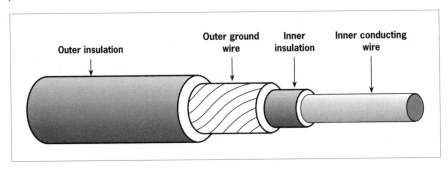

**Figure 1.5: Coaxial cable**

**Fiber-optic cable**    *Fiber-optic cables* (see Figure 1.6) transmit data as a beam of light. Certainly this is a fast transmission method, but reliability and distance are the main reasons for using fiber-optic cabling; it is feasible to connect network nodes using fiber-optic cable over a mile long. Also, fiber-optic cable does not pick up static or energy from external sources.

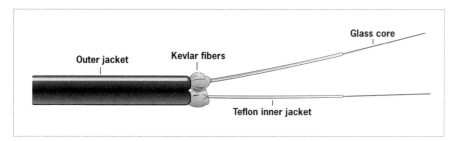

**Figure 1.6: Fiber-optic cable**

In addition to these assets, fiber-optic cables are very secure. It is possible to tap into a coaxial cable and read the data being sent over it, because the cabling radiates electronic signals as it transmits them; in fact, you can even read the signals from outside the cable. In contrast, a fiber-optic cabling system is much more controlled, because light does not leak out of the cable; nor can the cable be tapped into without breaking the connection. Hence, fiber-optic cable is often used in situations where security is a vital concern.

**Hubs and repeaters**    Depending upon the network configuration and the distance between each workstation and the server, a *hub* or *repeater* may be necessary. These allow a single cable from the server to service multiple workstations. They also can be used to boost the signal and extend the distance between workstations.

There are two kinds of hubs available: active and passive. An *active hub* (or concentrator) boosts the signal from the cable and passes it along; a *passive hub* merely passes the signal on. Hubs are used with ArcNet cards and cabling. A repeater serves the same purpose as an active hub for Ethernet cards and cabling. Both repeaters and hubs have ports to connect to the cables that run into them.

## THE FILE SERVER

As mentioned earlier, the server is the primary computer in a network system. It controls the shared resources and handles the data requests. These shared resources (the server's hard disk and printers) are monitored and made available to other computers by the network. Most servers have large hard disks and plenty of RAM. In order to maintain good performance, the RAM is used to buffer disk requests. A server may be *dedicated*, which means it runs only the network operating system, or it may be *nondedicated*, which means it can function as both a server and a workstation. A nondedicated server has twice the work to do, and is typically used only in smaller networks and peer-to-peer networks.

As you can see in Figure 1.3, the file server also requires a network adapter card and access to the cabling.

# NETWORK SOFTWARE

In addition to the hardware described above, several software programs must be run on a network to coordinate communications between the workstations and the file server.

### THE NETWORK OPERATING SYSTEM

The network operating system runs on the file server. The operating system's primary function is to accept data requests from the workstations and to respond by providing the requested data or results. Most network operating systems can also handle printers and other peripherals, and have extensive built-in security systems.

Although the server runs the network operating system, the server is rarely used to its full capacity. When a FoxPro application requests data from the network, the network sends all of the file's data to the requesting workstation, which then pulls out the data it needs. In a client/server relationship, however, the server becomes an intelligent piece of hardware. Instead of just shuffling data around, the server analyzes data requests and sends only the appropriate subset of data. Because less data is sent from the server to the workstation, throughput is greatly improved.

### IPX PROTOCOL

IPX (for Internet Packet Exchange) is a protocol that transmits data through cables among workstations on Novell networks. The IPX file contains the software to handle the data transmissions. The IPX software implements simple communication capabilities that provide the minimum service for network traffic between the network shell (NETX, discussed just below) and the network interface card.

For most applications, IPX is sufficient. However, a superset of communication commands and functions known as SPX can be added to IPX. Among other things, SPX can confirm that transmitted data has actually been received. (Both IPX and SPX are specific to Novell networks.)

### NETWORK SHELL PROGRAMS

Most networks have what is known as a *network shell*, which is the program that remaps the DOS file-access routines to its own code. Some network shells also remap DOS printer routines, date and time services, and so on. In this manner, the network can appear transparent to a wide variety of applications running on the workstation.

For example, the network shell for Novell networks is a program called NETX. Let's examine the memory map for a workstation with the NETX shell installed:

```
MCB     PSP    Files   Bytes  Owner    Hooked Interrupts
09C3    0008       0    7840  Config
0BAE    0BAF       0    3376  Command  22 23 2E
0C82    0000       0      48  Command
1091    1096       1   39312  NETX     1B 20 21 24 27 CE CF F0
```

You can see that NETX has taken DOS interrupt 21H (33 decimal) and remapped it. This means all DOS service requests will be passed to the shell for processing. NETX also takes over the DOS fatal-error and program-termination interrupts. Notice also that the shell uses some of DOS's memory, so less will be available for your FoxPro application. (In the next section, we will discuss how to maximize the amount of memory available for your FoxPro program.)

NETX is the current release of the Novell Netware shell that works with all versions of DOS. Older versions are NET3, NET4, and NET5, which work with DOS 3.0, 4.0, and 5.0, respectively. There are also versions of the network shell that work in expanded memory. See Appendix C for more information.

## NETWORK MEMORY OPTIMIZATION

DOS versions 5.0 and above, as well as certain add-on products, allow the network shell to be loaded into memory above the 640K available to DOS. If your application is tight on memory, even in a single-user system, we strongly recommend that you consider obtaining software to place the network shell into high memory. Also, DOS versions 5.0 and above allow you to load DOS itself into high memory. The ability to load programs into memory above the 640K limit can mean a dramatic increase in the amount of memory available for your FoxPro application.

## LOADING INTO HIGH MEMORY

Tables 1.1 and 1.2 represent two memory maps. Table 1.1 describes the network software installed in the base 640K memory, and Table 1.2 shows what happens when DOS's LOADHIGH program is used to place the network software above the 640K limit. You will see that the second arrangement increases memory available to your FoxPro program by 55,000 bytes.

**Table 1.1: Network Software Loaded in Conventional Memory**

| Name | Size in Decimal | |
| --- | --- | --- |
| MSDOS | 16,544 | (16.2K) |
| COMMAND | 3,392 | (3.3K) |
| IPX | 16,656 | (16.3K) |
| NETX | 43,728 | (42.7K) |
| FREE | 64 | (0.1K) |
| FREE | 574,976 | (561.4K) |
| Total FREE: | 575,040 | (561.5K) |
| Largest executable program size: 574,976 (561.4K) | | |

**Table 1.2: Network Software Loaded in High Memory**

| Conventional Memory | | | Upper Memory Blocks | | |
| --- | --- | --- | --- | --- | --- |
| **Name** | **Size in Decimal** | | **Name** | **Size in Decimal** | |
| MSDOS | 16,544 | (16.2K) | SYSTEM | 167,472 | (163.5K) |
| HIMEM | 1,072 | (1.0K) | IPX | 16,656 | (16.3K) |
| EMM386 | 3,232 | (3.2K) | NETX | 43,728 | (42.7K) |
| COMMAND | 3,392 | (3.3K) | FREE | 64 | (0.1K) |
| FREE | 64 | (0.1K) | FREE | 32,768 | (32.0K) |
| FREE | 630,768 | (616.0K) | FREE | 1,344 | (1.3K) |
| Total FREE: | 630,832 | (616.1K) | Total FREE: | 34,176 | (33.4K) |
| Largest executable program size: 630,768 (616.0K) | | | | | |

Be aware that the memory savings offered by loading NETX into high memory will come at the price of reducing network performance somewhat. This is due to the extra processing done by the upper-memory manager. If you are using FoxPro in Extended mode, you should leave NETX in lower memory, because FoxPro does not need much of the 640K to run applications or access data. If you are not running FoxPro in Extended mode, however, you should weigh the memory gain against the performance decrease, to see what is best for your environment.

IPX.COM can be loaded high with very little impact on performance.

**CONFIG.SYS requirements**   To use high memory, you must load the high-memory device drivers and then specify that DOS should be placed into the high-memory area. Here is a suggested setup for your CONFIG.SYS file:

```
DEVICE=C:\DOS\HIMEM.SYS
DEVICE=C:\DOS\EMM386.EXE NOEMS
DOS=HIGH,UMB
```

> **Note:**   You can obtain more details about CONFIG.SYS in your DOS manual. If Microsoft Windows is installed on the workstation, you might need to specify additional device drivers.

**Adding LOADHIGH to AUTOEXEC.BAT**   Once the high-memory device drivers are loaded, any network software can be loaded into high memory, using the DOS LOADHIGH command. Here is a simple AUTOEXEC.BAT file that loads the NETX network shell and IPX programs into high memory:

```
@ECHO OFF
LOADHIGH C:\NETWORK\IPX
LOADHIGH C:\NETWORK\NETX
```

If you do not want your network users to boot directly into the network, you can create a separate batch file to load the network software. Keep in mind that if the software cannot be loaded into high memory, DOS will place the software into conventional memory below the 640K limit.

## OTHER MEMORY MANAGEMENT PROGRAMS

DOS is not alone in its ability to move programs into high memory. Two popular programs, QuarterDeck's QEMM and Qualitas's 386Max, also provide memory configuration. If you are in a network environment, you will want to explore ways to maximize available memory for FoxPro, which can use every bit of memory you can acquire for it.

# Network programming concepts

Programming on a network can best be described as the art of designing systems to circumvent Murphy's Law. (That is, if something can go wrong, it will do so, and at the worst possible moment.)

To understand the programming considerations for a network environment, we first need to understand what the network operating system is doing for us. An analogy we find useful is to think of the network as a massive file cabinet. In front of this file cabinet is one dedicated secretary. His name is Jake; he is 6' 4" tall and weighs in at 280 pounds, and you are not going to get anything from the files unless he lets you. So you have to tell Jake what you want to use and how you want to use it. Unfortunately, Jake's vocabulary is limited, so you must tell him exactly what you want in precisely the right terms.

## MAY I HAVE A FILE, PLEASE?

In order to access any information at all from the file cabinet, you have to tell Jake the name of the file you want, and whether other people can use it while you are working with it. You do this with the FoxPro USE command, whose syntax is

USE <*file_name*> EXCLUSIVE (or SHARE)

The USE command instructs Jake to let you work with a file. If you do not want anybody else to use the file while you have it, you should request that the file be EXCLUSIVE. If you want to allow other people to work with it also, tell Jake to SHARE the file. Jake first determines whether he can give you the file, by checking his list to see if anyone else is using the file. If not, it's all yours. Jake writes your name on his pad of paper next to the file cabinet.

If someone else wants to use your file, Jake checks his pad of paper. When he discovers your name next to the file, he checks to see if you are using the file exclusively. If not, he then asks if the other person is willing to share the file or if he/she needs it exclusively. If you are both willing to share, Jake lets the other person have the file. If either of you refuses to share, however, Jake will not give the second person the file until you are finished with it. "First come, first served" is Jake's motto when it comes to files.

## CHECKING FOR ERRORS WITH ON ERROR

Now that we know how to ask Jake for files, we need to know how to figure out his answer. Unfortunately, USE is a command rather than a function, and commands do not return values, so we cannot expect a direct answer. At least, however, if Jake cannot give us the file we have requested, an error will occur, which will result in the "File is not available" message being displayed.

```
ON ERROR DO CHECKOPEN WITH ERROR()
USE customer EXCLUSIVE IN 1    && Jake, may I use the CUSTOMER
                               && file all by myself please?


ON ERROR                       && Restore original error handler

IF USED(1)                     && Jake said OK!
   &&   Do something with
   &&   the file
ELSE                           && Jake said NO!
   && Tell the end-user
   && Jake said NO
ENDIF
RETURN


PROCEDURE CHECKOPEN
PARAMETERS ERRNUMBER
IF ERRNUMBER = 108  OR ERRNUMBER = 3
   WAIT "FILE IS NOT AVAILABLE" WINDOW TIMEOUT 30
ENDIF
RETURN
```

**Caution!** Each and every time you open a file in a network environment, you must remember to check and see whether you were successful. If the file open was unsuccessful, you can either wait a few seconds and try again, or perform some other operation that does not require that file. In Chapter 3, we will design a function that you can use to smoothly handle all file-opening operations.

## EXCLUSIVE FILES VS. SHARED FILES

Why would you want to open a network file exclusively? The answer is, in most situations you don't want to—after all, nobody else will be able to use the file until you are done. (If you have a sadistic streak, you might code an application to randomly open files exclusively, so that the hapless clerk could unknowingly lock out the president of the company.)

The main reason for opening a file exclusively is when you need to use it with any of the following five FoxPro commands:

INDEX (when creating or deleting a tag in a compound index)

INSERT [BLANK]

PACK

REINDEX

ZAP

Inserting a new index key into a compound index, or inserting a blank record into the database both require changes to the entire index file or database file. FoxPro can only perform these actions if exclusive use of the file is obtained. You should carefully weigh the use of these commands in a network environment.

You will want to avoid the REINDEX command, since it will not correct index files with corruption in the header, and REINDEX can easily be replaced with the INDEX ON command.

The PACK and ZAP commands are used very infrequently, so your corresponding need for exclusive use of a file should be equally infrequent.

INSERT [BLANK] is a very slow method of adding a record to the file, and you should use APPEND BLANK, instead. If the file's physical order is important, INSERT [BLANK] might be required, but for many applications, the index files control the file's order and it is not necessary to physically order the file, as well.

## OK, I'VE GOT THE FILE OPEN

Once your USE command is successful, you can perform one of two general operations: (1) read information from the database; or (2) write information to it. From FoxPro's view of the network, the only time you need to lock the file or a portion of the file is when you need to write to it. Yet there *are* times when locks are needed—even though you are not writing to the file.

**Locks?** What are *locks*? Remember Jake? In addition to opening the files for you, he will allow you to change a file's contents—but he will allow only one person at a time to change a file (or a record from a file). Jake does this by maintaining a *lock table*, an area of memory in the network operating system that lists all sections of the file cabinet that currently are reserved by a user.

Each user may have one of two types of locks active: a *file lock* or a *record lock*. FoxPro programs may have several records locked per work area at any given time. You can mix file locks and record locks in separate work areas. For example, you might have a file lock on the CUSTOMER database at the same time that you have locks on the first and fifteenth records in the PARTS database.

A file's entry in the lock table prevents other users from writing to that file or record. They may still read from the file, but they cannot update the data in a locked record.

**File locks**   Locking a file is similar to obtaining exclusive use of a file for a brief period of time. No other users can update any information in the file until you release the lock. The significant difference between a file lock and exclusive use is that other users can continue to read information from a locked file; however, they are not at liberty to change it.

Locking an entire file should be done judiciously. If you need to change only a single record, for instance, file locking is definitely overkill. On the other hand, if you need to change multiple records as part of one process, then FoxPro will require a file lock. Here are examples of both situations:

```
* File lock here is overkill
SELECT customer
IF FLOCK()
   GOTO 15
   REPLACE name WITH "Grumpfish"
   UNLOCK
ENDIF
* File lock here is required
SELECT customer
IF FLOCK()
   REPLACE ALL status WITH "LATE" FOR age > 3Ø
   UNLOCK
ENDIF
```

Use a file lock only when more than one record will be affected by your operation. Remember that if you lock a file, no one else can update that file until you release the lock.

The FLOCK() function in FoxPro attempts to obtain a file lock for the current work area. It makes one attempt, and returns a logical value indicating the success or failure of the attempt.

**Record locks**   A record lock allows you to update a single record in the database. It also denies any other user the ability to update that record until you release the lock. As with file locks, another user can read a locked record but cannot change it. Whenever you need to update only a single record, use the record lock to avoid interfering with other users.

The RLOCK() function in FoxPro attempts to obtain a record lock for the current work area. It makes one attempt, and returns a logical value indicating the success or failure of the attempt.

In Chapter 2 we will explore FoxPro's locking commands in much more detail. We will also discuss FoxPro's automatic locking capabilities.

# NETWORK PROGRAMMING GUIDELINES

Regardless of the programming language you use for developing applications, keep in mind the following guidelines when programming on a network.

### START NETWORKING FROM THE BEGINNING

When you are designing and writing a FoxPro program, plan right from the start for the program to run on a network. Although it might not be specified that the program is to be designed for a network, the program will probably have to run in a network environment at some point. It is much easier to write all your programs for a network than it is to go back and modify existing code to make it network ready.

If you run your program on a single-user machine, the network locks will always succeed, because no other process is contending for them. You can always run a network application on a single-user machine; however, it is rare that you will be able to run a single-user application in a network environment. With networks becoming more and more common in the workplace, it's a good idea to design all applications with the capability to run well on a network.

### DO NOT MAKE ASSUMPTIONS

One of the mistakes most frequently made when programming for a network is that the code assumes all network locking will be successful. For example, the following code from an actual application produces no run-time errors:

```
SELECT customer
m.cust_code = id_code
IF RLOCK( )
   REPLACE balance WITH balance + m.nAmount
ENDIF
SELECT trans
IF RLOCK( )
   REPLACE amount WITH m.nAmount,;
           who    WITH m.cust_code
ENDIF
SELECT taxes
IF RLOCK( )
   REPLACE amt_due with amt_due + (m.nAmount * .06 )
ENDIF
```

The lack of run-time errors in this code means that a far worse error can occur: data corruption. In this situation, three files are updated each time the code is executed. Almost every time this program is run, the correct results are obtained. However, *almost* is not good enough. The correct results must be obtained every time.

Let's take a look at what our databases will contain if the second record lock in this example is not successful. The CUSTOMER database will contain the proper balance and the TAXES database will be up-to-date, but the TRANS database will contain the wrong information. When this customer's record is displayed, the total of the transactions will not equal the balance in the customer's account. If the TAXES file is not updated, then the amount of money paid for sales tax will be understated, which will not please the state government.

Now examine a corrected version of the foregoing function; this one reports to the user that data may have been corrupted. (In Chapter 6, we will discuss transaction processing, which would treat the three file updates as a single unit.)

```
SELECT customer
m.cust_code = id_code
IF RLOCK()
   REPLACE balance    WITH  balance + m.nAmount
   SELECT trans
   IF RLOCK()
      REPLACE amount WITH m.nAmount,;
              who    WITH m.cust_code
      SELECT taxes
      IF RLOCK()
         REPLACE amt_due WITH amt_due + (m.nAmount * .06 )
      ELSE
         WAIT "ERROR: Tax file not updated" WINDOW TIMEOUT 30
      ENDIF
   ELSE
      WAIT "ERROR: Trans/taxes not updated" WINDOW TIMEOUT 30
   ENDIF
ELSE
   WAIT "ERROR: Transaction not recorded!!" WINDOW TIMEOUT 30
ENDIF
RETURN
```

Although the error messages here are somewhat terse and there are no instructions for recovery procedures, at least we have taken the extra step to notify the user that something went wrong with this transaction.

## ASK FOR PERMISSION

Another important network characteristic to keep in mind is that other people are probably using the same files that you are using. Someone like Jake is in charge of all these files.

Among other things, you must ask if it is okay for your application to continue. For example, the following code does not ask for permission before erasing a transaction file:

```
SELECT customer
* Some update work
USE trans EXCLUSIVE IN 1
*
* Remove prior transactions
*
ZAP
SELECT customer
*
* More code
*
```

For the most part, this code will execute correctly. However, when another user tries to open the transaction file, he/she will be unsuccessful. As a result, a run-time error will occur, which, though slightly better than erasing the wrong database file, is nonetheless quite disconcerting.

Following is the same code, but this time we include an extra step to ask for permission to open the transaction file. Although users might be surprised when they encounter the error message, this is certainly better than possibly zapping the wrong file.

```
SELECT customer
* Some update work
ON ERROR DO CHEKOPEN WITH ERROR()
USE trans EXCLUSIVE IN 1
ON ERROR
IF NOT USED(1)
    WARN "Cannot open the TRANS file.." WINDOW TIMEOUT 30
    RETURN
ELSE
    *
    * Remove prior transactions
    *
    ZAP
ENDIF
SELECT customer
*
* More code
*
RETURN

PROCEDURE CHEKOPEN
```

```
PARAMETER ERRNUMBER
IF ERRNUMBER = 108 OR ERRNUMBER = 3
   WAIT "FILE IS NOT AVAILABLE..." WINDOW TIMEOUT 30
ENDIF
RETURN
```

**Note:** Always ask for permission from the network before attempting to do any operation. This is particularly important when you are preparing for operations that will affect a large number of records in the file.

## PLAN FOR CONFLICTS

Certainly the three foregoing guidelines deal with ensuring that the data is properly updated, but they also assume that the user has nothing better to do than wait until the computer is finished with its processing. Your application should assume that *every* record lock or file lock request will fail.

If we write our applications based on this assumption, we must also consider appropriate courses of action. If a file open request fails, what options should the user be offered? In some cases, the program should simply tell the user it cannot run, because the files are not available. In other cases, the program might switch to another database. For example, consider an application that allows the user to get the name of a person to call for a survey. If all the names are in one file, the only appropriate action in the event of a file open failure is to tell the user that the file is unavailable. However, if the names are spread across ten files, then failure to open one of them should be followed by an attempt to open the next one.

It is vitally important to design your application with the assumption that every attempt to open a file will fail and that the program will not be able to obtain any record locks. Does your program handle these conditions gracefully by alerting the user and offering other options? Does it merely report the failure and abort the procedure? Or, worse yet, does it ignore the problem and just update what it can? In this book, you will see how to design programs that run effectively on a network, but not by simply wrapping record locks around the appropriate sections of code.

# SUMMARY

This chapter introduced basic network concepts, including how a network communicates with its workstations. You learned some general guidelines to keep in mind when programming on a network. In subsequent chapters, we will expand on those guidelines and provide practical working code that you can use to write robust, network-ready applications.

# Basic FoxPro Network Commands

Opening files: exclusive or shared mode?

Specifying how to open files

Opening a database

File locking concepts

Global settings

Basic networking commands and functions

Optimizing FoxPro to run on a network

# Chapter 2

F oxPro's commands and functions operate the same way on a stand-alone or networked computer. In this chapter we will cover the concept of exclusive use versus shared use when handling files. We will also discuss the functions and commands that are necessary for working with shared files. Finally, we will discuss how to fine-tune your configuration options for optimal network performance.

## OPENING FILES: EXCLUSIVE OR SHARED MODE?

FoxPro provides two methods of opening database files, to control whether or not other programs can also read from or write to the file. The *exclusive mode* allows only the current program to access the file. *Shared mode* allows other applications to access the file at the same time as the current program.

### EXCLUSIVE MODE

When a program is the only one with access to a file, it can pretty much do as it pleases with that file. The program will greedily open the file and not allow anyone else to use it until that program is finished. This approach works well for word processing and spreadsheet applications, but it is inadequate for networked database files. This is because databases are generally edited at the record level (only a portion of the file as opposed to the entire file).

There are some FoxPro commands that operate on the entire file, and thus require exclusive use of the file. These commands are

INDEX (when adding or deleting compound index tags)

INSERT BLANK

MODIFY STRUCTURE

PACK

REINDEX

ZAP

All of these commands can make substantial changes to a file's contents or its structure, which is why exclusive use is required. If you attempt to use one of these commands when the file is not opened exclusively, you will get an error message to that effect.

> **Note:** When INDEXing a database, FoxPro expects a static database during the entire process.

Files that are opened exclusively can only be changed by the current program. FoxPro takes advantage of this fact and can offer extraordinary performance when a file is opened exclusively. Since disk operations are generally the slowest, FoxPro has built-in techniques to perform many of these operations entirely in memory. When the file is being changed only by the current program, FoxPro can do much more work from its memory copy of the data, instead of from disk (which is considerably slower).

FoxPro prefers to open files exclusively for performance reasons and will go to great lengths to do so. If FoxPro determines that no one else can access a file (for example, because the file is not on a network drive and the DOS SHARE utility is not loaded), it will open the file exclusively even when you do try to open it shared.

### SHARED MODE

For most network applications, exclusive use of a file is too restrictive. The files will need to be opened in a shared mode so that other users can access them.

Files opened as shared require some coordination when it comes to writing data into the file. Imagine the chaos if everyone sharing a file could write to that file without notifying other users of the changes. To handle this coordination, FoxPro requires that, whenever you are going to write to a file, you must lock either the entire file or the record you intend to change. The lock serves as a message to other FoxPro programs that part of the file is being updated.

Most of FoxPro's commands and functions automatically perform the minimum required lock when writing data. In addition, there are commands that allow you to manually lock the record and/or file.

Shared file access will operate a bit more slowly than exclusive use. Because the data can be changed by other users, FoxPro cannot boost performance by relying on its memory copy of the data. In shared mode it is very possible that the next record you need to read has been changed, and FoxPro must be sure to fetch the data again from the disk in order to give you the most current information. (FoxPro provides the SET REFRESH command, which allows you to control how often the disk file is accessed when using a shared file.)

## Specifying how to open files

The SET EXCLUSIVE command is used to specify how all subsequent file openings should be handled. The default value, ON, causes all files to be opened for exclusive use. SET EXCLUSIVE OFF causes all files to be opened in shared mode. The syntax for the command is

SET EXCLUSIVE ON | OFF

This command does not affect any files that are already open. You can also override the SET setting by using the SHARE or EXCLUSIVE option in conjunction with the USE command. Keep in mind that FoxPro prefers to open files exclusively. So if you are writing a program primarily for network use, add the following line at the top of your program:

```
SET EXCLUSIVE OFF
```

You can also change the default to EXCLUSIVE OFF by entering the command

```
EXCLUSIVE=OFF
```

in your CONFIG.FP file.

## Opening a database

The USE command is used to open a file into a *work area*. A work area is a portion of memory that is set aside to hold information about the file, including a copy of the current record from the file. In addition to opening the files, USE can specify the indexes to be opened and updated with the file. The syntax of the USE command is

> USE <cFile> [ IN <nWorkArea> ]
>
>     [ AGAIN ]
>
>     [ INDEX indexfilelist>][ORDER <options> ]
>
>     [ ALIAS <cAlias> ]
>
>     [ EXCLUSIVE | SHARE ]
>
>     [ NOUPDATE ]

<cFile> indicates the name of the .DBF file you wish to open. It is not necessary to include a .DBF extension. If there is a problem (such as the file not existing or being used exclusive elsewhere), the ON ERROR condition will occur. (In Chapter 3 we will provide a file-opening routine that can be used in place of the USE command.)

<nWorkarea> indicates the work area in which you want to open the file. If another file is already open in that area, that file will be closed. If you specify the number zero, the next available work area will be used.

The optional AGAIN keyword allows you to open the same file in multiple work areas. If you open a file in another work area, it will assume the attributes of the first work area in which the file was opened. It will also use that work area's alias by default, although you are free to specify a new alias.

The INDEX clause should be followed by a list of index files that should be opened in conjunction with the database. Each index file in the list is opened in the same access mode as the database. The first index in the list will serve as the controlling index, which is used to determine the display order of the records.

The optional ORDER clause can be used after INDEX in several ways:

▶ If you are using the INDEX clause with a list of file names, ORDER <nOrder> specifies a controlling index file other than the first one in the list. If you specify ORDER 0, the records in the database are displayed in physical order, although the indexes will remain open. This is useful if you do not particularly want the database to be in any sort order, yet you want to be certain to update the index files.

▶ Without the INDEX clause, ORDER <cFilename> can be used to specify an .IDX index file as the controlling index.

▶ Without the INDEX clause, ORDER <cTag> [OF <cFilename>] specifies which tag to use to determine the sort order of the database. If you do not use the optional OF *<cFilename>* clause, *<cTag>* must exist in the structural (production) compound index file that was opened automatically along with the database. The OF *<cFilename>* clause allows you to specify a tag from any open compound index (.CDX) file.

If you are using the ORDER clause, you may also include either the ASCENDING or DESCENDING keywords. These specify the order in which to display the database records. Using these keywords does not change the index file or tag; it merely alters the order in which the records are accessed and displayed.

The ALIAS keyword is used to specify a name for the work area. The default alias is the file name, but you can specify a different alias of up to ten letters and beginning with a letter. You can use this alias name with many of FoxPro's commands to refer to the work area. Using memorable alias names produces much more readable code than referring to the work areas by numbers.

The optional EXCLUSIVE and SHARE keywords determine which method to use for opening the file. If you do not specify either of these, the file will be opened in accordance with the current value of the SET EXCLUSIVE command. For most network applications, files will be opened in shared mode. For safety we recommend that you always specify the open mode on the USE command. This will prevent another part of the program from affecting the way your files are opened.

The NOUPDATE keyword can be used to prevent changes from being made to the .DBF table or its structure. If you specify NOUPDATE and set the file's read-only attribute at the DOS level, FoxPro will recognize this condition and buffer the file so that overall performance can be enhanced. If you have small tables containing read-only data (such as tax tables or state codes), consider using the NOUPDATE option and setting the file to read-only.

**Note:** Since there are substantial performance improvements when a file is used exclusively, you should look for opportunities to use files exclusively whenever feasible. Any temporary files, such as transaction files, will automatically be candidates for exclusive use.

## FILE LOCKING CONCEPTS

FoxPro requires that you lock either the record or the file before you write any data to it. FoxPro will implicitly attempt a lock if the requested operation requires one, and if there is not already an explicit (that is, user-initiated) lock in place. The automatic locking can be a blessing or a curse, depending upon your application. Since you cannot disable FoxPro's implicit locking, it is important to understand the meaning of record locks so that you can design your program appropriately.

### A LOCK IS A SIGNAL

The bare-minimum requirement is that the lock be placed around the RE-PLACE statements when a shared file is in use. However, this method does not consider the implication of a failed lock. A lock will fail if another user has locked either the entire file or the record you wish to update.

A failed lock should be considered a signal that your program needs to act upon. You will need to determine how to handle the failure. In some cases, the proper action might be to try another record. For example, imagine a telephone survey program that randomly chooses a person to call. If that person's record cannot be locked, it is a signal that someone else is calling that person. The appropriate action would then be to try to find another person to call. In other cases, the failed lock is a critical error and should be treated as such.

Carefully review each lock in your program to determine the most appropriate action when the lock fails.

### DEVELOPING A LOCKING STRATEGY

Record-lock timing is an important issue to consider when writing a network application. There are two times when the lock can be requested.

The first is to attempt to lock the file before the user is allowed to edit the record, and to keep it locked for the duration of the edits. This is referred to as the LOCK-EDIT-WRITE-UNLOCK cycle.

The second option, EDIT-LOCK-WRITE-UNLOCK, is to read the record into memory and allow the person to edit it. The record will not be locked until the instant that the person has to write the changes back to the file. This is the bare-minimum locking that FoxPro requires.

Each locking scheme merits further discussion.

**LOCK-EDIT-WRITE-UNLOCK**   This is the safest approach when allowing multiple programs to update a file. The lock serves as a signal to other applications that this record is currently being updated and is hence off limits to other programs. If you consider the lock a method of communication between programs and not a database requirement, this approach is the only one you should use.

With this method, you should first locate the record and attempt to lock it. If the lock succeeds, keep the record locked and allow the user to update it. After the user is finished updating the record, you should replace the data and unlock the record.

The following listing shows an example of this approach. You can use this code fragment as a template for editing records in this fashion.

```
USE customer INDEX customer SHARE && or USE customer ORDER customer SHARE
SEEK cust_id
IF FOUND()
   IF LOCK()
      SCATTER MEMVAR
      **
      ** Update the memory variables
      **
      READ TIMEOUT 60
      IF LASTKEY() <> 27
         GATHER MEMVAR
      ENDIF
      UNLOCK
   ELSE
     WAIT "Someone's editing the customer" WINDOW TIMEOUT 30
   ENDIF
ELSE
   WAIT "Customer not found" WINDOW TIMEOUT 30
ENDIF
```

**Note:**   The READ command in the above listing has a TIMEOUT option of 60 seconds. This is to circumvent one of the dangers of the LOCK-EDIT cycle, namely, the "lunch-time lock." This unpleasant phenomenon occurs when the user calls up the customer on the screen, thus locking the record, and then goes off to lunch, unwittingly leaving the lock intact to frustrate other users.

**EDIT-LOCK-WRITE-UNLOCK**    This approach keeps the record locked for the shortest possible time and is the minimum lock duration required. It is also the more dangerous of the two locking methods, because another user might read the record, update it, and write it back again between the moment that your program reads the record and the moment it attempts to write the record to the disk. Following is an example of this approach to record locking:

```
USE customer INDEX customer SHARE
SEEK cust_id
IF FOUND()
   SCATTER MEMVAR
   **
   ** Update the memory variables
   **
```

```
      READ TIMEOUT 60
      IF LASTKEY() <> 27
         IF LOCK()
            GATHER MEMVAR
            UNLOCK
         ELSE
            WAIT "Cannot lock this customer" WINDOW TIMEOUT 30
         ENDIF
      ENDIF
ELSE
   WAIT "Customer not found" WINDOW TIMEOUT 30
ENDIF
```

The placement of the lock is the only real difference between the two foregoing record lock versions. If you choose to use the LOCK-LAST cycle, please keep the following two cautions in mind:

▶ Do not rely on SCATTER and GATHER. Since these commands grab every field and replace every field, there is an increased likelihood that you will overwrite a field. If your program is only updating the customer's balance field, for example, then edit and replace only that field. Then, if another user has updated the address field, you will not overwrite those changes.

▶ Consider implementing a semaphore field (such as SIGNATURE). When you plan to edit the record, lock it and increment this field, save the value, and then unlock the record. When you go to write the data to disk, first check the SIGNATURE field. If the value is the same as the number you saved previously, then you will know that it is safe to update. If another user has incremented the SIGNATURE field, the values will not be the same and you can take corrective action.

**Caution!**   Make sure your locking strategy deals properly with failed locks. A failed lock is a message that must not be ignored!

## Global settings

FoxPro has a number of global command settings that can be used to control how your application operates on the network. For the most part you should include these settings at the beginning of your program file and leave them alone after that. In this fashion you will always know the behavior of the commands that are affected by these settings.

## SET LOCK

When FoxPro performs certain operations that read a large number of records, it is possible that users can update these records while FoxPro is reading them. This introduces the potential of FoxPro's reading inaccurate data. Certainly you can wrap these commands in a file lock, but FoxPro can also place an implicit lock *before* the command. The SET LOCK command is used to tell FoxPro whether or not to place the implicit lock. The implicit lock ensures that the results obtained match the database, but also affects the performance of other programs that are waiting to update the table.

The commands affected by SET LOCK are

| | |
|---|---|
| AVERAGE | JOIN (both files are locked) |
| CALCULATE | LIST |
| COPY TO | LABEL |
| COPY TO ARRAY | REPORT |
| COUNT | SORT |
| DISPLAY (when used with a scope) | SUM |
| INDEX | TOTAL |

The syntax for the command is:

SET LOCK ON | OFF

If you set LOCK to ON, implicit locking is enabled before the above-listed commands. If you set LOCK to OFF, which is the default, no lock will be implicitly performed.

## SET MULTILOCKS

In early releases of dBASE, programmers were limited to one record lock per work area. This is also the default lock operation in FoxPro. However, there are times when you might need to lock several records in a work area. FoxPro provides the MULTILOCKS setting to allow you this option. The syntax for this command is

SET MULTILOCKS ON | OFF

The default setting of OFF retains the single-lock-per-work-area restriction. Setting MULTILOCKS to ON allows several records to be locked within the same work area. The LOCK( ) and the RLOCK( ) functions are the only two functions affected by the MULTILOCKS setting.

You should include the statement

```
SET MULTILOCKS ON
```

in the beginning of your program file. This will allow you the most flexibility in your locking strategies.

### SET REFRESH

The SET REFRESH command determines how often data is read from the network and how often your screen display is updated. Its primary effect is upon the BROWSE, CHANGE, and EDIT commands (see Chapter 4).

When you are viewing data in a shared file, it is possible that other users will be editing records while they are displayed on your screen. You might also have a copy of a record in your computer's memory. It is therefore necessary to have the computer periodically update both the screen and your computer's memory buffers.

The SET REFRESH command controls how often this update process gets done. The more frequently it is performed, the slower the program will run. You can use the SET REFRESH command to determine the proper mix between performance and accuracy of displayed data. If you choose to edit a record that has been changed, FoxPro will be sure to give you the most current copy of the record. (The most current record is always given for editing, regardless of the setting of SET REFRESH or the screen display.)

The syntax for SET REFRESH is

SET REFRESH TO <*nWindow*> [, <*nBuffer*> ]

The <*nWindow*> number determines how often the browse or edit windows are updated. It can range from 0 (never), which is the default, to 3,600 seconds (once every hour). The lower the setting, the slower the browse window performs. Higher settings improve performance, but can cause the display to be out of sync with the actual data. (Remember that the edit data will be current even if the screen display is not.)

The <*nBuffer*> portion of the command determines how often the local memory buffers are to be updated with network data, from 0 seconds (never) to 3,600 seconds. The default is 5 seconds, or the same as <*nWindow*> if you specify only the <*nWindow*> setting. If you set <*nWindow*> to 0 and do not specify the <*nBuffer*>, then the default of 5 seconds is used. You can alter your program's performance by using this setting: The higher the setting, the better the performance.

Although your network environment and program needs will determine the proper settings, it is best to include the SET REFRESH command in the beginning of your program.

## SET REPROCESS

The SET REPROCESS command is used to determine how many times Fox-Pro will retry a failed lock. You can specify a number of retries or an amount of time to wait for a lock. The syntax for the command is

SET REPROCESS TO <*nTime*> [ SECONDS ]

[ AUTOMATIC ]

<*nTime*> indicates the number of times a lock should be retried. If you add the keyword SECONDS after the time, it indicates the number of seconds to continue to retry. The default value is 0, which causes FoxPro to retry the lock for an infinite period of time.

The SET REPROCESS setting should be very carefully considered as part of your overall locking strategy. If you employ the EDIT-LOCK-WRITE-UNLOCK cycle discussed above, then you should never try the lock more than once, because the lock is a signal that the data may have changed. Trying the lock multiple times until it is successful will cause another user's data to be overwritten.

If you employ the LOCK-EDIT-WRITE-UNLOCK cycle, then it makes sense to try the lock a few times. Thus you might use

```
SET REPROCESS TO 30 SECONDS
```

and

```
SET STATUS ON
```

so a message will appear informing the user to wait for the lock. At this point, the user will have the option of either pressing the Esc key to abort, or waiting until the other person is done before proceeding with updates.

**A dangerous combination!**   You can use a

```
SET REPROCESS TO AUTOMATIC (or -1)
```

which causes an indefinite number of retries. If SET STATUS is OFF, the lock will be continually retried without any message to the user indicating what is going on. Consider the impact of the following identical code fragments, each running on separate computers against the same customer file:

| PC 1: The CEO | PC 2: The Data Entry Clerk |
|---|---|

```
PC 1: The CEO
SET REPROCESS TO -1
SET STATUS OFF
SELECT customer
IF LOCK()
   SCATTER MEMVAR
   **
   ** Update memory
   ** variables
   **
   READ
   IF LASTKEY() <> 27
      GATHER MEMVAR
   ENDIF
   UNLOCK
ELSE
   WAIT "Nope" WINDOW
ENDIF
```

```
PC 2: The Data Entry Clerk
SET REPROCESS TO -1
SET STATUS OFF
SELECT customer
IF LOCK()
   SCATTER MEMVAR
   **
   ** Update memory
   ** variables
   **
   READ
   IF LASTKEY() <> 27
      GATHER MEMVAR
   ENDIF
   UNLOCK
ELSE
   WAIT "Nope" WINDOW
ENDIF
```

Most of the time, the foregoing code will run fine, since the LOCK is obtained. However, imagine the scenario where the data entry clerk is updating the record (and hence has it locked) and decides to go to lunch. Because there is no timeout feature, the record stays locked until the clerk returns from lunch. Meanwhile, the CEO runs the same program to add an important new contact name to the client file. Since the record cannot be locked and FoxPro is retrying it constantly, the CEO will think her computer is hung and will either reboot or call and complain about the buggy software someone has written for her. Neither prospect is pleasant!

**Implicit locks**  If an implicit FoxPro lock fails, FoxPro handles communication with the user, offering the option of continuing to wait for the lock or of pressing Esc to abort the attempt. If Esc is pressed or the lock is not available, an error message appears indicating that the record or file is in use, and the command is not performed.

**Explicit locks**  If either RLOCK( ) or FLOCK( ) is used, FoxPro assumes that the programmer is responsible for handling communication with the user and will thus not display any messages while waiting for a lock. If you are using

REPROCESS and RLOCK( ) or FLOCK( ), be sure to keep the user informed of what is going on. Never let the user think the computer is hung simply because you are waiting to lock a record!

> **Caution!**    When working with locks, and particularly the SET REPROCESS command, be sure to rigorously follow these two rules:
>
> (1) Always tell the user when you are waiting to lock a record or file and (preferably) offer the option to abort the operation.
>
> (2) NEVER, EVER allow a record to be locked indefinitely during a wait state (a command where the computer is waiting for input from the user). Be sure to use the TIMEOUT option with any command that can lock a record!

## BASIC NETWORKING COMMANDS AND FUNCTIONS

This section describes a number of other commands and functions, in addition to the global SET commands, that FoxPro has available for the network programming environment.

### FLOCK()

The FLOCK( ) function makes a single attempt (or more if the SET REPROCESS command is used) to lock the file, and returns TRUE if successful or FALSE if the lock is not granted. A failed FLOCK( ) does not generate an error condition.

The syntax for FLOCK( ) is

> *<logical>* = FLOCK( [*nWorkarea* | *cAliasName*] )

The optional parameter can be either a numeric work area or a character alias name. If the parameter is not used, the lock is attempted on the file in the current work area.

If FLOCK( ) is successful, then the current program has both read and write access to the file, while other programs only have read access for the duration of the lock. The lock can be released by issuing the UNLOCK command or by closing the table.

If FLOCK( ) cannot lock the table, it returns FALSE. It does not generate an error condition but merely continues to the next line of code.

FLOCK( ) should only be used for operations that will update a large number of records (such as REPLACE ALL). In many situations you can avoid locking the entire file by simply locking the individual records that are going to be changed. Keep in mind that if you lock the entire file, you are preventing *all* other users from updating the file until you are done.

FoxPro will perform an implicit FLOCK() for the following commands:

APPEND

APPEND FROM

DELETE  *<scope>* (if *<scope>* is more than one record)

RECALL  *<scope>* (if *<scope>* is more than one record)

REPLACE *<scope>* (if *<scope>* is more than one record)

UPDATE

As mentioned above, always carefully consider the need for FLOCK(), because some file lock operations can be replaced with multiple record locks. You might also want to consider the implications of locking a file during a report or some other process that reads the entire database. If you are running a report on an unlocked file, other users are free to change the file between the start and end of the report. If the file is updated during this time, your report could contain inaccurate information. Is the accuracy of the report worth the contention caused by locking the file?

### FLUSH

The FLUSH command instructs FoxPro to save all database and index updates to disk. This action ensures visibility of the changes to other programs and is done automatically by FoxPro when the database is closed or the file or record is unlocked.

The FLUSH command takes no parameters.

Flushing the data to disk, either explicitly using FLUSH or implicitly, guarantees that other workstations will see the changed data. Most networks, however, use disk caches to improve performance and may not physically write the data to disk. The FLUSH command should be used to instruct DOS to give the data to the network. Since the file server is generally less likely to go down and is usually protected by an uninterrupted power supply, getting the information to the server improves data integrity should the workstation go down.

The FLUSH command is not normally necessary, but does provide a way to make changes visible to other records without releasing the file or record locks.

### LOCK() and RLOCK()

The LOCK() and RLOCK() functions make a single attempt (or more if the SET REPROCESS command is used) to lock the current record. These commands return TRUE if successful or FALSE if the lock is not granted. A failed record lock will not generate an error condition.

The syntax for both RLOCK( ) and LOCK( ) is

$$<logical> = RLOCK( [nWorkarea \mid cAliasName] )$$

$$( [nRecList,nWorkArea\mid cAliasName] )$$

$<nWorkarea>$ or $<cAliasname>$ refer to the work area or alias name in which you wish to lock the record. If you do not use any parameters, FoxPro attempts to lock the current record in the current work area.

$<nRecList>$ is a character string consisting of a series of record numbers separated by commas. This parameter can only be used if MULTILOCKS is set to TRUE.

If RLOCK( ) is successful, then the current program has both read and write access to the specified records, as compared with other programs' having only read access for the duration of the lock. The lock can be released by issuing the UNLOCK command or by closing the table.

If RLOCK( ) cannot lock the records, it returns FALSE. It does not generate an error condition and merely continues to the next line of code.

FoxPro will perform an implicit RLOCK( ) for these commands:

APPEND MEMO

BROWSE

CHANGE

DELETE $<scope>$ (when $scope$ is one record)

EDIT

GATHER

MODIFY MEMO

READ $<fields>$ (when GETs are done on $fields$)

RECALL $<scope>$ (when $scope$ is one record)

REPLACE $<scope>$ (when $scope$ is one record)

SHOW GETS

## SYS(0)

The SYS(0) function returns the machine name and number when you are attached to a network. If the network has not assigned a name or if the workstation shell has not been loaded, then SYS(0) returns a string of 15 spaces followed by a pound sign, a space, and the number 0.

### SYS(3)

The SYS(3) function, useful when creating temporary files, returns a unique file name. A different file name is returned each time SYS(3) is called. You can use SYS(3) in conjunction with SYS(2023) to create temporary files in the temporary directory.

### SYS(2011)

This function returns a string that indicates the lock status of the current record or work area. It merely reports the status and does not make an attempt to lock the record. It also reports only on whether the current program has the record or file locked and does not indicate whether another program may have done so.

### SYS(2023)

This function returns the drive and path name where temporary files are stored. You can use this function when you need to create a temporary file from within your application program. For example,

```
cPath = SYS(2023)
cFile = SYS(3)
cFN   = cPath+cFile
SELECT trans
COPY STRUCTURE TO &cFN.
```

This code would copy the structure of the transaction file to the temporary drive with a temporary file name.

### UNLOCK

The UNLOCK command releases all record locks or a file lock from the current or specified work area. UNLOCK also instructs the network to update the work area buffers to disk. With this command, you can unlock all work areas or merely a single work area.

The UNLOCK syntax is

UNLOCK [ IN <*nWorkArea*> | <*cAliasName*> ]

[ ALL ]

If the optional IN and ALL clauses are not specified, the current work area is unlocked. You can unlock other work areas by specifying the IN clause and the work area name or number. The ALL keyword causes all work areas to be unlocked.

# OPTIMIZING FOXPRO TO RUN ON A NETWORK

FoxPro provides a wide variety of configuration options that can be used to fine-tune your application's performance. Some of these options are particularly important when you are running FoxPro on a network.

However, before we explain these configuration options, let us examine the differences between the types of drives that are available to the various FoxPro files.

### RAM DRIVES

A RAM drive is a temporary drive created in your workstation's random access memory. Since it is entirely in RAM, this is by far the fastest type of drive available. However, its size cannot exceed the amount of available memory on the workstation, and its contents are irrevocably lost if the workstation hangs or reboots. The RAM drive is generally good for small scratch files that FoxPro can use to boost performance.

You can create a RAM drive by adding the following line to your CONFIG-.SYS file:

```
DEVICE=C:\DOS\RAMDRIVE.SYS /e 1024
```

The /e option indicates that the RAM drive is to be created in extended memory rather than expanded or conventional memory. The /a option specifies expanded memory rather than extended. The 1024 indicates the size of the drive in kilobytes. Some versions of DOS may require slightly different syntax for this DEVICE-statement, and you may wish to consult your DOS manual to be sure.

If you have extra memory in your computer, you might want to consider a RAM drive. Be aware, however, that FoxPro takes advantage of all the memory it can find and could probably make better use of the memory than if you assigned it to a RAM drive. You might need to experiment a bit to discover a good memory mix between FoxPro and the RAM drive.

### LOCAL DRIVES

A local drive is one that is part of the workstation and therefore not available to other network users. If a data file resides on your workstation's local hard disk, then the operating system merely instructs the disk controller to transfer a portion of the file into the computer's RAM whenever a program requests the file. Since the operating system is already loaded into memory, this operation can be performed very quickly. Usually the disk drive access time is the slowest part of the operation.

The local drive is a good place for temporary files and scratch work areas—particularly if you have a fast hard drive, as do most new computers.

### NETWORK DRIVES

When files are stored on the network, the operating system has to accept the request for a file and hand it off to a network card. The network card then creates data packets to be sent along the cable to the file server. The server then finds the file on its hard disk, converts it into packets, and sends it back to the workstation. The network card in the workstation receives the packets and converts them into the data that the program requested.

All of this overhead can slow down the network drive's performance. If your network cards and cabling are good, and the server is not too busy, the network drive generally performs quite well. However, as more users access the server and network traffic increases, performance may degrade.

The network drive is generally the place for all shared files; it is the *last* place you should put any temporary files. Consider using the network drives if your local hard drive is very slow and the network traffic is not too heavy.

### CONFIGURATION OPTIONS FOR OPTIMUM PERFORMANCE

The CONFIG.FP file is used to control the FoxPro configuration options (CONFIG.FPW for FoxPro for Windows). When FoxPro starts, it will first search the FOXPRO directory (that is, the directory where the FOXPRO executable files are stored) and then the DOS path for these configuration files. You can also start FoxPro with the –C option to specify the configuration file name and path. Additionally, the DOS environment variables FOXPROCFG and FOXPROWCFG can be used to specify the name of the configuration file.

You should create a default FOXPRO configuration file and store it in the FoxPro directory. If any users need a customized configuration file, place the default file on the local disk and have users modify their AUTOEXEC.BAT file to set the appropriate environment variables.

The following configuration settings should be carefully considered to maximize FoxPro's performance.

**PROGWORK: The program cache**   The program cache is a temporary file that FoxPro creates while your program is running. FoxPro attempts to keep this file under 256,000 bytes, although the file can grow larger. This file should not be placed on the file server, or your application will spend a lot of time sending data back and forth over the network cables. The ideal location is a RAM drive, since the file is small and disk access speed is critical to performance. If a RAM drive is not available, try to put this file on the fastest possible local hard drive.

For example, the line

```
PROGWORK = D:\RAMDRIVE
```

specifies the D:\RAMDRIVE directory, which is presumably a RAM drive.

**SORTWORK: Sort and index work files**   FoxPro needs temporary disk space whenever it is indexing or sorting a database. Unfortunately, this space can easily exceed a RAM disk's size, so you should configure the sort/index work files to the fastest local drive available. The line

```
SORTWORK = C:\TEMP
```

specifies the C:\TEMP directory to hold the sort work files. Be sure there is plenty of free space, since these temporary files can grow to as much as twice the size of the original file.

**EDITWORK: Text editor work files**   This scratch area holds the files you are editing. Although this option is important for program development, it is not often used during execution of a program. Set this to one of your local drives, so that network traffic is reduced while you are editing a PROGRAM file.

**TMPFILES: Temporary files**   This option specifies where temporary files will be placed (if nothing else is specified). The PROGWORK, SORTWORK, and EDITWORK options will override this option.

# SUMMARY

In this chapter, we have covered the basic concepts necessary for using FoxPro in a network environment. We also discussed the importance of interpreting a lock as a signal, rather than as a database requirement. Finally, we looked at how to optimize your FoxPro configuration to get the best possible performance while using FoxPro on a network.

To optimize your network performance, keep two rules in mind:

▶ Don't share unless you have to!

▶ Limit your use of network files as much as possible!

FoxPro is like a greedy little child: It doesn't like to share. It will work well with shared files, but will perform substantially better when it doesn't have to.

# Designing and Working with Files and Indexes

DESIGNING DATABASES

FILE OPENING AND INTEGRITY CHECKING

# 3

FoxPro is a very powerful programming language with the ability to manipulate database (.DBF) files. It offers two improvements over other xBASE dialects: It can store memos more efficiently, and it has powerful indexing capabilities. FoxPro allows you to update your database files, change their structure, sort them, add new indexes, and so on—all without writing any code. With this power, however, comes a degree of responsibility to the programmer. Files should be designed to ensure data integrity. Your application should make sure the files are opened and indexed properly, and should be able to accommodate structure changes and old indexes.

In this chapter we will talk about how you should design your files and indexes. We will also describe functions for opening files and recovering from any problems that might occur.

## DESIGNING DATABASES

A file is a collection of records that contain information about a group of things such as customers, transactions, products, and the like. The database structure serves as the template for each record. Though it might be possible to create a file containing a field for every item of information that could ever prove necessary, taking that approach would result in many drawbacks. A much better strategy is to design multiple files that are related to each other. This group of related files is called a database, and it keeps track of both the files and their relationships.

FoxPro does not contain any functions to create databases per se, but it does contain the necessary components to create files and relate them. It is up to your program to maintain these file relationships and keep your database intact.

## DATA NORMALIZATION

*Data normalization* is a methodology used to design databases from a collected group of files and indexes. It is based upon work done in 1970 (and subsequently updated in 1990) by E.F. Codd, a theoretical mathematician. Codd described the *relational database model* with the goals of data independence and data integrity. *Data independence* means that the relational model is not dependent upon the physical format used to store the data. *Data integrity* means that the files avoid inconsistent and improper information when processing the data. (For more information, refer to Codd's article, "A Relational Model of Data for Large Shared Data Bands," published in the June 1970 issue of *Communications of ACM*.)

Codd's relational model is based upon sound mathematical theorems. By using the rules of data normalization, you can define a coherent and consistent database. Before we discuss the steps to normalize your files, however, we need to cover some basic concepts and definitions. Keep in mind that these definitions were created long before FoxPro existed, although you will clearly see that FoxPro can easily work within this framework.

**Tables** A *table* in the relational model is a series of rows and columns that contain some data that we wish to track. Each column has a name (also known as an *attribute*) and a number of possible entries (known as the *domain*). In FoxPro terms, the rows are *records,* and the columns are *fields*. The domain is determined by the data type and size. For example, a *numeric field* with a width of three can contain the numbers 0 through 999 (we will discount negative numbers for the time being). A *logical field* has only two entries in its domain, TRUE or FALSE. Each table is assigned a name (usually the file name) and consists of the list of columns (the names of the fields in a database).

**Keys** Each row in the table must be uniquely identifiable by some number of columns. If only one column is used, this is called a *simple key*. If multiple columns are needed to identify the record, then those columns form a *composite key*. Sometimes several keys (combinations of columns) are created to uniquely identify a record; however, one combination should be chosen to serve as the *primary key*. The primary key is the combination that is used to link tables together. If possible, the primary key should be a simple key value, although this is not a strict requirement.

You can also have *secondary keys,* which provide alternate ways of finding the unique record. For example, the table shown in Figure 3.1 has a simple primary key of Initials (assuming the Initials value is unique) and a composite secondary key of Last_Name and First_Name.

| Table: PEOPLE | | | | | |
|---|---|---|---|---|---|
| | **COLUMNS** | | | | |
| | **Initials** | **First_Name** | **Last_Name** | **Birthdate** | **Married?** |
| **ROWS** | JDB | Joseph | Booth | 07/05/58 | Yes |
| | BLH | Brianne | Hoffler | 12/21/79 | No |
| | JRT | Rick | Tyma | 10/03/49 | Yes |

*Primary Key:* Initials (column 1)
*Secondary Key:* Last_Name + First_Name (columns 2 and 3)

**Figure 3.1: PEOPLE table with two keys**

If a primary key cannot be found in the table, then you should create one. In the above example, we are assuming that the Initials values are unique, which will often not be the case in reality. One solution is to assign a numeric primary key each time a record is added, and use that key for all related tables. This key would never change, and your users need not know that it exists. This way, if Brianne gets married and changes her last name, the created primary key will stay the same. On the other hand, if her initials were to serve as the primary key, then all *foreign keys* (described just below) in the database would have to be checked and updated if they contained the letters BLH.

**Foreign keys**   Data normalization in the relational model depends upon the ability of tables to be related to one another. To relate tables, you include a column in one table that contains the primary key of another table; this column is referred to as a *foreign key*. For example, Figure 3.2 shows a table that contains employment information for the table in Figure 3.1.

**Integrity rules**   There are two rules that must be enforced with primary and foreign keys to ensure data integrity. *Entity integrity* means that any column that is part of the primary key must be unique and cannot be blank. *Referential integrity* requires that any foreign key must refer to an existing primary key or must be left blank. Though FoxPro does not provide built-in support to enforce these rules, the FoxPro language is powerful enough to allow you to have your program enforce them.

| TABLE: EMPLOY | | | | | |
|---|---|---|---|---|---|
| | COLUMNS | | | | |
| | **Initials** | **Company** | **Start** | **Position** | **Active** |
| **ROWS** | JDB | Ronin Corp. | 10/01/87 | Controller | No |
| | BLH | Heart Assn. | 03/04/92 | Bookkeeper | Yes |
| | JRT | PEP, Inc. | 01/02/84 | President | Yes |

*Primary Key:* Initials + Company
*Foreign Key:* Initials (relates to PEOPLE table)

**Figure 3.2: Employment table**

### NORMALIZING YOUR FILES

With understanding of the foregoing basics, you can proceed to *normalize* your files. The starting point for this process is the un-normalized file, which is a collection of the fields that the system must track. (The fields are only loosely grouped into files at this point.) The first three forms of normalization, referred to as the First, Second, and Third Normal forms, are examined next. We will also discuss the steps necessary to take the un-normalized data into the Third Normal form. (There are actually several more forms of data normalization beyond the Third Normal form, but for most applications Third Normal is a sufficient level of normalization.)

**First normal form: Eliminate recurring entries**   First Normal form is the step that eliminates recurring entries and places them into a separate table. For example, imagine a file that keeps track of the departments in which an employee has worked. Figure 3.3 shows the structure of an employee file that can be used to keep track of the information.

The structure in Figure 3.3 will work, but it has a few problems. For instance, if most employees have only worked in one department, then 70 extra bytes of storage are being wasted for each employee because the Dept_2 and Dept_3 fields will be empty. Also, this table cannot handle the owner's son-in-law, who started in the mail room and has worked in every department (all 12 of them).

To convert this file into First Normal form, you need to move the repeating fields into a separate table. You also need to add a field (the foreign key) that refers back to the employee. We will use the employee initials as our foreign key. Figure 3.4 shows the EMPLOYEE file broken into two tables.

| File Name: EMPLOYEE | | | | |
|---|---|---|---|---|
| # | Field Name | Type | Width | Description |
| 1 | Initials | Char | 3 | Employee initials (primary key) |
| 2 | Employee | Char | 25 | Full name |
| 3 | Started | Date | 8 | Date of hire |
| 4 | No_Depts | Num | 2 | Number of departments |
| 5 | Mgr_Init | Char | 3 | Manager's initials |
| 6 | Mgr_Ext | Char | 4 | Manager's telephone extension |
| 7 | Dept_1 | Char | 15 | First department worked in |
| 8 | Start_1 | Date | 8 | Date started in first dept. |
| 9 | Position_1 | Char | 12 | Job title in first department |
| 10 | Dept_2 | Char | 15 | Second department worked in |
| 11 | Start_2 | Date | 8 | Date started in second dept. |
| 12 | Position2 | Char | 12 | Job title in second dept. |
| 13 | Dept_3 | Char | 15 | Third department worked in |
| 14 | Start_3 | Date | 8 | Date started in third dept. |
| 15 | Position_3 | Char | 12 | Job title in third dept. |

**Figure 3.3: EMPLOYEE table, un-normalize**

You will also want to define a primary key for the EMP_DEPT file. The index key could be the Initials field, plus the Start field (converted from date to string with the DTOS() function). This will allow the data for each employee to be shown in chronological order.

With the first normalized form structure, less space is wasted (70 bytes are saved for most employees), yet employees who have worked in more than three departments (such as the owner's son-in-law) can easily be accommodated. The owner's son-in-law will have 12 records in the EMP_DEPT file, and most other employees will only have one.

**Note:**   Before discussing Second and Third Normal forms, we would like to point out that in some cases it is easier to query data while it is still in First Normal form.

| File Name: EMPLOYEE | | | | |
|---|---|---|---|---|
| **#** | **Field Name** | **Type** | **Width** | **Description** |
| 1 | Initials | Char | 3 | Employee's initials |
| 2 | Employee | Char | 25 | Full name |
| 3 | Started | Date | 8 | Date of hire |
| 4 | No_Depts | Num | 2 | Number of dept. worked in |
| 5 | Mgr_Init | Char | 3 | Manager's initials |
| 6 | Mgr_Ext | Char | 4 | Manager's phone extension |

| File Name: EMP_DEPT | | | | |
|---|---|---|---|---|
| **#** | **Field Name** | **Type** | **Width** | **Description** |
| 1 | Initials | Char | 3 | Employee's initials |
| 2 | Dept | Char | 15 | Department worked in |
| 3 | Start | Date | 8 | Date started in dept. |
| 4 | Position | Char | 12 | Job title in dept. |

**Figure 3.4: EMPLOYEES table in First Normal form**

## SECOND NORMAL FORM: ELIMINATE REDUNDANT DATA

Second Normal form is the step that removes redundancy from your files. The tables must already be in First Normal form before you can proceed with this step. For a database to be in Second Normal form, there should be no duplicate information except for foreign keys. Unfortunately, redundancies can hide in many places, and you should attempt to ferret them all out. Let's go back to our EMPLOYEE and EMP_DEPT files to look for redundancy.

**EMP_DEPT table** This simple file contains only four fields, yet it is possible that two of them will be redundant. Initials is a foreign key, so its redundancy is acceptable. The Start date field probably will contain the same value, but here it is unique to the individual and department, so it is not redundant. The Dept and Position fields, however, could both be redundant. If we assume that there are 13 departments and several hundred employees, it is a safe bet that department names will be repeated at least several times in this file.

To break the EMP_DEPT table into Second Normal form, you create two new tables called DEPTS and POSITION. Each file will have a primary key and the department name. The EMP_DEPT table now consists of the three FoxPro .DBF files, shown in Figure 3.5.

| \#  | Field Name | Type | Width | Description |
|-----|------------|------|-------|-------------|
| **File Name: EMP_DEPT** | | | | |
| 1 | Initials | Char | 3 | Foreign key to EMPLOYEE |
| 2 | Dept_No | Num | 3 | Foreign key to DEPTS table |
| 3 | Start | Date | 8 | Date started in department |
| 4 | Position | Char | 12 | Job title in department |

| \#  | Field Name | Type | Width | Description |
|-----|------------|------|-------|-------------|
| **File Name: DEPTS** | | | | |
| 1 | Dept_No | Num | 3 | Primary key |
| 2 | Name | Char | 15 | Department name |

| \#  | Field Name | Type | Width | Description |
|-----|------------|------|-------|-------------|
| **File Name: POSITION** | | | | |
| 1 | Pos_No | Num | 3 | Primary key |
| 2 | Job_Title | Char | 20 | Job title |

**Figure 3.5: EMP_DEPT table in Second Normal form**

This may seem like a lot of extra work and files to create, but consider the ramifications of a department name change. Under the First Normal form, you would have to replace all occurrences of the Dept field with the new department name. In a network application, this process could require locking the entire file, or updating each record individually and hoping that you will be able to lock the record to change it. If every applicable record does not get changed, your database will no longer be accurate, because some EMP_DEPT records will refer to departments that do not exist. In contrast, in Second Normal form, you need to change only the record in the DEPTS file that contains the department name, and the EMP_DEPT records will automatically be up-to-date.

**EMPLOYEE table**   At first glance it may appear that none of the fields in the new EMPLOYEE table is redundant. Yet there is a redundancy in the No_Depts field, because this value can be obtained by counting the total number of EMP_DEPT records for the employee. Although it may seem more convenient to track the number of departments in a field rather than having to calculate it each time, remember that wherever there is redundancy, there exists the possibility of a data integrity problem. If someone adds a record to the EMP_DEPT table and does not update the No_Depts field in the EMPLOYEE table, the database is no longer accurate. A common example of this type of redundancy occurs in invoice tables that have been normalized into a separate invoice table and an items table. The invoice table will often contain the total dollar value of the items ordered.

Figure 3.6 shows an example invoice table.

| File Name: INVOICE | | | | |
|---|---|---|---|---|
| **#** | **Field Name** | **Type** | **Width** | **Description** |
| 1 | Customer | Char | 8 | Foreign key to CUSTOMER |
| 2 | Invo_Numb | Num | 6 | Primary key (invoice number) |
| 3 | Total_Pric | Num | 12.2 | Total invoice value |
| 4 | Total_Cost | Num | 12.2 | Total invoice cost |

| File Name: ITEMS | | | | |
|---|---|---|---|---|
| **#** | **Field Name** | **Type** | **Width** | **Description** |
| 1 | Invo_Numb | Num | 6 | Foreign key to INVOICE |
| 2 | Item_Nbr | Num | 3 | Invoice line item |
| 3 | Cost | Num | 10.2 | Item's cost |
| 4 | Price | Num | 10.2 | Item's price |

**Figure 3.6: INVOICE table, normalized**

By putting the Total_Pric and Total_Cost fields into the INVOICE file, we have a database structure that can allow invalid information. If one program reads through the INVOICE file and sums the Total_Pric and Total_Cost fields, and another sums the Cost and Price fields from the ITEMS file, it is possible to produce reports with two different results.

Many applications will accept this redundancy to improve performance, but you should be aware of the possible data integrity problems. FoxPro is a speed demon, so the performance advantage had better be significant to justify the potential data integrity problem. If you want to allow this redundancy, then you will probably end up spending time writing a program to recalculate the fields.

**Other tables**    Check integrity among not only the related tables, but also other tables that exist. For example, our EMPLOYEE table does not contain any salary information, so presumably a PAYROLL table exists somewhere. That PAYROLL table might contain a foreign key into the EMPLOYEE table, or it might duplicate the employee name and start date fields. If it does duplicate some information, be sure to correct the tables into Second Normal form.

## THIRD NORMAL FORM: REMOVE INDEPENDENT FIELDS
Third Normal form begins with tables that are at least in Second Normal form. Third Normal moves to a separate table any data that is not descriptive of the record. For example, in the EMPLOYEE table in Second Normal form, as shown in Figure 3.7, notice the field Mgr_Ext.

| File Name: EMPLOYEE | | | | |
|---|---|---|---|---|
| # | Field Name | Type | Width | Description |
| 1 | Initials | Char | 3 | Employee's initials |
| 2 | Employee | Char | 25 | Full name |
| 3 | Started | Date | 8 | Date of hire |
| 4 | Mgr_Init | Char | 3 | Foreign key into MANAGERS |
| 5 | Mgr_Ext | Char | 4 | Manager's phone extension |

**Figure 3.7: EMPLOYEE table in Second Normal form**

The Mgr_Ext field is not related to the employee directly, but rather to the employee's manager. As such, it should be moved into the MANAGERS table. If you need to know an employee's manager's phone extension, you first find the employee and then look for his or her manager in the MANAGERS file—you get the manager's extension from the MANAGERS file, not the EMPLOYEE file.

> **Tip:** Use this simple rule of thumb: If you need two apostrophes to describe the field (as in "employee's manager's extension"), it does not belong in the table and should be moved into another table.

You may find that after you have completed Second Normal form, you do not encounter this type of redundancy. This is often the case if you are very thorough and aggressive in removing redundancy—that is, when you can often go directly from First to Third Normal form.

### DATA NORMALIZATION SUMMARY

Figure 3.8 shows the original EMPLOYEE table from Figure 3.3, and compares it with the normalized database we have defined. Check carefully to see if you can find a way to maintain the integrity rules and still produce erroneous data into the new database design.

Eventually you will find normalization to be second nature. As previously mentioned, you will often move directly from simple data into Third Normal form with little effort. The benefit of normalization is that it produces a database design that is very resistant to data corruption. Of course, your FoxPro program must then ensure that the normalization rules are enforced and the data is properly updated, but at least the data structures will withstand the onslaught of information.

## FILE OPENING AND INTEGRITY CHECKING

Once you have completed the normalization process and produced a solid database design, you should realize that each single file is only part of the overall database. When your program updates a table, it is necessary to open all the files that make up that table. If all of the files cannot be opened, then the table itself should not be updated.

FoxPro does not contain built-in integrity checks and enforcement, but you can easily program them into your application. In the remaining parts of this chapter, we will describe how to set up a program to handle all file opening and integrity checking.

### DESCRIBING THE DATABASE WITH ARRAYS

In order to have FoxPro understand the underlying database design, we need to tell FoxPro what the design is, by creating three public arrays that describe the database. These arrays are used by the opening programs to make sure all required files and indexes get opened whenever you need to update the files.

| Un-normalized EMPLOYEE File | Third Normal Form EMPLOYEE Database |
|---|---|
| **Table: EMPLOYEE**<br><br>1 Initials<br>2 Employee<br>3 Started<br>4 No_Depts<br>5 Mgr_Init<br>6 Mgr_Ext<br>7 Dept_1<br>8 Start_1<br>9 Position_1<br>10 Dept_2<br>11 Start_2<br>12 Position2<br>13 Dept_3<br>14 Start_3<br>15 Position_3 | **Table: EMPLOYEE**<br><br>1 Initials<br>2 Employee<br>3 Started<br>4 Mgr_Init<br><br>**Table: EMP_DEPT**<br>1 Initials<br>2 Dept_No<br>3 Started<br>4 Pos_No<br><br>**Table: Depts**<br>1 Dept_No<br>2 Name<br><br>**Table: Position**<br>1 Pos_No<br>2 Job_Title<br><br>**Table: Managers**<br>1 Mgr_Init<br>2 Full_Name<br>3 Extension |

**Figure 3.8: Comparison between databases**

**AFiles_: File array**    This array describes each table name (or *alias* in FoxPro terms), its actual .DBF file name, and all index files that must exist for that file. Each file is one element in the array, and the components are separated by semicolons. Figure 3.9 shows the AFiles_ array for the EMPLOYEE table discussed earlier. Note that the .DBF name can be preceded by the path name, so it is possible to access files in other directories.

**AIndex_: Index key array**    The AIndex_ array describes each index file and the key expression that is used to create it. This array is used to allow the file-opening functions to create any missing index files. Figure 3.10 shows the AIndex_ array for the EMPLOYEE table.

**ARelat_: File relations**  The ARelat_ array describes each logical table and the .DBF files that must be opened to access that table. In our example, we have only one logical table, called EMPLOYEE. To access that table, you must open five .DBF files. Figure 3.11 shows an example ARelat_ array for our EMPLOYEE table.

|  | **Alias** | **.DBF Name** | **Index File Names** |
|---|---|---|---|
| AFiles_[1] = | "EMPLOYEE; | F:\APP\EMPLOYEE ; | EMP_INIT,EMP_NAME" |
| AFiles_[2] = | "EMP_DEPT; | F:\APP\EMP_DEPT ; | EMP_LINK" |
| AFiles_[3] = | "DEPTS  ; | F:\PAY\DEPTS  ; | DEPTS" |
| AFiles_[4] = | "POSITION; | F:\PAY\POSITION ; | POSITION" |
| AFiles_[5] = | "MANAGERS; | F:\PERS\MANAGERS; | MGRS" |

**Figure 3.9: AFiles_ array**

|  | **Index** | **Expression** |
|---|---|---|
| AIndex_[1] = | "EMP_INIT; | INITIALS" |
| AIndex_[2] = | "EMP_NAME; | EMPLOYEE" |
| AIndex_[3] = | "EMP_LINK; | INITIALS+DTOS(STARTED)" |
| AIndex_[4] = | "DEPTS  ; | DEPT_NO" |
| AIndex_[5] = | "POSITION; | POS_NO" |
| AIndex_[6] = | "MGRS   ; | MGR_INIT" |

**Figure 3.10: AIndex_ array**

|  | **Logical Table** | **Required files** |
|---|---|---|
| ARelat_[1]= | "EMPLOYEE; | EMPLOYEE,EMP_DEPT,DEPTS,POSITION, MANAGERS" |

**Figure 3.11: ARelat_ array**

**Creating the arrays**    You can create a FoxPro function to define these three public arrays. This function would be called once at the beginning of the application. When you attempt to open the files using the SHARED( ) and NONSHARED( ) functions (discussed later in this chapter), these arrays are used to open the proper files.

The following program listing shows a FoxPro function called INITDB( ), which is used to create the three public arrays for the EMPLOYEE table. In this example, the table structure is hard-coded into the function. You can also create a version that will read a dictionary file to load the arrays. Our preference, however, is to make the program self-contained and thus not require any additional files to run it.

INITDB( ) would be created for any new application, to describe the file relationships for the database that you have designed once you have normalized the files.

```
**********************************************************************
*  Function:  INITDB()
*      Purpose:  Initialize database structure arrays
*       Syntax:  InitDB()
* Arguments:  <NONE>
*      Returns:  .T.
*
*       Notes:  This function is used to create two public
*               arrays that the opening programs use to make
*               sure that all necessary files are opened when
*               you need to access a table.
*
**********************************************************************

PUBLIC AFiles_[5]
PUBLIC ARelat_[1]
PUBLIC AIndex_[6]


*                 Alias        .DBF Name      Index File Names
*                 --------     ----------     ------------------
AFiles_[1]  = "EMPLOYEE; F:\APP\EMPLOYEE ; EMP_INIT,EMP_NAME"
AFiles_[2]  = "EMP_DEPT; F:\APP\EMP_DEPT ; EMP_LINK"
AFiles_[3]  = "DEPTS   ; F:\PAY\DEPTS    ; DEPTS"
AFiles_[4]  = "POSITION; F:\PAY\POSITION ; POSITION"
AFiles_[5]  = "MANAGERS; F:\PERS\MANAGERS; MGRS"
*
*                 Index        Expression
*                 -------      ----------
AIndex_[1]  = "EMP_INIT;  INITIALS"
AIndex_[2]  = "EMP_NAME;  EMPLOYEE"
```

```
AIndex_[3]  = "EMP_LINK;  INITIALS+DTOS(STARTED)"
AIndex_[4]  = "DEPTS    ;  DEPT_NO"
AIndex_[5]  = "POSITION;  POS_NO"
AIndex_[6]  = "MGRS     ;  MGR_INIT"
*
*                Logical
*                Table      Required Files
*                --------   --------------
ARelat_[1]  = "EMPLOYEE; EMPLOYEE,EMP_DEPT,DEPTS,POSITION,MANAGERS"
*
return .T.
```

### OPENING THE TABLES

After you have called INITDB( ) and created the arrays, you can open any tables that you need to use with the SHARED( ) or NONSHARED( ) functions. These functions accept a list of tables as a parameter and will attempt to open all required files. If all required files are opened, the functions return TRUE; if any files are not available, they will return FALSE. This next listing is the OPENEM.PRG procedure file, which contains the SHARED( ) and NONSHARED( ) functions. The SHARED( ) and NONSHARED( ) functions take care of opening files and creating missing or corrupt index files. These functions provide fairly robust code to make sure that all required files are opened and that all indexes are available.

```
************************************************************
*  Function: SHARED()
*   Purpose: Open a list of tables in shared mode
*    Syntax: <logical> = Shared( cTable(s) )
* Arguments: cTable  - Name of logical table(s) to open
*   Returns: .T.     - If files were opened ok
*             .F.     - If the files could not be opened
*
************************************************************
FUNCTION Shared
PARAMETERS cTab1,cTab2,cTab3,cTab4,cTab5,cTab6,cTab7,;
           cTab8,cTab9,cTab10
PRIVATE all_ok,x
DECLARE aFlist_[ PARAMETERS() ]

FOR X = 1 TO PARAMETERS()
   tmp = "CTAB"+ALLTRIM(STR(X,2))
   aFLIST_[X] = &tmp
NEXT
all_ok = OPENLIST(.F.,@AFLIST_)

return all_ok
```

```
*************************************************************
*
*  Function:  NONSHARED()
*   Purpose:  Open a list of tables in exclusive mode
*    Syntax:  <logical> = NonShared( cTable(s) )
* Arguments:  cTable  - Name of logical table(s) to open
*   Returns:  .T.     - If files were opened ok
*             .F.     - If the files could not be opened
*
*************************************************************
FUNCTION NonShared
PARAMETERS cTab1,cTab2,cTab3,cTab4,cTab5,cTab6,cTab7,;
           cTab8,cTab9,cTab10
PRIVATE all_ok,x
DECLARE aFlist_[ PARAMETERS() ]

FOR X = 1 TO PARAMETERS()
   tmp = "CTAB"+ALLTRIM(STR(X,2))
   aFLIST_[X] = &tmp
NEXT
all_ok = OPENLIST(.T.,@AFLIST_)

return all_ok
*************************************************************

FUNCTION OPENLIST
PARAMETERS isExcl,FilesToDo
PRIVATE x,y,z
PRIVATE tmp,cFile
PRIVATE all_ok
SET EXACT OFF

FOR X = 1 TO ALEN(FILESTODO)
   Y = ASCAN(ARELAT_,FILESTODO[X])   && Look for this table
   IF Y = 0                          && File name does not exist
   CLOSE DATABASES                   && in our database, so we
    RETURN .F.                       && return FALSE
   ENDIF
   tmp     = ARELAT_[Y]              && Extract the information
   Y       = AT(";",tmp)
   tmp     = SUBSTR(tmp,Y+1)+","     && Get required files
   Z       = AT(",",tmp)
   DO WHILE Z > 0
      cFile  = ALLTRIM(SUBSTR(tmp,1,Z-1)) && Extract each name
      all_ok = OPENFILE(cFile, isExcl)    && and try to open it
      IF NOT all_ok                 && File could not be opened
         CLOSE DATABASES            && so we close any open
         RETURN .F.                 && files and return FALSE
```

```
           ENDIF
           IF z < LEN(tmp)
              tmp    = SUBSTR(tmp,Z+1)
              z      = AT(",",tmp)
           ELSE
              z      = Ø
           ENDIF
        ENDDO
        IF NOT all_ok
           CLOSE DATABASES
           RETURN .F.
        ENDIF
NEXT
RETURN .T.
************************************************************
FUNCTION OpenFile
PARAMETER cFileName, is Excl
PRIVATE y,z,tmp
PRIVATE cDBFname,cIndx
PRIVATE all_ok
PRIVATE cPath
cPath  = ""
all_ok = .T.

y = ASCAN( aFiles_,cFileName )
ON ERROR DO OPENERR WITH cFilename,cDBFName
IF y > Ø
   tmp  = aFiles_[y]
   y    = AT(";",tmp)
   tmp = SUBSTR(tmp,y+1)
   y    = AT(";",tmp)
   cDBFname = SUBSTR(tmp,1,y-1)
   z        = RAT("\",cDBFname)
   if z > Ø
      cPath = substr(cDBFName,1,z)
   endif
   tmp      = alltrim(SUBSTR(tmp,y+1))+","
   IF NOT USED( cFileName )
      IF is Excl
        USE & cDBFName IN Ø ALIAS & cFileName EXCLUSIVE
      ELSE
        USE & cDBFName IN Ø ALIAS & cFileName SHARE
      ENDIF
      IF USED( cFileName )              && File was opened ok
         *
         * DEAL WITH THE INDEX FILES
         *
         SELECT &cFileName
```

```
       Z   = AT(",",tmp)
       DO WHILE Z > 0
           cIndx  = cPath+ALLTRIM(SUBSTR(tmp,1,Z-1))
           SET INDEX TO &cIndx ADDITIVE
           IF NOT all_ok
              ** RECREATE THE INDEX FILE
              zz = ASCAN(AIndex_,ALLTRIM(SUBSTR(tmp,1,Z-1)) )
              IF zz > 0
                 temp2 = aIndex_[zz]
                 zz    = AT(";",temp2)
                 temp2 = ALLTRIM(SUBSTR(temp2,zz+1))
                 INDEX ON &temp2 TO &cIndx
                 all_ok = .T.
                 SET INDEX TO &cIndx ADDITIVE
              ELSE
                 CLOSE DATABASES
                 RETURN .F.
              ENDIF
           ENDIF
           IF z < LEN(tmp)
               tmp    = ALLTRIM(SUBSTR(tmp,Z+1))
               Z      = AT(",",tmp)
            ELSE
               Z      = 0
            ENDIF
         ENDDO
         SET ORDER TO 1
      ENDIF
   ENDIF
ELSE
   RETURN .F.
ENDIF
ON ERROR
RETURN USED( cFileName )
****************************************************************
FUNCTION OPENERR
PARAMETER cAlias,cDBF
PRIVATE nError
PRIVATE cMessage
nError = ERROR()
cMsg   = MESSAGE()
DO CASE
**
** These errors handle missing or corrupt index files
**
CASE nError = 1 .or. nError = 114 .or. nError = 19
   all_ok = .F.
ENDCASE
```

```
RETURN
****************************************************************
```

The following code fragment shows how you can use SHARED() and NON-SHARED() to open your databases.

```
*  Program: Employee Update
*
INITDB()                    && Create PUBLIC arrays
SET PROCEDURE TO OpenEm     && Get the Opening functions
IF Shared( "EMPLOYEE" )     && Try to open EMPLOYEE table
   *
   * Do some update code
   *
ELSE
   WAIT "EMPLOYEE Table is not available..." WINDOW TIMEOUT 3Ø
ENDIF
```

## CHECKING DATABASE STRUCTURE WITH AFIELDS()

Once you have opened the databases needed, you must check whether the structure has been changed. If new fields have been added to the structure without your knowledge, your program probably will be able to work with the data but will not update these fields. On the other hand, if the size or data type of a field has been changed, or if a key field has been removed, then your program will undoubtedly encounter a run-time error when you attempt to use those fields.

You can use FoxPro's AFIELDS() function to check on the name, type, and size of any field within a work area. If your program is being run in an environment where people have access to the database files outside of your application, consider adding some code to check the key fields' sizes and types.

Following is a listing of a program that checks to make sure the Initials field in the EMPLOYEE file is character data and is three digits long:

```
SELECT employee
all_ok = .F.
DECLARE aStruct[1]
=AFIELDS(aStruct)
x = ASCAN(aStruct,"INITIALS")
IF x > Ø
   IF aStruct[x+1]="C" .and. aStruct[x+2]=3
      all_ok = .T.
   ENDIF
ENDIF
IF NOT all_ok
   WAIT "Somebody has changed the EMPLOYEE structure" WINDOW
```

```
    QUIT
ENDIF
```

Although this extra step might seem unnecessary, it can save you from the inevitable phone call when your program produces an error message because the newest employee decided to change the Initials field to five characters.

### HANDLING FILE-OPENING ERRORS

The error handler in the OPENEM.PRG procedure file is limited to detecting file sharing problems and missing/corrupt index files. It can easily be expanded to deal with other kinds of errors, as well. Table 3.1 lists some possible file-opening errors and the steps you might take to recover from them.

**Table 3.1: File-Opening Error Codes and Recovery Actions**

| Error Number | Possible Recovery Action |
| --- | --- |
| 6-Too many files | This generally requires modifying the CONFIG.SYS or SHELL.CFG file and increasing the number of file handles available. |
| 15-Not a DBF file | Check the file for corruption and if needed, re-create it. |
| 41-Memo file invalid | You can create an empty memo file using FoxPro's low-level functions, but be careful that you do not cause the existing memo file to be destroyed. Remember the physician's first rule: Do no harm! |
| 56-Not enough space | If this is truly a disk space problem, you cannot do much short of buying more disk space to recover. However, the Netware operating system sometimes gives this misleading message if you are trying to increase the size of a file that has no owner. |
| 1707-Missing CDX index | Re-create the production index for this database by using the INDEX ON command. |

# SUMMARY

We have covered a lot of ground in this chapter. You should now be familiar with how to use database normalization to design solid relational databases, and how to describe those databases to FoxPro. By using the SHARED( ) and NONSHARED( ) functions introduced in this chapter, you can open your tables reliably while dealing with any unexpected problems that might occur.

# Concurrency and FoxPro

CONCURRENCY

REFRESHING THE DATA

NETWORK VISIBILITY

THE BROWSE COMMAND

CHANGE/EDIT COMMAND

# Chapter 4

F oxPro provides two commands, BROWSE and EDIT, that allow you to view databases and edit their contents. The mind-boggling array of options supported by these commands allow displaying and editing your files in any way imaginable. In this chapter we will discuss the BROWSE and EDIT commands, and particularly how they operate on a network. We will also show several examples of the flexibility that these commands offer to the network programmer. First, however, we need to cover a few relevant network topics.

# Concurrency

*Concurrency* exists when several users can use the databases simultaneously. While your application is viewing the data in a browse screen, another program might be updating the very information you are browsing. This concept is essential in a network environment, but it also affects some of the design issues you must contend with when writing a program. In this section, we will discuss how to write programs while heeding concurrency issues.

## TAKING THE GREEDY APPROACH

The simplest solution to concurrency is that of utter greed: Open all the files in exclusive mode, thus preventing anyone else from using the files. This approach solves the concurrency problem by making it go away altogether—at least for your program; of course, other users might not appreciate this tactic. There are, however, times that files should be opened in exclusive mode. In Chapter 2, we discussed FoxPro commands that required exclusive use of a file. There may also be application-specific times when it makes sense to prohibit other users from any access to one or more files, as described next.

**Single-entity files**  A single-entity file is a file that contains only information about one logical unit; the entire database file is treated as a single logical unit. Spreadsheets or word processing documents are good examples. Single-entity files are not as common in database files, in which each record represents an entity in and of itself. When the single entity is being edited, it may make sense to prohibit other users from using the data.

Let's consider an example that uses a single-entity file. Imagine a file structure for tracking vehicles that are being designed. Each engineer keeps a file of drawings and designs for any vehicle in progress. This file contains detailed notes in a memo field, as well as a general field to hold object links. When the engineer runs a FoxPro program to work with this file, it is used exclusively, to improve performance and offer the maximum flexibility. A master file keeps track of all vehicles being designed by the company. This file serves as a master index to the other files. Figure 4.1 shows the database structures of the files for this single-entity database.

| File: MASTER - Index file | | | |
|---|---|---|---|
| **#** | **Name** | **Type** | **Size** |
| 1 | MAKE | Char | 15 |
| 2 | MODEL | Char | 20 |
| 3 | DET_FILE | Char | 12 |
| 4 | MANAGER | Char | 3 |

| File: DET_FILE - All information about one project | | | |
|---|---|---|---|
| **#** | **Name** | **Type** | **Size** |
| 1 | PHASE | Char | 12 |
| 2 | DESC | Memo | 10 |
| 3 | OBJNAME | General | 10 |
| 4 | START_DATE | Date | 8 |
| 5 | DUE_DATE | Date | 8 |
| 6 | COST | Numeric | 12.2 |

**Figure 4.1: Example of single-entity database**

The DET_FILE field in the MASTER file contains the name of the .DBF file that stores the make and model's design drawings. The following code example illustrates how a program might work with this file design:

```
CLEAR
USE master SHARE IN 1
PUSH KEY CLEAR
ON KEY LABEL ENTER DO DisplayProj
DEFINE WINDOW pbrowse FROM 2,10 TO 10,40  ;
      SHADOW DOUBLE
DO WHILE .T.
   BROWSE WINDOW pbrowse FIELDS project=make+" "+model ;
        NOEDIT TITLE "Project list"
   IF LASTKEY() = 27
      EXIT
   ENDIF
ENDDO
POP KEY ALL
RELEASE WINDOW pBrowse
CLOSE DATABASES


PROCEDURE DisplayProj
   ON ERROR DO InUse WITH ERROR(),MESSAGE()
   USE (master.det_file) EXCLUSIVE IN 2 ;
      ALIAS details
   IF USED(2)
      SELECT 2
      DEFINE WINDOW details FROM 12,1 TO 19,55 ;
            TITLE 'Project details'
      ACTIVATE WINDOW details
      BROWSE IN WINDOW details
      DEACTIVATE WINDOW details
   ENDIF
RETURN


PROCEDURE InUse
PARAMETER nErrNo,cErrMsg
IF nErrNo = 108 OR nErrNo = 1705
   WAIT "Project is being worked on" WINDOW
ELSE
   WAIT cErrMsg WINDOW
ENDIF
RETURN
```

In this example, the fact the file is not available for exclusive use tells the main program that the file is being used by one of the engineers.

Why is the engineer's file used exclusively? Perhaps the FoxPro program employed by the engineers was written for single-user mode, and the source code is no longer available. Or perhaps the file is considered a work file and is frequently packed, zapped, or reindexed. Whatever the reason, if the file is considered a single entity, rather than a collective series of records, it might make sense to only allow one person to use it at a time.

**Critical operations**   Another situation where exclusive use is appropriate is when a critical business operation is being performed. For instance, suppose a physical count is being taken of the inventory, and the counts will be updated from one workstation. Obviously, allowing another program to update inventory during the physical count will defeat the purpose of counting the inventory in the first place! Moreover, since the inventory count is performed to get an accurate value, reports that are run during the counting process will not be accurate.

This next listing shows code that can be used to run the inventory update program, except during the physical inventory (assuming that is the only reason for the inventory file to be used exclusively).

```
ON ERROR DO InUse WITH ERROR(),MESSAGE()
USE invent EXCLUSIVE IN 1
IF USED(1)
   SELECT 1
   REPORT FORM priclist ALL NOCONSOLE ;
        TO PRINTER
ENDIF
RETURN


PROCEDURE InUse
PARAMETER nErrNo,cErrMsg
IF nErrNo = 108 OR nErrNo = 1705
   WAIT "Physical inventory being done" WINDOW
ELSE
   WAIT cErrMsg WINDOW
ENDIF
RETURN
```

In summary, although the greedy approach is usually overkill, there may be times when it is appropriate. When you do choose to utilize it, make sure that your program, if it cannot open a file, reports to the user that some other process is currently using the file.

## LETTING OTHER USERS READ THE DATA ONLY

Instead of opting for exclusive use of a file, preventing other users from any access to the data, you can be less restrictive by using a *file lock*. A file lock prevents other users from updating the data file, although they can still read the file.

The FoxPro FLOCK( ) function is used to request a file lock. The function returns TRUE if the lock is obtained, or FALSE if it is unsuccessful. Once the lock is obtained, your program has full read-and-write access to the file; other FoxPro programs will be able to only read from it. If you want to use FLOCK( ) to restrict other concurrent users, the function should be attempted at the beginning of the program. If FLOCK( ) fails, it will be because someone else has already locked the file or one of its records. (If you retry FLOCK( ) and are successful, imagine the consternation for the other user, who will swear the file was available just a second ago!)

More often than not, you will want to use FLOCK( ) to restrict other users for a brief period of time, and not for the entire time your program is running. Consider the following example of code from an actual system. This FoxPro program produces an executive overview window, which shows the company president the status of overall operations.

```
1    USE orders IN 1 SHARE
2    SUM ALL tot_price TO tot_sales
3
4    USE lineitem IN 2 SHARE
5    SUM ALL item_cost * quantity TO tot_cost
6
7    DEFINE WINDOW overview FROM 2,10 TO 11,40 SHADOW DOUBLE
8
9    ACTIVATE WINDOW overview
10   @ 1,2 SAY "Total sales..: "
11   @ 2,2 SAY "Total cost...: "
12   @ 3,2 SAY "Gross profit.: "
13   @ 5,2 SAY "Profit margin: "
14
15   @ 1,16 SAY tot_sales            PICTURE "9,999,999.99"
16   @ 2,16 SAY tot_cost             PICTURE "9,999,999.99"
17   @ 3,16 SAY tot_sales-tot_cost   PICTURE "9,999,999.99"
18
19   profit = (tot_sales-tot_cost)
20   margin = (profit/tot_sales)*100
21
22   @ 5,21 SAY margin               PICTURE "999.99%"
23
24   IF margin < 25
25      @ 6,2 SAY "WARNING -LOW MARGIN!!!"
```

```
26   ENDIF
27
28   WAIT
29   DEACTIVATE WINDOW overview
30   RELEASE WINDOW overview
```

This code will run for the most part without any problems, but let us imagine that another user is adding a new order while the report is being run. The new order gets added to the LINEITEM file first, which is totaled and added to the ORDERS file. Here is the code fragment being performed by the user adding the order:

```
1    total_price = 0
2    USE lineitem IN 1 SHARE
3    FOR x = 1 TO ALEN(aQuantity)
4       APPEND BLANK
5       REPLACE item_cost WITH aCost[x],;
                 quantity  WITH aQuantity[x]
6       total_price = total_price + aPrice[x]
7    NEXT
8    USE orders IN 2 SHARE
9    APPEND BLANK
10   REPLACE tot_price WITH total_price
```

Since the two foregoing programs are running concurrently, the database updates can happen at any time. If the executive overview program completes lines 1–2 while the order entry program completes lines 1–7, the data in the executive overview program will be incorrect; the new sale will not be reflected in TOT_SALES but will be reflected in TOT_COST. If this is a large sale, it is very possible that the president will be concerned with the company's profit margin. Instead, the executive overview code can be written to attempt to lock both files before producing the overview screen. This will force the other program to wait for the lock, but it will also make sure the executive overview is completely accurate.

This simple example will give you sufficient reason to carefully consider the implications of allowing file updates while running reports or totals against those files.

**An important FLOCK/RLOCK caveat**   FLOCK( ) and RLOCK( ) suffer from one drawback that does not occur with files used exclusively. Other FoxPro programs will recognize the file as locked; however, other xBASE products, such as CA-Clipper, will not. To understand why this is the case, let's review exactly what takes place when FoxPro performs a file (or record) lock.

DOS 3.1 introduced a new function that could be used by programs to control shared access to files. This LOCK/UNLOCK function takes four parameters: file handle, offset, size, and a flag indicating a lock or unlock. When the lock is obtained, all access to that section of the file is denied.

But wait a minute…if all access is denied, then how can FoxPro read a locked record? The answer to this very good question is that the FoxPro designers took advantage of the fact that the LOCK does not have to be physically within the bounds of the file. When FoxPro locks a record, it computes the offset into the file by taking the size of the header, plus the record size, times the record number (minus one). It then adds 40 million hexadecimal (or 1,073,741,824) bytes to the offset, and locks the next record size bytes. It does not lock an offset within the file itself. This allows read access to the file, while coordinating write access between FoxPro programs.

The developers of CA-Clipper used a similar strategy to allow reading of locked records. Unfortunately, they chose 1 billion as the offset (instead of 40 million hex). And CA-Clipper only locks one byte, not the record size bytes. Therefore, if CA-Clipper is used to lock record 10, and FoxPro locks record 10 as well, the operating system thinks there are two locks, one at offset 1,000,000,010, and the second at another offset. The operating system sees no problem with this, and allows the FoxPro and CA-Clipper programs to lock the same record. As you can imagine, this will wreak havoc in a database that is accessed from both FoxPro and CA-Clipper.

## SHARE WITH EVERYBODY

This approach to concurrency is the most common and usually the most appropriate for use in a network environment. It also requires careful design to allow concurrent use of the file while still maintaining file integrity. When you open a file in shared mode, you are allowing other programs to have read-and-write access to the file, simultaneously with your program.

To achieve the necessary balance between concurrent data access and data integrity, you need to design a locking strategy for your application. When devising a locking plan for shared data, you should plan to use record locking as much as possible. This allows most of the file to be used by other concurrent users.

To devise your locking strategy, look at all files that the program needs to work with. You need to determine

▸ The minimal level of locking that each file requires

▸ How to resolve a failed lock

**Temporary files**    If a file is used only by the current program (for instance, a transaction file), that file should be opened in exclusive mode. For example, imagine an accounting application in which users enter batches of journal entries. When a journal entry is complete and balanced, it is posted into the master journal. Since FoxPro is so fast with exclusive files, a good solution would be to create an empty file, using the journal file's structure, and use this empty file exclusively. This will reduce contention for the actual journal file and give the users very good performance.

If you create temporary files from within your program, you can use the SYS(3) function to come up with a unique file name and the SYS(2023) function to determine the directory where temporary files will be placed. The following code fragment shows how to create a temporary file to hold the work journal:

```
USE journal SHARE IN 1
tmp = SYS(2023) + "\" + SYS(3)
COPY STRUCTURE TO &tmp.
USE &tmp. ALIAS WorkJrnl IN 2 EXCLUSIVE
```

You should never need to worry about file contention in the temporary file because your application has created it and is using it exclusively. Just remember to clean up after yourself and erase any temporary work files you create.

**Multirecord updates**    The next group of files to be considered are files in which multiple records within the same file need to be updated. You can either use FoxPro's multiple-record locking capability, or a file lock. A file lock operates faster than locking many records; however, as mentioned previously, it will also reduce concurrency for the duration of the lock. Though they are slower, multiple record locks keep most of the file available, except for the locked records.

Consider your environment carefully. What is the impact of locking the entire file, even briefly? In our work journal example, attempting to lock the file briefly to add the records from the work file is probably acceptable, since each user does not finish a batch at the same time. If you plan to use the file lock, it is more likely that you will not succeed and have to retry. So the retry option should be set to several tries. In this case, the message from the failed lock is not that *your* records have changed, but that *some* records in the file have been changed.

If you use the multirecord lock strategy, a failed lock attempt indicates that the very records you are attempting to update may have been changed. You might want to consider implementing some type of semaphore system between processes to ensure that two users are not updating the same records concurrently.

**Single-record updates**   The most frequent type of update is that of a single record. You should design your program to keep these records locked for the shortest time possible. While the only requirement is that the lock be placed before the REPLACE statements, it is often more appropriate to lock the record prior to the edit session. Keep in mind that the lock is a hands-off signal to other FoxPro programs. (The duration of the lock should be kept to a reasonable amount of edit time, using the TIMEOUT option on the READ command, in the event that the user brings up an editing screen just before leaving for a two-hour lunch meeting.)

If the lock fails when you are attempting to lock a single record, be sure to get the fresh data from the network. Do not blindly retry a failed record lock. Though FoxPro allows this behavior, it is usually an inappropriate course of action.

# REFRESHING THE DATA

*Buffering* is one of the techniques that FoxPro uses to achieve its renowned speed. Rather than access the slower disk or network drives, FoxPro transfers a number of records into the RAM memory on the workstation and displays the data from there. This approach has the benefit of speed, but it also allows the possibility of redundant data. Figure 4.2 illustrates how the buffering works.

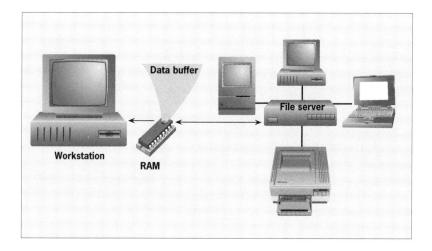

**Figure 4.2: Buffering**

Notice in Figure 4.2 that the data is now available from two spots: the workstation's RAM and the actual network drive. For display purposes, FoxPro reads the data from the workstation's RAM. For edit purposes, FoxPro retrieves the most current copy of the data from the disk.

In a network environment with shared files, plan on updating the records that are displayed on your screen. This slows performance somewhat, but it also ensures you have the most up-to-date data displayed. FoxPro will update its buffer for single records any time you attempt to lock the record or move from it to another record. Issuing a SKIP 0 command causes the current record to be reread from the network or local drive. You can also use the SET REFRESH command to automatically keep your screen display and buffers refreshed.

## THE SET REFRESH COMMAND

The SET REFRESH command is used to determine how frequently FoxPro updates its buffered copy of the data. As indicated in Chapter 2, this syntax of this command is

```
SET REFRESH TO <nWindow> [, <nBuffer> ]
```

The $<nWindow>$ parameter determines how often the browse or edit windows are updated. The $<nBuffer>$ parameter determines how often the local memory buffers are updated with network data. See Chapter 2 for more discussion of the parameters.

SET REFRESH has significant impact on network performance. If the settings are too low, FoxPro spends most of its time reading data from the network and updating the screen display. Imagine how long a book would take to read if you had to get a new copy from the library after every page! Higher settings for this command can cause misleading data to be displayed on the screen. If the screen is primarily an edit screen, where the user will select a record to work with, higher settings are acceptable because a new copy of the record will be obtained before FoxPro allows the record to be edited. FoxPro always reads the network when it is getting a record for editing.

If the screen is designed to convey information to make decisions, then the screen should be refreshed frequently. At the very least, suggest that the user press a key to get an updated view of the data. If refresh were turned off ($<nWindow>$ set to zero), a user could easily read data from an hour ago that is no longer current.

# NETWORK VISIBILITY

When you lock a record, FoxPro performs two steps. First, it attempts to lock the appropriate region of the file. If this is successful, FoxPro then reads the data from the disk and places it into a memory buffer. The lock is maintained and you can edit the memory buffer copy of the data. Since FoxPro is working on a memory copy, it is necessary to instruct FoxPro to write the information back to the network to ensure that your changes will be made visible to other users. FoxPro keeps your changes in memory until you either move to another record, unlock the current record, or close the file. Once any of these commands are performed, the changed information is sent back to the network.

You can also use the FLUSH command to force the changed data back to the network without unlocking the record or moving to another record.

Once the data is written back to the network, other programs will see the changed data. Any browse or edit windows that are displaying this data (and using the appropriate refresh options) will be updated at that time.

# THE BROWSE COMMAND

The BROWSE command is one of the most powerful commands in FoxPro's arsenal. BROWSE has global control that applies to the entire browse screen, and field level control over each column in the browse. Nearly any type of table view can be created using BROWSE. Unfortunately, since this command can display a large amount of data, it requires careful understanding of what is happening in order to optimize browses for network use.

## RECORD MOVEMENT

When a BROWSE command is executed, it operates on the current work area, displaying as many records as there are rows in the browse window. Each row causes FoxPro to read another record from the disk. FoxPro also moves the current record pointer to the last record it processes in the browse screen.

The BROWSE command supports both SET RELATION and SET SKIP while it is displaying the data.

**The SET RELATION command**   SET RELATION establishes a one-to-one relationship between the parent work area and the child work area. The specified expression indicates the field used to form the link. The syntax for SET RELATION is

```
SET RELATION TO <cExpression> INTO <cAlias | nAlias>
```

As you browse through a file, FoxPro moves the record pointers for the current work area and for any related files. In a complex system with many related tables, it is likely that several files are being moved each time a single row is updated in the BROWSE operation.

**The SET SKIP command**   SET SKIP is used to establish one-to-many relationships between already related files. When SET SKIP is active, the parent record stays positioned until all records in the child database have been read. If you are using SET SKIP, be sure to include fields from the child work area in the browse screen so that the user knows the browse is working. If SET SKIP were on and only fields from the parent were included in the BROWSE operation, the screen might easily be mistaken for a frozen screen when the program was browsing through a database with a large number of child records.

## BROWSE OPTIONS FOR NETWORK CONSIDERATION

The BROWSE command has several options that are useful when you are browsing in a network setting.

**The NOREFRESH option**   A browse screen will be refreshed as often as specified in the SET REFRESH command. If you want a stagnant browse screen, you can disable the refresh for the browse without changing the SET REFRESH command, with NOREFRESH. Specifying the NOREFRESH option substantially improves performance and should always be used when browsing a read-only file. However, even if the NOREFRESH option is used, the most current data will be read when the user chooses to edit a record.

**The TIMEOUT option**   Always use the TIMEOUT clause of a BROWSE screen! Even if you set the timeout to an hour, it is better than allowing the browse to sit and request updates from the network. Users inevitably get called away from their workstations at the most inopportune moments, and your software should recognize that. Do not allow an unattended workstation to slow down performance by constantly refreshing the display screen when no one is there to watch it.

## OPTIMIZING BROWSE PERFORMANCE

There are several steps that you can take to improve performance of a BROWSE operation. By reducing the amount of work that FoxPro needs to do on each row, we can gain tangible speed improvements when browsing network data. These steps are described in this section.

**Reduce the number of columns**    Often, BROWSE is written without the field list, which causes every field from the table to be included in the BROWSE. Only the first few fields will be displayed in the screen, although the users can move to the other fields. Generally, however, the users neither know nor care about the fields that are not displayed. By limiting the BROWSE to the minimum number of fields required, you can improve performance, because FoxPro will need to send less data to the screen.

**Reduce the number of rows**    Keep the number of rows that can be displayed on the browse screen as small as possible. The fewer rows FoxPro has to update, the faster BROWSE will complete the screen update.

**Unlink the relations**    If the data you are displaying on each browse row comes from the current file only, consider turning off your relations during the browse and manually seeking the keys when you are ready to edit a record.

For example, consider the database structures shown in Figure 4.3.

One approach to browse this structure could make use of the SET RELATION command, as follows:

```
USE employee IN 1 SHARED
USE emp_dept IN 2 SHARED
USE depts    IN 3 SHARED
USE position IN 4 SHARED
USE managers IN 5 SHARED

SELECT employee
SET RELATION TO initials INTO emp_dept
SET RELATION TO mgr_init INTO managers ADDITIVE

SELECT emp_dept
SET RELATION TO dept_no  INTO depts
SET RELATION TO pos_no   INTO position

DEFINE WINDOW eBrowse

SELECT employee
BROWSE FIELDS emp_line = initials+" "+employee+" "+; DTOC(started)+"
       "+mgr_init IN WINDOW eBrowse
```

With this approach, five tables are repositioned each time a single row is updated during the browse. Although this has the benefit of each file being properly positioned for each line of the browse, it adds considerable overhead to the browse process.

| Table: Employee-Primary Browse Table | | | |
|---|---|---|---|
| # | Name | Type | Size |
| 1 | INITIALS | Char | 3 |
| 2 | EMPLOYEE | Char | 25 |
| 3 | STARTED | Date | 8 |
| 4 | MGR_INIT | Char | 3 |

**Secondary Lookup Tables:**

| Table: EMP_DEPT | |
|---|---|
| # | Name |
| 1 | INITIALS |
| 2 | DEPT_NO |
| 3 | STARTED |
| 4 | POS_NO |

| Table: POSITION | |
|---|---|
| # | Name |
| 1 | POS_NO |
| 2 | JOB_TITLE |

| Table: DEPTS | |
|---|---|
| # | Name |
| 1 | DEPT_NO |
| 2 | NAME |

| Table: MANAGERS | |
|---|---|
| # | Name |
| 1 | MGR_INIT |
| 2 | FULL_NAME |
| 3 | EXTENSION |

**Figure 4.3: Related tables**

Instead of using the relations, you can use the ON KEY LABEL command to allow the user to press a key for more information about a record. When the key is pressed, you can than seek the related records. Since the related databases are repositioned only when the user requests the additional information, performance will be substantially better. The following code illustrates this approach.

```
USE employee IN 1 SHARED
USE emp_dept IN 2 SHARED
USE depts    IN 3 SHARED
USE position IN 4 SHARED
USE managers IN 5 SHARED


DEFINE WINDOW eBrowse
PUSH KEY CLEAR
ON KEY ENTER DO DispEmploy

SELECT employee
BROWSE FIELDS emp_line = initials+" "+employee+" "+; DTOC(started)+"
        "+mgr_init IN WINDOW eBrowse

POP KEY
*
* Establish relations after done browsing
*

SELECT employee
SET RELATION TO initials INTO emp_dept
SET RELATION TO mgr_init INTO managers ADDITIVE

SELECT emp_dept
SET RELATION TO dept_no  INTO depts
SET RELATION TO pos_no   INTO position


PROCEDURE DispEmploy

SELECT emp_dept
SEEK Employee.Initials

SELECT managers
SEEK Employee.mgr_init

SELECT depts
SEEK emp_dept.dept_no
```

```
SELECT position
SEEK emp_dept.pos_no

*
* Display employee information
*

SELECT Employee
```

**Control the refresh rate**    The higher you set the refresh rate, the better the performance of the BROWSE operation. If a browse screen has to spend all of its time updating the data displayed, obviously performance will suffer.

Consider the following two questions to determine the proper setting for SET REFRESH:

- ▶ How likely is it that the displayed fields will change?
- ▶ Does it affect the program operation if the fields change?

If the displayed fields are updated infrequently (for example, customer name and address), then you can set the refresh rate to a high number (300 seconds or more). FoxPro will give the updated customer information when the record is edited, so it is not necessary to constantly update the screen.

On the other hand, if records are selected from the browse screen based on what is displayed, then the screen should be frequently updated (at least every few seconds). For instance, imagine a screen in a credit department used to select customers to be contacted regarding past-due balances. As deposits are received and balances are changed, the screen should be carefully updated to reflect the changes. This will prevent one user from selecting (and needlessly bothering) a customer for whom a check was posted by another user just moments before.

**Physically sort the database**    FoxPro is not alone in its intelligent use of caches and buffers; most network operating systems use disk caches to boost performance. When you request a record from a .DBF file, FoxPro converts your record number into an offset in the file. It then asks the network for data from the offset for the record-size number of bytes. The network fulfills the request, but also copies the sector into its own internal cache. If the network sector size is 4,096 bytes, for example, and the record size is 64 bytes, then the sector transferred into the cache contains the current record and the next 47 records.

If you ask for the records in natural order or record number order, the network will only need to access the disk drive after every 48 records, which will substantially improve performance. When you are reading through an index file, the record numbers might be scattered throughout the file, reducing the chance that record requests can be handled directly from the cache. By sorting the database on the browse key, or by reading through the file in natural order, you can greatly increase the number of network cache hits, resulting in a great increase in performance.

# CHANGE/EDIT COMMAND

The CHANGE and EDIT commands of FoxPro use a record-oriented screen (that is, all fields are stacked vertically), rather than the table-oriented display of BROWSE. These commands, which operate identically, share many of the same features and network concerns of the BROWSE command. One important difference, however, is the lack of a NOREFRESH option. When you are changing data, the REFRESH option still works to update the screen. To disable the refresh during CHANGE or EDIT, you will have to set the refresh to 0 on the SET REFRESH command.

Whatever approach you use for displaying and editing data, keep the performance and concurrency rules in mind. They will allow you to reach a good mix between concurrent data access, performance, and data integrity.

## SUMMARY

In this chapter we have discussed the concept of concurrency, and how/when locks should be applied. We looked at how FoxPro makes changes visible to other network users. Finally, we discussed how to use the BROWSE, CHANGE, and EDIT commands on a network. In Chapter 5, we will discuss techniques for communicating between concurrent applications.

# Communicating Between Programs

Messaging

Event-driven programming

Handling messages

Using Dynamic Data Exchange (DDE)

O ne of the hottest computing trends today is *messaging:* the capacity
for programs to send and receive information ("messages") amongst
themselves. In fact, vendors of e-mail programs are scrambling to devise a standard messaging convention that will enable all e-mail packages to
peacefully coexist.

The concept of messaging can extend far beyond simple mail communication, however. You can embed commands in your messages that will cause another program to perform some action. Imagine sending a message from a
FoxPro program on one workstation to another FoxPro program elsewhere in
the network, instructing that program to change its video display mode or
print its screen. The possibilities are indeed endless.

In this chapter, we will discuss how FoxPro allows you to pass messages between processes that are under control of a main module. We will also explore
how you can implement messages on a network, and write event-driven programs so that your messaging system can be plugged in easily. Finally, we will
examine the use of DDE (Dynamic Data Exchange) when programming with
FoxPro for Windows. DDE is a powerful messaging component built into Fox-
Pro and many other Windows applications.

## MESSAGING

Programs running on workstations often need to communicate, and you can
design your FoxPro programs to use a common database file that serves as a
communications buffer. When two workstations are running such a FoxPro

application, each program can check this common file during idle time to see if any messages have been added and not yet read. If a new message is found, the program can handle the message and mark it as received, and then continue execution. How the program responds to the message is entirely up to you. If the message file contains only display messages, you can display them on the screen and wait for a keypress. You can also store commands in the message file which the program would process. As mentioned earlier, the possibilities are limited only by your imagination.

First, let's look at a simple method of passing messages using a database (.DBF) file. This can be implemented in either the DOS or Windows versions of FoxPro. If you are using FoxPro for Windows exclusively, the DDE functions can be used to expand messaging even further, to other Windows products such as Excel and Word. (See the later section, "Using Dynamic Data Exchange.")

### THE MESSAGE FILE

MESSAGES.DBF will serve as our message file. Its structure is shown in Figure 5.1.

| Field | Type | Size |
|---|---|---|
| USER_ID | Char | 12 |
| FROM_USER | Char | 12 |
| MESSAGE | Char | 60 |
| RECEIVED | Logical | 1 |

**Figure 5.1: Message file structure**

If you anticipate that the file will store a large number of messages you might want to consider keeping a production index on the USER_ID field. This will enhance performance during message lookups. The key would be as follows:

```
UPPER(user_id)+IIF(received,"Y","N")
```

This key allows one seek to determine if there are any unread messages for a user.

### RETRIEVING A MESSAGE

The GETAMSG() function is used to check for messages that have not yet been received. If one is found, it is placed into a public variable, and the record in the file is flagged as received.

The GETAMSG() function first checks whether a production index file exists. If so, it is used to accelerate message checks. If the index file does not exist, the program resorts to using the LOCATE command, instead. (The program assumes that the public variable, LASTMSG, will have been created in the main menu procedure.)

Following is the source code for the GETAMSG() function:

```
**********************************************************
*   Program:  GETAMSG.PRG
*   Authors:  Joseph D. Booth and Greg Lief
* Function:  GetaMsg()
*   Purpose:  Retrieve a message from the message file
*    Syntax:  GetaMsg()
**********************************************************

PRIVATE oldarea,cUser

SET LIBRARY TO BLNET ADDITIVE
SET PROCEDURE TO BINDERY

oldarea = SELECT()
cUser   = N_whoami()              && From Chapter 8

USE messages SHARE IN Ø          && Open the file
SELECT messages
IF SYS(22) = ""                   && No production index
   LOCATE ALL FOR UPPER(messages.user_id) = UPPER(cUser) ;
        AND NOT messages.received
ELSE
   SEEK UPPER(cUser) + "N"
ENDIF
IF FOUND()
   IF RLOCK()
      REPLACE messages.received WITH .T.
      FLUSH
      UNLOCK
      m.lastmsg = messages.message
   ENDIF
ENDIF
USE
SELECT (oldarea)
RETURN
```

### CREATING A NEW MESSAGE

The PUTAMSG() function, whose source code follows, is self-explanatory; it
puts a message into the message file for retrieval.

```
***********************************************************
*    Program:   PUTAMSG.PRG
*    Authors:   Joseph D. Booth and Greg Lief
*    Function:  PutaMsg()
*    Purpose:   Places a message into the message file
*     Syntax:   PutaMsg(cUserID,cMessage)
***********************************************************

function PutaMsg
PARAMETERS   cToUser,cMessage
PRIVATE oldarea,cUser,is_ok

SET LIBRARY TO BLNET ADDITIVE
SET PROCEDURE TO BINDERY

oldarea = SELECT()
cUser   = N_whoami()              && From Chapter 8
is_ok   = .F.

USE messages SHARE IN 0     && then open the file
SELECT messages
APPEND BLANK
REPLACE messages.user_id   WITH cToUser,;
        messages.message   WITH cMessage,;
        messages.from_user WITH cUser,;
        messages.received  WITH .F.
FLUSH
UNLOCK
is_ok = .T.
USE
SELECT (oldarea)
RETURN is_ok
```

**Note:** In the two examples just above, we retrieve the USER_ID value
through a function described in Chapter 8. This function, N_whoami(), works
with Novell's NetWare system to obtain the User ID code. Other network operating systems may have other functions available for determining the User
ID. If you are using something other than NetWare, be sure to use the function appropriate to your network operating system.

FoxPro makes it easy to communicate between two network workstations, provided they are both running FoxPro programs. Since Clipper and dBASE can both access the MESSAGES.DBF file, you can adapt the code to share messages between Clipper, FoxPro, and other xBASE-compatible applications fairly easily.

Now that we have defined the message file structure and some simple functions to access it, we will discuss how the program can check for messages and react to them. This discussion introduces *event-driven programming*.

# EVENT-DRIVEN PROGRAMMING

An *event-driven program* is one that responds to a variety of events, not just to keystrokes or mouse clicks. These events can include new messages in the MESSAGES.DBF file.

FoxPro allows you to create event-driven programs easily. To write event-driven code with FoxPro, you must first understand the various *READ* mechanisms provided in FoxPro.

### THE REGULAR READ COMMAND

The READ command instructs FoxPro to begin processing any pending @..GET commands. With linear code, you would program the READ after any series of GETs you want to edit. This next listing shows how multiple GETs and READs can be combined to work together:

```
*
*
CLEAR
PUBLIC running,lastmsg
DIMENSION aChoices(2)
PRIVATE nOption

aChoices(1) = "Customer Update"
aChoices(2) = "Employee Update"

running = .T.
lastmsg = ""
*
DO WHILE running

   @ 5,10 MENU aChoices,2 TITLE "Update menu"
   READ MENU TO nOption

   =DOMSG()                   && Call the routine to
```

```
                              && process a message
DO CASE
CASE nOption = Ø
   running = .F.
CASE nOption = 1           && Customer update
   *
   USE customer SHARE IN Ø
   DEFINE WINDOW Customer FROM 1, 1 TO 12, 40 ;
         TITLE "Customer Update"
   ACTIVATE WINDOW Customer
   @ 1,1 SAY " ID CODE: " GET cCustId
   READ
   IF LASTKEY() <> 27      && Not the Esc key
      SEEK cCustId
      IF FOUND()
         cName = customer.company
         cWho  = customer.contact
         nRec  = RECNO()
      ELSE
         cName = space(25)
         cWho  = space(25)
         nRec  = Ø
      ENDIF
      @ 2,1 SAY " COMPANY: " get cName
      @ 3,1 SAY " CONTACT: " get cWho
      READ
      IF LASTKEY() <> 27
         IF nRec = Ø
            APPEND BLANK
         ENDIF
         REPLACE customer.id_code WITH cCustId,;
                 customer.company WITH cName,;
                 customer.contact WITH cWho
         FLUSH
         UNLOCK
      ENDIF
   ENDIF
   RELEASE WINDOW Customer
   USE
   *
 CASE nOption = 2           && Employee update
    *
   USE employee SHARE IN Ø
   DEFINE WINDOW Employee FROM 1, 1 TO 12, 40 ;
         TITLE "Employee Update"
   ACTIVATE WINDOW Employee
```

```
      @ 1,1 SAY " ID CODE: " GET cEmplId
      READ
      IF LASTKEY() <> 27      && Not the Esc key
         SEEK cEmplId
         IF FOUND()
            cName = employee.name
            cSoc  = employee.soc_sec
            nRec  = RECNO()
         ELSE
            cName = space(25)
            cSoc  = space(11)
            nRec  = 0
         ENDIF
         @ 2,1 SAY "    NAME: " get cName
         @ 3,1 SAY " SOC SEC: " get cSoc  PICT "999-99-9999"
         READ
         IF LASTKEY() <> 27
            IF nRec = 0
               APPEND BLANK
            ENDIF
            REPLACE employee.id_code WITH cEmplId,;
                    employee.name    WITH cName,;
                    employee.soc_sec WITH cSoc
            FLUSH
            UNLOCK
         ENDIF
      ENDIF
      RELEASE WINDOW Customer
      USE
      *
   ENDCASE
ENDDO
CLOSE ALL
RETURN


FUNCTION DOMSG
=GETAMSG()                         && See if any messages
IF NOT EMPTY(lastmsg)              && If message was found
   WAIT m.lastmsg WINDOW TIMEOUT 600 && then display and
                                    && wait for a keypress
   lastmsg=""                      && then clear the msg
ENDIF
RETURN .T.
```

In the foregoing example the message function is called before the menu option is displayed. Once the user is inside the READ statement, the message will not be called. You could, however, include the VALID option on the READ commands to cause the message routine to be called after *every* READ statement:

```
READ VALID DoMsg
```

Since DoMsg( ) always returns TRUE (.T.), the READ will also be allowed to exit, but the message routine will be processed first.

### THE MULTIPLE GETS/READ

The *multiple GETs/READ* is a single READ command that controls multiple windows. It is a very different approach to the traditional @..GET/READ method. Each window is prepared using @..GET, but no READ command is issued immediately. When the READ command is issued, it is followed by the CYCLE option, which causes the READ to loop through the windows. Following is an example of the multiple GETS/READ at work. This code will continue to cycle between the two windows until the Esc key is pressed to terminate the READ.

```
DEFINE WINDOW Customer FROM 1, 1 TO 12, 40 ;
                TITLE "Customer Update"
ACTIVATE WINDOW Customer
@ 1,1 SAY " ID CODE: " GET cCustId
@ 2,1 SAY " COMPANY: " get cName
@ 3,1 SAY " CONTACT: " get cWho

DEFINE WINDOW Employee FROM 2, 41 TO 12, 79 ;
                TITLE "Employee Update"
ACTIVATE WINDOW Employee
@ 1,1 SAY " ID CODE: " GET cEmplId
@ 2,1 SAY "    NAME: " get cName
@ 3,1 SAY " SOC SEC: " get cSoc   PICT "999-99-9999"

READ CYCLE

CLEAR ALL
```

You can also add the ACTIVATE clause to the READ command, which allows you to specify a user-defined function to be executed between windows. As long as the function returns TRUE (.T.), you will be allowed to switch between the windows.

Following is an example of the multiple GETs/READ with the DoMSG() function. This will allow our message processing to take place each time the user moves between windows.

```
DEFINE WINDOW Customer FROM 1, 1 TO 12, 40 ; PUBLIC lastmsg
               TITLE "Customer Update"
ACTIVATE WINDOW Customer
@ 1,1 SAY " ID CODE: " GET cCustId
@ 2,1 SAY " COMPANY: " get cName
@ 3,1 SAY " CONTACT: " get cWho

DEFINE WINDOW Employee FROM 2, 41 TO 12, 79 ;
               TITLE "Employee Update"
ACTIVATE WINDOW Employee
@ 1,1 SAY " ID CODE: " GET cEmplId
@ 2,1 SAY "    NAME: " get cName
@ 3,1 SAY " SOC SEC: " get cSoc  PICT "999-99-9999"

READ CYCLE ACTIVATE DOMSG()

CLEAR ALL

    FUNCTION DOMSG
    =GETAMSG()                        && See if any messages
    IF NOT EMPTY(lastmsg)             && If message was found
       WAIT m.lastmsg WINDOW TIMEOUT 600  && then display and
                                      && wait for a keypress
       lastmsg=""                     && then clear the msg
    ENDIF
    RETURN .T.
```

# HANDLING MESSAGES

In the foregoing READ examples, the only action we took on the message was to display it in a window and wait for a keypress. However, we can have the message routine do much more than this. For example, let's assume the message consists of a command, followed by a colon, and then by a parameter. We can have our message handler recognize the following commands:

SHOW: *cMessage*    The SHOW command merely pops up a window and displays the message text. It then waits for a keypress. Once the user reads the message and presses any key, the program resumes execution at the point after the SHOW command.

| | |
|---|---|
| VAR: *variable=value* | The VAR command updates a variable with a new value. Any public variable that is part of the system can be updated through this command. For example, imagine a scenario in which the maximum credit limit is stored in a public variable called MAX_LIMIT. A supervisor who wants to allow a customer to override that limit can send a message to the workstation instructing it to change the MAX_LIMIT value. |
| PROC: *procedure name* | This command causes FoxPro to run the named procedure. If the procedure does not exist, an error message will appear. If the procedure is on disk or otherwise available to the current application, it will be executed. |
| MOUSE: ON \| OFF | This command allows the mouse to be turned on or off from another PC. |
| CLOCK: *row,column* | This command turns the clock on at the specified screen location. |

## THE DOMSG() PROGRAM

The expanded DoMSG() function in the following program implements the five options described just above. This is but a small sampling of messaging control. You can expand upon this by building keyboard macros and saving them to a file, and then allowing these macros to play back on the workstation that is receiving the message.

```
FUNCTION DOMSG
PRIVATE x,cVar,cExpr
PRIVATE cCommand,cRest

=GETAMSG()                              && See if any messages
IF NOT EMPTY(lastmsg)                   && If message was found
   x = AT(":",lastmsg)
   IF x = Ø
     WAIT m.lastmsg WINDOW TIMEOUT 6ØØ
   ELSE
     cCommand = UPPER(SUBSTR(m.lastmsg,1,x-1))
     cRest    = SUBSTR(m.lastmsg,x+1)
     DO CASE
     CASE cCommand = "SHOW"
```

```
        WAIT m.cRest WINDOW TIMEOUT 600
    CASE cCommand = "PROC"
        DO &cRest.
    CASE cCommand = "VAR"
        x     = AT("=",cRest)
        cVar  = SUBSTR(cRest,1,x-1)
        cExpr = SUBSTR(cRest,x+1)
        &cVar = &cExpr.

    CASE cCommand = "CLOCK"
        SET CLOCK TO &cRest.
        SET CLOCK ON
  *
  * Turn the mouse either ON or OFF
  *
    CASE cCommand = "MOUSE"
        IF AT("ON",UPPER(cREST)) > 0
            SET MOUSE ON
        ELSE
            SET MOUSE OFF
        ENDIF
    ENDCASE
  ENDIF
  lastmsg=""                         && then clear the msg
ENDIF
RETURN .T.
```

# Using Dynamic Data Exchange (DDE)

With the advent of Dynamic Data Exchange (DDE), FoxPro is no longer an is-
land when running under Windows, but rather an integral component in the
environment. FoxPro for Windows can control other applications by passing
messages to them, and this messaging capability greatly enhances FoxPro's
power and flexibility.

   With DDE, messages are passed between two applications. One application is
called the *server* and the other application is the *client*. Although FoxPro for Windows can act as a server, we will focus on using it as a client. A server performs
tasks at the request of the client. We could, for example, have our FoxPro for
Windows program request that Excel calculate a formula and return the results.

### CREATING A SERVER

In order to create a server process, the server program has to be running at the
same time the FoxPro for Windows program is running. You can do this either

by using the Windows Task Manager or by calling the server program from within your FoxPro for Windows application. The RUN command in FoxPro for Windows allows you to open a program under the control of the application. This program can then act as a server to the FoxPro client.

## ESTABLISHING THE CONNECTION WITH DDEINITIATE()

The DDEInitiate() function tells FoxPro to attempt to establish a link between FoxPro and the requested application. This function requires two parameters: the name of the program to link with, and a topic to send to that program. The syntax is

```
m.channel = DDEInitiate( cProgram, cTopic )
```

The *cProgram* value might be EXCEL or WINWORD (Word for Windows). Borland's Quattro Pro for Windows and Lotus Improv and 1-2-3 for Windows are other examples of programs that support DDE and can be accessed from FoxPro. The *cTopic* text can be SYSTEM, or the name of any document or spreadsheet.

> **Note:**   Consult the specific program's documentation to determine the program name and available topics.

For example, the command

```
DDEInitiate( "EXCEL", "SHEET1" )
```

requests a link to Excel and assumes that Excel has already opened the spreadsheet named SHEET1. This command

```
DDEInitiate( "WINWORD", "DOCUMENT1" )
```

creates a link to Word for Windows and opens the DOCUMENT1 file.

If the link is established, then the *m.channel* variable will contain the channel number for communication. If the link fails, the channel number will be –1. You can determine the reason for the failure by using the DDELastError() function, which returns the last DDE error encountered.

If you plan to have FoxPro open the program you wish to link to, you need to understand some additional FoxPro commands, described in the following paragraphs.

**DDESetOption()**   When you issue the DDEInitiate() function, FoxPro first verifies that the requested application is already running. If the program is not running, FoxPro will ask if it should start the program. You can disable this dialog box by turning off the DDE safety option. This is done with the DDESetOption() function. Its syntax is

DDESetOption( "SAFETY", <*logical*> )

If the <*logical*> value is TRUE, then the dialog box will appear whenever Fox-Pro cannot get a response from the server application. If the value is FALSE, FoxPro will not prompt the user with a dialog box. In this case, you would depend upon the value returned from DDEInitiate() to determine whether the link has been established.

**The RUN command**    The RUN (or !) command is used to start another program from within FoxPro. RUN searches the DOS path for the program you specify, first looking for a .PIF (Program Information File), and then an .EXE (executable) file. If FoxPro finds either one, it starts the requested program. If the program file is not found, FoxPro uses the FOXRUN.PIF file stored in the FoxPro for Windows directory. You can configure this .PIF file to the most appropriate settings for your environment.

You also need to specify the /N (or NO WAIT) option in the RUN command for the program you request. This emulates the behavior of opening the program via the Windows Program Manager. If necessary, you can then switch tasks between this new program and FoxPro.

> **Caution.**    When using the RUN /N command, the program you open becomes the active program. You will need to create the link and then instruct the running program to make FoxPro the active application. You can do this using the DDEExecute() function with the APP.ACTIVE() and the APP.MINIMIZE() commands.

**All together now**    The following example shows how to run Excel from within your FoxPro application. This code makes the assumption that EXCEL.EXE can be found within the DOS path. If this is not the case, you must include the full path name as part of the RUN command.

```
**********************************************
*    Program:  Link2Xls()
*    Authors:  Joseph Booth and Greg Lief
*
**********************************************

=DDESetOption("SAFETY",.F.)              && Prevent dialog box
m.nChan    = DDEInitiate("EXCEL","SYSTEM")  && Try to link
```

```
IF m.nChan < Ø                              && Problem occurred
   run /N C:\EXCEL\EXCEL.EXE                 && Run Excel
   m.nChan = DDEInitiate("EXCEL","SYSTEM")   && Try again
   IF m.nChan >= Ø
      =DDEExecute(m.nChan,;
         '[APP.ACTIVATE("FoxPro",1)]')        && Activate FoxPro
      =DDEExecute(m.nChan,;
         '[APP.MINIMIZE()]')                  && Minimize Excel
   ENDIF
ENDIF
RETURN m.nChan
```

## COMMUNICATION WITH THE SERVER

Once the channel has been established, you can send messages to the server process using the DDEExecute() and the DDEPoke() functions. You can retrieve information from the server using the DDERequest() function.

**Sending data to the server**   The DDEPoke() function is used to send data to the server application, which then merely writes it to the requested location. The syntax for DDEPoke() is

$$<logical> = DDEPoke( nChannel, cLocation, xData )$$

The *nChannel* parameter is the channel number that was returned from the DDEInitiate() function call. The *cLocation* is used to refer to a spot in the server's work area. (For Excel spreadsheets, you can use the Row/Column notation to indicate the cell address you want to write to.) The *xData* value represents the actual data that should be placed into the specified *cLocation*.

For example, the following program computes a median by loading the data into Excel and asking Excel to compute the median via a DDE link:

```
=DDEPoke(nChannel, "R1C1", "12750")
=DDEPoke(nChannel, "R2C1", "25000")
=DDEPoke(nChannel, "R3C1", "50000")
=DDEPoke(nChannel, "R4C1", "80000")
=DDEPoke(nChannel, "R5C1", "=Median(A1..A4)")
```

If you were to examine the SHEET1 spreadsheet after running these five lines of code, you would find the value 37,500 in cell A5. Since Excel recalculates cells automatically, the DDEPoke() function causes Excel to recalculate a new value to be written into cell Row 5, Column 1.

You can readily see that by using DDE, the entire realm of Excel functions are now available to your FoxPro for Windows program.

**Giving the server a task**    The DDEExecute() function is used to request that the server application performs some task. The task must be some function that the server knows how to perform. The syntax for DDEExecute() is:

*<logical>* = DDEExecute( *nChannel, cCommand* )

The *nChannel* is the channel number that was returned from the DDEInitiate(). The *cCommand* is the command that you are requesting the server program to execute. Valid commands vary by application.  In Excel, all command-equivalent functions can be passed via DDE.  For example, Excel's macro language includes the OPEN() function, which acts exactly like the File Open dialog in Excel. You could use OPEN() as a command to instruct Excel to open a particular spreadsheet.

Here is sample code to open a spreadsheet called PAYROLL.XLS and change the Social Security rate in cell A1 (row one, column 1). The entire process is controlled by FoxPro using DDE.

```
PRIVATE  x
PRIVATE nRate

nRate = 7.5165

x = Link2Xls()            && discussed earlier
IF x >= 0
   =DDEExecute(x,'OPEN("PAYROLL.XLS")')
   =DDEPoke(x,"R1C1",str(nRate) )
   =DDEExecute(x,'CLOSE.ALL()')

   =DDETerminate(x)
ENDIF
```

**Getting information from the server**    The DDERequest() function is used to request data from the server application. The data must be specified by item name, which might be a Bookmark in Word for Windows, or a cell address in Excel. The syntax for DDERequest() is

*<xData>* = DDERequest( *nChannel, cAddress* )

The *nChannel* is the channel number that was returned from DDEInitiate(). The *cAddress* is the location from which to get the data. The location must be understood by the server application. If the server application is Excel, use the R1C1 notation to refer to cells.

To retrieve the median that we calculated earlier in the DDEPoke() example, we would simply add the following line:

```
x = VAL( DDERequest(nChannel,"R5C1") )
```

Notice that the data is returned as character type, so we need to convert it to numeric.

### ENDING THE LINK

Once you have finished using the server application, you can terminate the DDE link. This leaves the server application still running but with no connection to your FoxPro program. The DDETerminate() function is used to terminate the link to the server application. The syntax is

$$<logical> = \text{DDETerminate}(nChannel)$$

The *nChannel* is the channel number that was returned from DDEInitiate().

### A DDE EXAMPLE

The following program shows an example of DDE at work. Suppose you have collected a database of results, and you need to compute some statistics against this database. The following program opens a DDE link to Excel, loads the data, lets Excel compute the statistics, and returns with all the credit:

```
PRIVATE  x
PRIVATE cRange
PRIVATE nAverage,nMedian,nSum,nStdDev

x = Link2Xls()            && discussed earlier
IF x >= 0
  *
  * Put the data from the stats file into Excel
  *
  USE stats
  GO TOP
  DO WHILE !EOF()
    =DDEPoke(x, "R"+alltrim(str(recno())))+"C1",;
                STR(stats.datapoint) )
    SKIP +1
  ENDDO
  *
  * Put some formulas into Excel
  *
  y      = RECCOUNT()
  cRange = "A1:A"+ALLTRIM(STR(y)) =DDEPoke(x,"R"+ALLTRIM(STR(y+1))+"C1",;
                "=AVERAGE("+cRange+")" )
```

```
        =DDEPoke(x,"R"+ALLTRIM(STR(y+2))+"C1",;
                     "=SUM("+cRange+")" ) =DDEPoke(x,"R"+ALLTRIM(STR(y+3))+"C1",;
                 "=MEDIAN("+cRange+")" )
     =DDEPoke(x,"R"+ALLTRIM(STR(y+4))+"C1",;
                 "=STDEV("+cRange+")" )
   *
   * Get the results from the spreadsheet
   *
   m.nAverage =  VAL(DDERequest(x,"R"+ALLTRIM(STR(y+1))+"C1" ))
   m.nSum     =  VAL(DDERequest(x,"R"+ALLTRIM(STR(y+2))+"C1" ))
   m.nMedian  =  VAL(DDERequest(x,"R"+ALLTRIM(STR(y+3))+"C1" ))
   m.nStdDev  =  VAL(DDERequest(x,"R"+ALLTRIM(STR(y+4))+"C1" ))
   *
   * Close the spreadsheet and terminate the link
   *
   =DDEExecute(x,'CLOSE.ALL()')
   =DDETerminate(x)
ENDIF
```

The foregoing examples have only briefly touched upon the power of DDE. All Windows applications that are DDE-aware are now available from within your FoxPro for Windows application.

## SUMMARY

Messaging is a very powerful concept that you can implement in your DOS programs with a simple .DBF structure. You can decide how to handle any message the program receives. In the Windows environment, Dynamic Data Exchange (DDE) extends the messaging concept far beyond FoxPro. With DDE you can redirect tasks from your FoxPro application to the most appropriate Windows program, and let FoxPro collect the results.

# Transaction Processing

An example of transaction
  processing

Handling possible problems in
  transaction processing

Transaction processing and Netware

# Chapter 6

A FoxPro database system may contain any number of "logical views" that represent the various entities that the system is modeling. A logical view represents the user's view of the file. The .DBF files are the physical representation of that logical view. Depending upon the application, any number of physical .DBF files and relations among them might be required to represent one logical view.

In order to maintain data integrity in the logical views, it is necessary to treat each update to the physical files as a single unit, rather than a series of separate updates. This concept is known as *transaction processing,* and it is an important part of any database system. In this chapter, we will cover transaction processing and the appropriate format for FoxPro code to properly handle database transactions.

## AN EXAMPLE OF TRANSACTION PROCESSING

Let's imagine a logical view called CUSTOMER. It contains name and address information, an account balance, a series of charges and payments, and the amount of commission paid to the salesperson who obtained the order.

We have normalized CUSTOMER into three separate .DBF files. (See Chapter 3 for a discussion of data normalization.) One of the drawbacks of data normalization is that it often requires more than one file to represent a logical entity. While this drawback is certainly no reason not to normalize your files, it poses a slight difficulty when programming on a network.

The physical .DBF files to represent the logical CUSTOMER view are shown in Figure 6.1.

| File: CUSTOMER | | | |
|---|---|---|---|
| # | Name | Type | Size |
| 1 | ID_CODE | Char | 8 |
| 2 | COMPANY | Char | 30 |
| 3 | ADDRESS | Char | 35 |
| 4 | CITY | Char | 20 |
| 5 | STATE | Char | 2 |
| 6 | ZIP | Char | 10 |
| 7 | PHONE | Char | 14 |
| 8 | BALANCE | Num | 12.2 |
| 9 | REP | Char | 3 |
| File: TRANS | | | |
| # | Name | Type | Size |
| 1 | ID_CODE | Char | 8 |
| 2 | TYPE | Char | 3 |
| 3 | AMOUNT | Num | 11.2 |
| 4 | TRANS_DATE | Date | 8 |
| File: COMMIS | | | |
| # | Name | Type | Size |
| 1 | ID_CODE | Char | 8 |
| 2 | SALESPER | Char | 3 |
| 3 | AMT_DUE | Num | 11.2 |

**Figure 6.1: The .DBF files for the CUSTOMER logical file**

In order to record a sale properly, you need to update all three .DBF files, not just one file. If for some reason (such as a failed record lock) you cannot update one of the files, then you really don't want to apply the other updates. This requires an "all-or-none" approach that can require some tedious code. For example, the code in Listing 6.1 shows three files being updated, one at a time.

**Listing 6.1: Recording the sale in three separate file writes**

```
SELECT customer
IF RLOCK()
   REPLACE customer.balance WITH customer.balance +nAmount
ENDIF

SELECT trans
APPEND BLANK
IF RLOCK()
   REPLACE trans.amount      WITH nAmount,;
           trans.id_code     WITH customer.id_code,;
           trans.type        WITH "CHG",;
           trans.trans_date  WITH date()
ENDIF

SELECT commis
IF RLOCK()
   REPLACE commis.amt_due   WITH ;
           commis.amt_due + (nAmount * .06 )
   REPLACE commis.salesper  WITH customer.rep,;
           commis.id_code   WITH customer.id_code
ENDIF
UNLOCK ALL
```

This code will work in FoxPro, but it can produce erroneous data. If the record lock fails on the TRANS file, then the total amount of transactions will not agree with the customer balance nor the amount of commission due. Thus it is important in this type of an application to view the database updates *as a unit* rather than three separate file-writes. A modified version of the foregoing code is shown in Listing 6.2.

**Listing 6.2: Recording the sale as a single transaction**

```
SELECT trans
APPEND BLANK
all_locked = rlock( "CUSTOMER" ) .AND. ;
             rlock( "TRANS" )  .AND. ;
             rlock( "COMMIS" )
IF all_locked
   REPLACE customer.balance  WITH customer.balance +nAmount

   REPLACE trans.amount      WITH nAmount,;
           trans.id_code     WITH customer.id_code,;
```

**Listing 6.2: Recording the sale as a single transaction (Continued)**

```
            trans.type         WITH "CHG",;
            trans.trans_date   WITH date()

   REPLACE commis.amt_due      WITH ;
            commis.amt_due + (nAmount * .06 )
   REPLACE commis.Salesper     WITH customer.rep
ELSE
   WAIT "Couldn't record the sale..." WINDOW
ENDIF
UNLOCK ALL
```

In this second example, the three locks are attempted at the beginning of the database update. If all three locks are obtained, then the files are updated. If any lock is not obtained, then the error message is displayed.

This is an example of simple transaction processing, and represents the bare-minimum level of protection you should use when designing FoxPro network systems.

# HANDLING POSSIBLE PROBLEMS IN TRANSACTION PROCESSING

In our unit-based transaction processing code example, we assume that the only possible problem is a failed record lock. This would certainly be the most likely problem, but it is not the only difficulty that can occur. The workstation might freeze up between the database updates, or the server might go down. The user might turn off the PC, thinking it is not working...the list goes on and on.

## ROLLBACK PROCESSING

In order to handle any potential problems, you need to incorporate the concept of *rollback*. A rollback (also referred to as a *backout*) is the process of reverting the files back to their original state if the transaction does not complete.

Although FoxPro does not contain any provision to automatically perform rollbacks, it is possible to design your own rollback system. Such a system will slow down performance, but will also increase data integrity in the event of a hardware or software failure.

**Recording the transaction processing snapshot**    In order to perform a rollback, we need to take a "snapshot" of the files as they are before the transaction, and save the snapshot. If the transaction completes, then the snapshot can be erased. If any problem occurs, then the snapshot will still be on the disk. The next time the program is run, it will detect the snapshot and perform the rollback.

Here is the basic sequence of transaction processing:

```
BEGIN TRANSACTION
      Take a snapshot of databases
      Write snapshot to disk

      Lock required records
      Update the databases

      Erase the snapshot file
END TRANSACTION
```

With this sequence of events, the snapshot is written first. If the computer fails during the locking or update process, the snapshot file will still exist when the program restarts. If the computer completes the updates, it will then delete the snapshot file, so rollback is no longer possible nor necessary.

**Using log files**   There are two approaches you can employ to create database snapshots for recovery purposes. If your data can be recalculated easily, as in our single-unit example, then you only need to record the name of the customer. If the transaction fails, the name of the customer is stored in the *transaction log file.* When the system starts up, it checks the log file to see if there are any incomplete transactions. If any are detected, the appropriate code to recalculate the CUSTOMER file is performed.

Figure 6.2 shows the structure of the log file we can use to take the snapshot.

| File: LOG_FILE | | | |
|---|---|---|---|
| # | Name | Type | Size |
| 1 | ID_CODE | Char | 8 |
| 2 | ST_DATE | Date | 8 |
| 3 | ST_TIME | Char | 8 |
| 4 | END_DATE | Date | 8 |
| 5 | END_TIME | Char | 8 |
| 6 | COMPLETED | Logical | 1 |

**Figure 6.2: Log file structure**

Each time an update is performed, a record is added to the log file. The starting date and time of the update are recorded, along with the customer ID_CODE. When the transaction completes, the ending date and time are recorded and the completed flag is set to TRUE.

Listing 6.3 shows a transaction-based version of the database update code from Listing 6.2.

**Listing 6.3: Recording the sale with transaction processing**

```
SELECT trans
APPEND BLANK

all_locked = rlock( "CUSTOMER" ) .AND. ;
             rlock( "TRANS" ) .AND. ;
             rlock( "COMMIS" )
IF all_locked
   *
   * Begin the transaction
   *
   SELECT log_file
   APPEND BLANK
   REPLACE log_file.id_code WITH customer.id_code,;
           log_file.st_date WITH DATE(),;
           log_file.st_time WITH TIME()
   nWhere = RECNO()
   *
   * Update the files
   *
   REPLACE customer.balance  WITH customer.balance +nAmount

   REPLACE trans.amount      WITH nAmount,;
           trans.id_code     WITH customer.id_code,;
           trans.type        WITH "CHG",;
           trans.trans_date  WITH date()

   REPLACE commis.amt_due    WITH ;
           commis.amt_due + (nAmount * .06 )
   REPLACE commis.Salesper   WITH customer.rep,;
           commis.id_code    WITH customer.id_code
   SELECT log_file
   GOTO nWhere
   REPLACE log_file.completed  WITH .T.,;
           log_file.end_date   WITH DATE(),;
           log_file.end_time   WITH TIME()
```

**Listing 6.3: Recording the sale with transaction processing (Continued)**

```
ELSE
   WAIT "Couldn't record the sale..." WINDOW
ENDIF
UNLOCK ALL
```

The snapshot file may seem like extra work, but let's consider what happens now when the application starts up. Listing 6.4 shows the code that is performed each time the program starts.

**Listing 6.4: Recovering from incomplete transactions**

```
USE log_file EXCLUSIVE IN 1
LOCATE ALL FOR .NOT. completed
DO WHILE .NOT. EOF()
   DO FixBalance WITH log_file.id_code
   SELECT log_file
   DELETE
   CONTINUE
ENDDO
SELECT log_file
PACK
USE

*
* Start the main program
*

PROCEDURE FixBalance
PARAMETERS cust_id
PRIVATE nAmount
nAmount = 0
USE customer EXCLUSIVE IN 2
SEEK cust_id
USE trans    EXCLUSIVE IN 3
SEEK cust_id
DO WHILE .NOT. EOF() .AND. trans.id_code = cust_id
   IF trans.type = "CHG"
      nAmount = nAmount + trans.amount
   ELSE
      nAmount = nAmount - trans.amount
   ENDIF
   SKIP +1
ENDDO
```

**Listing 6.4: Recovering from incomplete transactions (Continued)**

```
REPLACE customer.balance WITH nAmount
USE commis EXCLUSIVE IN 4
SEEK cust_id
IF EOF()
   APPEND BLANK
   REPLACE commis.amt_due   WITH nAmount*.06 ,;
           commis.salesper  WITH customer.rep,;
           commis.id_code   WITH customer.id_code
ELSE
   REPLACE commis.amt_due   WITH nAmount*.06
ENDIF
USE
SELECT trans
USE
SELECT customer
USE
RETURN
```

The code in Listing 6.4 makes several assumptions— for example, that production indexes exist for the databases, and that the log file will remain small (hence our use of LOCATE rather than a SEEK). It does, however, illustrate how your program can detect incomplete transactions and automatically correct any invalid information that is recorded from them.

**Using snapshot files**   While the log file concept allows us to recover our data, it operates on the assumption that it is a relatively simple task to correct erroneous values and recover from transaction failures. In many systems, this may be the case, and the log file offers good performance while still providing recovery capabilities. On the other hand, there are times when you need a more robust approach.

A *snapshot file* is an image of the physical databases before the updates are made. In our example of the logical CUSTOMER file, we could create the snapshot file shown in Figure 6.3.

This file contains the unique fields from the CUSTOMER file and the COMMISSION file. It also contains a numeric field to hold the record number of the added transaction record. Before the transaction is written, a record is appended and the current values are written into the snapshot file. This allows recovery in the event of some problem. The code in Listing 6.5 illustrates this approach to rollback processing.

| File: Snapshot | | | |
|---|---|---|---|
| # | Name | Type | Size |
| 1 | ID_CODE | Char | 8 |
| 2 | COMPANY | Char | 30 |
| 3 | ADDRESS | Char | 35 |
| 4 | CITY | Char | 20 |
| 5 | STATE | Char | 2 |
| 6 | ZIP | Char | 10 |
| 7 | PHONE | Char | 14 |
| 8 | BALANCE | Num | 12.2 |
| 9 | REP | Char | 3 |
| 10 | TRANS_REC | Num | 6 |
| 11 | AMT_DUE | Num | 11.2 |

**Figure 6.3: Snapshot file**

**Listing 6.5: Rollback processing (1)**

```
SELECT trans
APPEND BLANK
SELECT Snapshot
APPEND BLANK

all_locked = rlock( "CUSTOMER" ) .AND. ;
             rlock( "TRANS" )   .AND. ;
             rlock ("SNAPSHOT") .AND. ;
             rlock( "COMMIS" )
IF all_locked
   *
   * Begin the transaction
   *
   SELECT snapshot
   APPEND BLANK
   REPLACE snapshot.id_code   WITH customer.id_code,;
           snapshot.balance   WITH customer.balance,;
           snapshot.trans_rec WITH recno("TRANS"),;
           snapshot.amt_due   WITH commis.amt_due,;
           snapshot.company   WITH customer.company,;
```

**Listing 6.5: Rollback processing (1) (Continued)**

```
         snapshot.address    WITH customer.address,;
         snapshot.city       WITH customer.city,;
         snapshot.state      WITH customer.state,;
         snapshot.zip        WITH customer.zip,;
         snapshot.phone      WITH customer.phone,;
         snapshot.rep        WITH customer.rep

  nWhere = RECNO()
  *
  * Update the files
  *
  REPLACE customer.balance  WITH customer.balance +nAmount

  REPLACE trans.amount      WITH nAmount,;
          trans.id_code     WITH customer.id_code,;
          trans.type        WITH "CHG",;
          trans.trans_date  WITH date()

  REPLACE commis.amt_due    WITH ;
          commis.amt_due + (nAmount * .06 )

  REPLACE commis.Salesper   WITH customer.rep,;
          commis.id_code    WITH customer.id_code

  UNLOCK ALL

  SELECT snapshot
  GOTO nWhere
  DELETE
ELSE
  WAIT "Couldn't record the sale..." WINDOW
ENDIF
```

Although this process will slow down the performance of the update operation, it will allow you to recover if the server or the workstation goes down
during the process. The code in Listing 6.6 looks for any snapshot files and
rolls the database back using the information from these files.

**Listing 6.6: Rollback processing (2)**

```
USE snapshot EXCLUSIVE IN 1
DO WHILE .NOT. EOF()
  DO RollBack
```

**Listing 6.6: Rollback processing (2) (Continued)**

```
   SELECT snapshot
   DELETE
   CONTINUE
ENDDO
SELECT snapshot
PACK
USE


*
* Start the main program
*

PROCEDURE RollBack
PRIVATE nWhere
nWhere = snapshot.trans_rec
USE customer EXCLUSIVE IN 2
SEEK cust_id
IF FOUND()
   REPLACE   customer.id_code    WITH snapshot.id_code,;
             customer.balance    WITH snapshot.balance,;
             customer.company    WITH snapshot.company,;
             customer.address    WITH snapshot.address,;
             customer.city       WITH snapshot.city,;
             customer.state      WITH snapshot.state,;
             customer.zip        WITH snapshot.zip,;
             customer.phone      WITH snapshot.phone,;
             customer.rep        WITH snapshot.rep
ENDIF
USE

USE trans     EXCLUSIVE IN 3
IF nWhere <= RECNO() .AND. nWhere > 0
   GOTO nWhere
   DELETE
   PACK
ENDIF
USE
USE commis EXCLUSIVE IN 4
SEEK cust_id
IF FOUND()
   REPLACE commis.amt_due    WITH snapshot.amt_due
ENDIF
USE
RETURN
```

The snapshot files can be assigned unique names and placed in a common directory. The start-up process should read through all of the files in the directory and roll back any appropriate information. You also might want to consider designing a system utility program that the administrator can run to perform the rollback process manually.

Performance will be affected by the snapshot or log file, but you should weigh that against the issue of data integrity. If your files are inaccurate, people will very quickly lose trust in the system.

## TRANSACTION PROCESSING AND NETWARE

If you are using FoxPro on a Novell network, you can take advantage of Netware's built-in *transaction tracking system* (or TTS for short). TTS provides transaction tracking and rollback processing for Netware applications. These functions can be accessed through the Netware API (which is discussed in more detail in Chapter 7). FoxPro 2.5 includes a file called NETWARE.PLB that contains a number of functions that can be used to access Netware's TTS API directly from within your FoxPro application.

> **Note:** The functions in NETWARE.PLB are not documented in the FoxPro manuals and are not considered part of the base language. In addition, there is no corresponding NETWARE.FLL file for FoxPro for Windows. NET-WARE.PLB might not appear in future releases of FoxPro.

### USING NETWARE.PLB

In order to use NETWARE.PLB, make sure it is in the FoxPro directory or path. Include the following line of code in the top of your program file:

```
SET LIBRARY TO NETWARE ADDITIVE
```

This will allow you to access the five TTS functions from within your FoxPro application. Keep in mind there is no NETWARE.FLL if you are writing a Fox-Pro for Windows application.

**TSSAVAIL()** The TTSAVAIL() function checks to see if transaction tracking is installed and available on the server. The syntax for TTSAVAIL() is

$<numeric>$ = TTSAVAIL()

This function returns the number 1 if transaction tracking is available. If TTS is not available, the function returns either a zero (indicating TTS is not available) or a 253 (TTS is installed but is currently disabled). TTS can be disabled explicitly by typing **DISABLE TRANSACTIONS** at the file console or it can be automatically disabled when the backout volume gets full.

**TTSATTRIB()**   Any transaction files used with TTS must be flagged as transactional. This can be done from the command line using Netware's FLAG command. You can also use the TTSATTRIB() function to flag the files from within FoxPro. The syntax for TTSATTRIB() is

<numeric>  = TTSATTRIB( <cFileName>,<logical> )

The <cFilename> is the name of the file to flag. You must include the file name extension—.DBF, .FPT, .CDX, and the like. All files within a transaction group must be marked as transactional.

The <logical> parameter indicates whether the file should be marked as transactional (parameter is TRUE) or not (the parameter is FALSE).

TTSATTRIB() will return zero to indicate that the file has been flagged as requested. If the function returns a nonzero value, the file was not changed. If the file is currently being used or if the user does not have sufficient rights (directory rights) to the file, then the file attribute will not be changed.

**BEGINTRAN()**   The BEGINTRAN() function instructs TTS to start an explicit transaction. Once you start, all changes are recorded so that a rollback can be performed if need be. In addition, all locks made by FoxPro are kept for the duration of the transaction, until either COMMIT() or RLLBACK() is issued.

The following code shows how to structure a series of updates to use Netware's TTS system:

```
=BEGINTRAN()           && Tell TTS to begin

SELECT trans
APPEND BLANK
all_locked = rlock( "CUSTOMER" ) .AND. ;
            rlock( "TRANS" )  .AND. ;
            rlock( "COMMIS" )
IF all_locked
   REPLACE customer.balance  WITH customer.balance +nAmount

   REPLACE trans.amount      WITH nAmount,;
           trans.id_code     WITH customer.id_code,;
           trans.type        WITH "CHG",;
           trans.trans_date  WITH date()

   REPLACE commis.amt_due    WITH ;
```

```
            commis.amt_due + (nAmount * .06 )
   REPLACE commis.Salesper   WITH customer.rep

   UNLOCK ALL
   =COMMIT()                 && Tell TTS to commit the changes

ELSE

   WAIT "Couldn't record the sale..." WINDOW
   UNLOCK ALL
   =RLLBACK()                && Tell TTS to roll things back

ENDIF
```

Keep in mind that FoxPro keeps a very tight lock on the records during the TTS transaction. If another user attempts to lock one of the records involved in another TTS transaction, that user will have to wait until the other transaction is completed. This can cause some confusion because the user is forced to wait until the TTS completes. With other record locks, the retry option lets the user know what is happening, and offers the option to abort.

**COMMIT()**   COMMIT() instructs TTS to write the changes to the disk files. In addition, the TTS rollback file is updated to indicate that the transaction has completed and rollback is no longer needed. The syntax for COMMIT() is

   *<numeric>* = COMMIT()

The return value for COMMIT() will normally be zero, indicating the transaction was committed; however, it can contain an error number if a problem occurs. Possible error codes are

255   There is no BEGINTRAN() transaction started...

254   Not all records in the transaction group have been unlocked.

253   TTS is not active...

Be sure to unlock all records in the group of transactions before you issue the COMMIT; TTS will not automatically release any record locks.

**RLLBACK()**   RLLBACK() instructs TTS to discard the changes and to roll back the original files. The syntax for RLLBACK() is

   *<numeric>* = RLLBACK()

The return value of RLLBACK( ) will normally be zero, indicating the transaction was rolled back; however, it can contain an error number if a problem occurs. Possible error codes are

255    There is no BEGINTRAN( ) transaction started…

254    Not all records in the transaction group have been unlocked.

253    TTS is not active…

### GUIDELINES FOR USING TTS ON NETWARE

In order to use Netware's TTS system, you must keep the following rules in mind:

▶ **Flag ALL files.** Be sure all files are marked as transactional, including the .DBF file, the .FPT memo file, and any .IDX or .CDX index files. If you were to flag the .DBF file as transactional but not the memo file, you could easily end up with a memo field change that does not reflect the actual record in the .DBF.

▶ **Enable TTS from the file server.** The calls to TTS will work even when transaction tracking is disabled. This allows you to safely code the transaction calls into the program and not be dependent upon TTS's availability. The downside is that you might assume that all transactions can be rolled back when in fact they cannot. TTS is enabled and disabled by the ENABLE TRANSACTIONS and DISABLE TRANSACTIONS commands at the file console.

▶ **Keep transactions small.** Try to make the amount of time and code between BEGINTRAN( ) and COMMIT( ) or RLLBACK( ) as small as possible. Do not allow any wait state commands, such as READ or WAIT, in the middle of a transaction. Keep in mind the tight locking that is done by TTS, and the unavailability of these locked files to other processes.

▶ **Make sure TTS is carefully installed.** While TTS is a reliable system, it adds an extra degree of complexity to both the workstation and the server. If you are going to rely on TTS to track transactions, take the time to install it correctly, and monitor its performance often.

## Summary

In this chapter we've explained transaction processing and how it can be implemented in FoxPro. We've also described how FoxPro can be made to access Netware's transaction tracking system using the NETWARE.PLB file. Finally, we outlined the steps necessary to get TTS installed on a Netware file system.

# Establishing a Network Library

DOS INTERRUPTS

NOVELL APPLICATION PROGRAM
   INTERFACES (APIs)

USING THE FP_INT86() FUNCTION TO
   ACCESS DOS INTERRUPTS

NETWARE(): A FUNCTION TO CALL
   NOVELL'S API

THE XLATE PROGRAM: CONVERTING
   DATA BETWEEN NETWARE AND FOXPRO

USING CONVERSION FUNCTIONS IN YOUR
   PROGRAMS

# Chapter 7

Although FoxPro provides a robust set of commands and functions for writing network applications, there are a host of other network services just waiting to be tapped. In this chapter we will discuss DOS interrupts and how to access network services through them. We will also provide the code necessary to allow FoxPro to communicate directly with one of the most popular network operating systems, Novell's NetWare.

The material discussed in this chapter is very technical in nature. If you simply want to use the FoxPro functions to access NetWare, you can skip this chapter. If you want to learn more about how NetWare and FoxPro can communicate, however, then give this chapter a careful reading.

## DOS INTERRUPTS

DOS provides many services that the programmer can access. These services, called *interrupts*, can tell you what program is running, the date and time stamp of any file, and many other useful bits of information. Unfortunately, FoxPro does not provide an easy way of accessing this information, and DOS is not exactly user friendly to the average FoxPro programmer. In order to access these services, then, you have to know how DOS operates. Much as FoxPro provides functions to which are passed parameters and return values, DOS services, too, take parameters and return values.

DOS communicates through its CPU *registers*. There are 10 registers that are used by DOS, each containing 16 bits of data. The 16 bits, or 2 characters, can be used as a whole or as two halves. For example, register 1 is called AX. It can be used as is or divided into a high and low portion, which are called AH and AL respectively. These registers are used to pass and retrieve information to and from DOS.

> **Warning!** Do not experiment with interrupts, or you might accidentally erase or destroy your hard disk!!

### REQUESTING A DOS SERVICE

To request a DOS service (that is, execute an interrupt), you follow these general steps:

**1** Load the appropriate registers.

**2** Execute the desired interrupt.

**3** Read the values you need from the registers.

For example, to determine whether SHARE.EXE has been installed, we can set register AX to 1000h (4096 decimal), execute interrupt 2Fh or 47 decimal, and look in AL to see the return value. If AL contains FFh (255 decimal), SHARE is installed; if AL contains a zero, then SHARE has not been installed.

# NOVELL APPLICATION PROGRAM INTERFACES (APIs)

Novell, Inc., publisher of NetWare, actively encourages developers to write applications that communicate with the network. To assist the developer, Novell has released a set of APIs that give programmers access to almost all information available with the operating system. In this book, we will use many of the functions available through this API set.

The API set is divided into a number of sections. Here are some of the common API groups of services:

Accounting

Apple File Talk

Bindery

Communication

Connection and workstation

Diagnostics

Directory

File

Messaging

Printing

Queue

Synchronization

Transaction tracking

# Using the FP_INT86() function to access DOS interrupts

All NetWare APIs are available through the DOS interrupt system. In order to access any of Novell's API functions, we need a function that allows FoxPro to directly call a DOS interrupt. This book uses a function called FP_INT86() to handle the communication with DOS.

FP_INT86() uses an array in the place of the CPU registers. To use FP_INT86(), you must first create an array that contains ten elements. You then initialize the registers by writing to the appropriate array element. Once the array is initialized, you then call the FP_INT86() function, passing to it the interrupt you wish to execute and the array of registers. If the function returns TRUE (.T.), the array will be updated to reflect the changed parameters.

As an example, let's use FP_INT86() to determine if a network shell is loaded. The following listing contains the function N_WHATNET(), which returns the letter N if NetWare is loaded, or L if the LANtastic network is loaded. If neither network is loaded, the function returns an empty string.

```
************************************************************
*   Program:   N_WhatNet()                               *
*   Authors:   Joseph D. Booth and Greg Lief             *
*   Purpose:   A function to determine which network, if *
*              any, is loaded.                           *
************************************************************
#define   AX    1
#define   SI    5
#define   DI    6
#define   DS    8
#define   ES    9

function N_WhatNet()
PRIVATE cReturn,nReturn
DIMENSION aRegs[10]
```

```
cReturn = ''
nReturn = 0
**
** First, lets check Novell's Netware
**
aRegs[ AX ] = 227 * 256              && Set AH to nService
aRegs[ DS ] = CHR(1)+CHR(0)+CHR(70)  && Request packet
aRegs[ SI ] = .T.
aRegs[ ES ] = SPACE(5)               && Send packet
aRegs[ DI ] = .F.

IF FP_INT86( 33, @aRegs )            && Call DOS interrupt
   nReturn =  aRegs[AX] % 256        && Extract low byte
   IF nReturn = 0
      cReturn = "N"
   ENDIF
ENDIF
IF EMPTY(cReturn)
   **
   ** Now we can check for Lantastic
   **
   aRegs[ AX ] = 47104
   IF FP_INT86( 47, @aRegs )
      IF (aRegs[AX] % 256) <> 0      && Extract low byte
         cReturn = "L"
      ENDIF
   ENDIF
ENDIF
RETURN cReturn
```

# NETWARE(): A FUNCTION TO CALL NOVELL'S API

Novell's NetWare API works with *packets*. A packet is a string that contains various information that the function call requires. There are two packets needed: Request and Reply. The two first bytes of both these packets contain the packet size. The remaining bytes and the packet size will vary, depending upon which function in the API you are calling.

Using FP_INT86() to handle the actual DOS call, you can write a general-purpose function to call a NetWare API. Calling an API consists of the following steps:

**1** Create a Request packet. This is a FoxPro string containing various information needed by the API.

**2** Create an empty Reply packet. This packet must be large enough to hold the data returned from the called API.

**3** Load the DOS registers, which include the API function to call and the pointers to the Request and Reply packets, with the appropriate function number.

**4** Execute the DOS interrupt.

**5** Remove the length bytes from the beginning of the Reply packet.

**6** Return the success or error code from the DOS call.

This next program contains a general-purpose function to execute the NET-WARE() API function call.

```
**************************************************************
* Program:   NetWare.prg                                  *
* Authors:   Joseph D. Booth and Greg Lief                *
* Purpose:   Interface between NetWare and FoxPro         *
**************************************************************
function NetWare
PARAMETERS nService,cRequest,cReply
DIMENSION aRegs[10]
PRIVATE nReturn

nReturn = -1

aRegs[ 1] = nService * 256
aRegs[ 8] = CHR(LEN(cRequest))+CHR(Ø) + cRequest
aRegs[ 5] = .T.
aRegs[ 9] = CHR(LEN(cReply))+CHR(Ø) + cReply
aRegs[ 6] = .F.
IF fp_int86( 33, @aRegs )
   nReturn = aRegs[1] % 256
   IF nReturn < Ø
      nReturn = nReturn +256
   ENDIF
ENDIF
cReply = SUBSTR(aRegs[9],3)
RETURN nReturn
**************************************************************
```

## THE XLATE PROGRAM: CONVERTING DATA BETWEEN NETWARE AND FOXPRO

In addition to the actual communication with the NetWare function call, we will need some functions to convert the NetWare results into a format that FoxPro can use. When NetWare returns a string value, it is terminated by a null byte. In order for FoxPro to work with this string, the null byte and all bytes beyond it must be stripped off. When strings are passed to NetWare, they must be padded to the required length with null bytes.

In addition to strings, there are three kinds of numbers that NetWare works with: bytes, integers, and long integers.

- ▶ A byte is a number between 0 and 255 and uses one character of storage. The FoxPro ASC() and CHR() functions can be used to translate single bytes.

- ▶ An integer uses two characters of storage and can be signed or unsigned. Signed integers range from –32,767 to 32,768, and unsigned integers are in the range from 0 to 65,535. Unlike DOS, NetWare stores the integer from left to right. DOS swaps the bytes, so that the left 8 bits represent the lower portion of the number, and the right 8 bits the higher portion. In the XLATE program, we will provide a function to convert integers back and forth.

- ▶ A long integer uses four characters of storage and can be signed or unsigned. The XLATE program provides methods for translating long integers to and from FoxPro numerics.

Here is the XLATE program, which contains the user-defined functions for converting NetWare data into a format usable by FoxPro.

```
************************************************************
* Program:  Xlate.prg                                     *
* Authors:  Joseph D. Booth and Greg Lief                 *
* Purpose:  Conversion between NetWare and FoxPro         *
************************************************************
**
**   Function:  CleanStr()
**    Purpose:  Removes all characters following the NULL
**              character, including the NULL itself.
**     Syntax:  <cString> := CleanStr(cNovellString)
**   Argument:  cNovellString - A string returned from one
**                              of the Novell API functions.
**
**    Returns:  cString    - A string will all NULL
```

```
**                          characters removed
**
**      Notes:   Strings returned from Novell's API calls
**               are usually filled with NULL bytes. FoxPro
**               doesn't like these bytes, so this function
**               removes them. This function is primarily
**               for internal use, but can be used if you
**               develop any of your own API functions.
**
**************************************************************
function cleanstr
PARAMETER cString
PRIVATE x
x = AT(CHR(0),cString)
RETURN IIF( x=0, cString, SUBSTR(cString, 1, x-1) )
**************************************************************

**   Function:   Lstring()
**    Purpose:   Pads a string with NULL characters.
**     Syntax:   <cLstring> := Lstring(cString,nSize)
** Arguments:    cString - Any string value
**               nSize   - Size of string to create
**
**    Returns:   cLstring   - A string with the size as
*                              the first byte and padded
**                             out with NULL characters.
**
**      Notes:   Strings passed to Novell's API calls
**               need to be passed with the first byte
**               being the size and NULL filled. This
**               function converts FoxPro strings into
**               Novell formatted strings.
**************************************************************
function Lstring
PARAMETERS cString, nSize
RETURN CHR(nSize)+PADR(ALLTRIM(cString), nSize, CHR(0) )
**************************************************************

**   Function:   Int2Fox()
**    Purpose:   Converts an integer string to a
**               FoxPro numeric value.
**     Syntax:   <numeric> := Int2Fox( cInteger )
** Arguments:    cInteger - Binary integer from Novell
**
**    Returns:   numeric  - The value of the integer
**
```

```
**      Notes:   Novell's API calls store integers as two-
**               byte strings in high-low order. Intel
**               microprocessors usually store integers in
**               low-high order.
**********************************************************
function Int2Fox
PARAMETER cInteger
PRIVATE nValue
nValue = 256 * ASC(cInteger) + ASC(SUBSTR(cInteger,2,1))
RETURN nValue
**********************************************************


**   Function:  Fox2Int()
**    Purpose:  Converts a FoxPro numeric to an integer
**              string value.
**     Syntax:  <Cinteger> := Fox2Int( numeric )
** Arguments:  numeric  - The value of the integer
**    Returns:  cInteger - Binary integer for Novell
**
**      Notes:   Novell's API calls store integers as two-
**               byte strings in high-low order. Intel
**               microprocessors usually store integers in
**               low-high order.
**********************************************************
function Fox2int
PARAMETER  nValue
RETURN CHR( nValue / 256) + CHR( nValue % 256 )
**********************************************************


**   Function:  Long2Fox()
**    Purpose:  Converts a long integer string to a
**              FoxPro numeric value.
**     Syntax:  <numeric> := Long2Fox( cInteger )
** Arguments:  cInteger - Binary long number from Novell
**    Returns:  numeric  - The value of the long
**
**      Notes:   Novell's API calls store longs as four-byte
**               strings in high-low order. Intel computers
**               usually store numbers in low-high order.
**********************************************************
function Long2Fox
PARAMETER cInteger
PRIVATE nValue
nValue  = ASC(SUBSTR(cInteger,1,1)) * 65536 +;
          ASC(SUBSTR(cInteger,2,1)) * 4096  +;
```

```
          ASC(SUBSTR(cInteger,3,1)) * 256   +;
          ASC(SUBSTR(cInteger,4,1))
RETURN nValue
****************************************************************


**   Function:  Fox2Long()
**    Purpose:  Converts a FoxPro numeric to a long
**              string value.
**     Syntax:  <cLong> := Fox2Long( numeric )
** Arguments:  numeric  - The value of the number
**    Returns:  cLong    - Binary long number for Novell
**
**      Notes:  Novell's API calls store integers as four-
**              byte strings in high-low order. Intel
**              microprocessors usually store longs in
**              low-high order.
****************************************************************
function Fox2Long
PARAMETER nValue
RETURN CHR( nValue/65536)        +;
       CHR( (nValue%65536)/ 4096) +;
       CHR( (nValue%4096)/ 256)  +;
       CHR( nValue % 256 )
****************************************************************


**   Function:  Six2Fox()
**    Purpose:  Converts a six-digit integer string to a
**              FoxPro numeric value.
**     Syntax:  <numeric> := Six2Fox( cInteger )
** Arguments:  cInteger - Binary long number from Novell
**    Returns:  numeric  - The value of the long
**
**      Notes:  Novell's API calls store longs as six-byte
**              strings in high-low order. Intel computers
**              usually store numbers in low-high order.
****************************************************************
function Six2Fox
PARAMETER cInteger
RETURN    ASC(SUBSTR(cInteger,1,1)) * 16777216 +;
          ASC(SUBSTR(cInteger,2,1)) *  1048576 +;
          ASC(SUBSTR(cInteger,3,1)) *    65536 +;
          ASC(SUBSTR(cInteger,4,1)) *     4096 +;
          ASC(SUBSTR(cInteger,5,1)) *      256 +;
          ASC(SUBSTR(cInteger,6,1))
****************************************************************
```

```
**   Function:  Fox2Six()
**    Purpose:  Converts a FoxPro numeric to a long
**              string value.
**     Syntax:  <cLong> := Fox2Six( numeric )
** Arguments:  numeric  - The value of the number
**    Returns:  cLong    - Binary long number for Novell
**
**      Notes:  Novell's API calls store some integers as
**              six-byte strings in high-low order. Intel
**              microprocessors usually store longs in
**              low-high order.
***************************************************************
function Fox2Six
PARAMETERS nValue
RETURN CHR( nValue/16777216)             +;
       CHR( (nValue%16777216)/ 1048576) +;
       CHR( (nValue%1048576)/65536)      +;
       CHR( (nValue%65536)/ 4096)        +;
       CHR( (nValue%4096)/ 256)          +;
       CHR( nValue % 256 )
***************************************************************
```

**Note:**  For the sake of convenience, we have included versions of the translation functions in the library, along with the FP_INT86() function. These versions are written in C for better performance and will be used by the functions we will write in later chapters.

# USING CONVERSION FUNCTIONS IN YOUR PROGRAMS

The FP_INT86() and various conversion functions are the base functions used by all our programs to access NetWare. In order to make these functions available, you will need to include the following line of code at the beginning of your FoxPro program:

```
SET LIBRARY TO BLNET ADDITIVE
```

This loads the library functions provided with this book into your FoxPro memory so that other functions can access them. If you forget to load the library, you will receive undefined function errors when attempting to use other functions.

In subsequent chapters, we will provide the following procedure files to access various aspect of NetWare:

BINDERY.PRG - Access NetWare's Bindery     (Chapter 8)

NETPRINT.PRG - Netware Printing Services     (Chapter 9)

MESSAGES.PRG - Messaging Across Stations     (Chapter 10)

SYSINFO.PRG - Various System Information     (Chapter 11)

For example, if you want to access one of the bindery functions discussed in Chapter 8, put the following two lines into your program:

```
SET LIBRARY TO BLNET ADDITIVE    && Load DOS interrupt functions
SET PROCEDURE TO BINDERY         && Load the bindery access code
```

## SUMMARY

In this chapter you read about DOS interrupts and how to use them. You also explored some new functions that allow you to communicate directly with NetWare. These functions will be used frequently in subsequent chapters.

# Bindery: NetWare's Database

NetWare provides a very secure system for storing your information. Learning how to take advantage of it will help improve your FoxPro programs' interaction with NetWare. In this chapter we will discuss how NetWare stores user information, and provide functions that allow you to use this information from within your FoxPro applications.

The functions that we have developed in this chapter should provide you with the ability to read any bindery information from any object. You can customize your applications to utilize the bindery much more fully.

*Note:* To use the functions in this chapter, you must include the following two lines of code in your FoxPro program:

```
SET LIBRARY TO BLNET ADDITIVE
SET PROCEDURE TO BINDERY
```

The complete source code to the bindery functions is included on this book's disk, in the file named BINDERY.PRG.

## WHAT IS THE BINDERY?

Each NetWare file server contains a database of information about its users, groups, print queues, and more. This database is called the *bindery*. NetWare uses the bindery to provide extensive security and accounting for all users who have access to the network, and to keep track of all services such as print queues and remote bridges.

Using the bindery, the file server checks User IDs, passwords, and authorization to queues and directories; it even controls the amount of disk space that each user can consume. The bindery files contain the databases needed to provide these security and accounting services.

Each server running NetWare creates its own bindery files, which contain the names and attributes of all entities on the network. Using these files, the file server can allow or restrict access to all services available on the network.

### WHY USE THE BINDERY?

If you have not yet developed a log-in and security system for your applications, consider the NetWare bindery. It is an excellent system, and NetWare provides utility programs to update it. Even if you have already developed a log-in/security system, you might want to use the bindery instead, for the following benefits:

▸ The bindery is very secure. The network opens the bindery files when the network is started, and leaves them open and locked at all times. Only a supervisor User ID (or a user with Supervisor rights) can close the bindery. If you access the bindery via Novell's published API calls (as we do in the programs of this chapter), each object has a read-and-write security automatically enforced by NetWare.

▸ NetWare comes with a program called SYSCON that allows update of bindery information in a very organized fashion. Network administrators and many users are comfortable working with SYSCON and other menu-driven NetWare utilities.

## HOW THE BINDERY IS ORGANIZED

The bindery is organized into a collection of objects. An object can be a *client* or a *server*; client objects use services provided by server objects. Users are clients, for example, and the printer queues are servers. Each object has a name, a type, and any number of properties. Each property can have a single value or multiple values associated with it.

Figure 8.1 shows the bindery structure.

### OBJECTS

Although the bindery can hold up to 65,000 objects, it should remain small (fewer than 1,000 objects) for optimum performance. An object may be a user, group, or resource. For example, SHARON might be a user in the PERSONNEL group who needs access to the LASER_PRINT_QUEUE. The network would

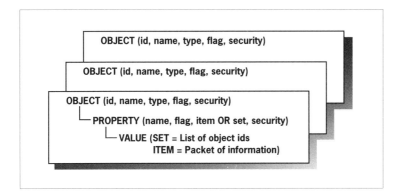

**Figure 8.1: Bindery structure**

use the bindery to determine if SHARON should be granted access and would also inform the other services that the LASER_PRINT_QUEUE is being used.

Each object has the following five pieces of associated information:

▸ *Object ID*—a unique number assigned by NetWare to each object added to the network. This is a 4-byte integer number.

▸ *Object Name*—a character string representing the name of the object. For a user object, it might be the person's initials. The name can be up to 47 characters long.

Objects are defined by both their name and type (explained next). Two objects may have the same name as long as their object types are different.

▸ *Object Type*—a numeric code indicating the type of object. The network expects certain characteristics based upon the object's type. The codes for the various object types are defined in Table 8.1.

**Table 8.1: Object Types**

| Code | Object Type |
| --- | --- |
| 1 | User |
| 2 | Group of users |
| 3 | Print queue |
| 4 | File server |
| 5 | Job server |

**Table 8.1: Object Types (Continued)**

| Code | Object Type |
|------|-------------|
| 6 | Gateway |
| 7 | Print server |
| 8 | Archive queue |
| 9 | Archive server |
| 10 | Job queue |
| 11 | Administration |
| 33 | NAS SNA gateway |
| 35 | Async gateway |
| 36 | Remote bridge server |
| 38 | Async bridge |
| 40 | X.25 bridge |
| 45 | Time synchronization server |
| 46 | Archive server |
| 71 | Advertising print server |
| 80 | Btrieve value-added Process |
| 83 | Print queue user |
| 162 | Bindery |
| 163 | Oracle DB server |
| 167 | Rconsole |

- ▶ *Object Flag*—indicates whether this object is static or dynamic. Dynamic objects are temporary and will be deleted when the network is brought down. Static objects remain in the bindery until they are specifically removed.

- ▶ *Object Security*—a read-and-write security associated with each object. This indicates which other objects have the ability to access this object. Security is a single byte; the first 4 bits indicate the write security, and the last 4 are the read security. The possible values for these 4 bits are as follows:

| Code | Value |
|------|-------|
| 0 | Anyone can access this object |
| 1 | Users logged in to the server |
| 2 | Only the current object |
| 3 | Supervisor only |
| 4 | NetWare operating system only |

**Finding objects**    NetWare provides an API function that can be used to obtain a list of all objects for a specified type. The function called N_SCAN-BINDERY(), listed below, takes an object type and an array as parameters. It returns the count of objects found. It also fills the array with all objects of that type. Note that the array must be passed by reference.

```
********************************************************
*  Function:  N_ScanBindery()
*   Purpose:  Scans the bindery for a given object type
*    Syntax:  nCount = N_ScanBindery( nType,@aObjects )
* Arguments:  nType      - Type of objects to be returned
*             aObjects   - Array of objects of the
*                            indicated type
*
*   Returns:  nCount     - How many objects were found
*
*     Notes:  This function is used to get a list of all
*             objects in a bindery type. For example,
*             type 4 is the servers, so N_ScanBindery(4)
*             would return all servers within the bindery.
*
********************************************************
function N_ScanBindery
PARAMETERS nType,aObjects

PRIVATE cBuffer,cRequest,nCount,cList
PRIVATE x,y,z
nCount    = 0
cBuffer   = SPACE(57)
cRequest  = CHR( 55)+CHR(255)+CHR(255)+;
            CHR(255)+CHR(255)+;
            CHR(0)+CHR(nType)+;
```

```
          Lstring("*",48)
cList    = ""

DO WHILE NetWare( 227,cRequest,@cBuffer ) == 0 AND ;
   LEN(TRIM(cBuffer)) > 0
   **
   ** Extract the object name and save in array
   **
   nCount = nCount +1
   cList  = cList +CleanStr(SUBSTR(cBuffer,7,48))+";"
   **
   ** Update the send buffer to get next member
   **
   cRequest = SUBSTR(cRequest,1,1)+SUBSTR(cBuffer,1,4)+;
              SUBSTR(cRequest,6)
ENDDO
IF nCount > 0
   DIMENSION aObjects[nCount]
   z  = 1
   FOR x = 1 TO nCount
      y = AT(";",cList,x)
      aObjects[x] = SUBSTR(cList,z,y-z)
      z = y+1
   NEXT
ENDIF
RETURN nCount
*************************************************************
```

The N_SCANBINDERY() function works by performing a wildcard lookup from the bindery for the specified object type. The function loops until a non-zero value is returned from NetWare, indicating the end of the list.

To use the N_SCANBINDERY() function in your FoxPro program, you declare an array to hold the results. Then call the N_SCANBINDERY() function, passing the object type and the array name by reference. The array will be automatically sized to reflect the number of objects that were found. By using the list of object types provided earlier in the chapter, you can easily create your own set of customized function calls to return a list of various object types.

The following code fragment shows how you can get a list of NetWare users:

```
DIMENSION aUsers(1)                 && Create an array
IF N_ScanBindery(1,@aUsers) = 0
   WAIT "There are no users..." WINDOW TIMEOUT 30
ENDIF
```

**Determining the security level**   In addition to scanning the bindery, you can determine the security level that the current workstation has to its logged object ID. The function called N_BINDLEVEL() listed below takes a single letter as a parameter and will return the appropriate result. The parameters may be

U   Get connection's User ID

R   Get connection's read security

W   Get connection's write security

```
*************************************************************
*   Function:   N_BindLevel()
*    Purpose:   Get workstation's access level to the bindery
*     Syntax:   xReturn = N_BindLevel( cOption )
* Arguments:   cOption = R -Read security
*                        W -Write security
*                        U -User id number
*
*************************************************************
function N_BindLevel
PARAMETERS cWhich
PRIVATE cBuffer,cRequest
PRIVATE xAnswer,y
IF PARAMETERS() = 0
   cWhich = "U"
ENDIF

cBuffer  = SPACE(5)
cRequest = CHR(70)
xAnswer  = -1
IF Netware(227,cRequest,@cBuffer) == 0
   DO CASE
   CASE cWhich = "R"
      y       = ASC(cBuffer)%16
      xAnswer = SUBSTR("ALOSN",y+1,1)
   CASE cWhich = "W"
      y       = INT(ASC(cBuffer)/16)
      xAnswer = SUBSTR("ALOSN",y+1,1)
   OTHERWISE
      xAnswer = Long2Fox(SUBSTR(cBuffer,2,4))
   ENDCASE
ENDIF
RETURN xAnswer
*************************************************************
```

The read-and-write security will consist of a letter that indicates the level for this object. Here are codes and their meanings:

| Code | Security Level |
|------|----------------|
| A    | Anyone can access this object |
| L    | Only users logged in to the server |
| O    | Only the current object |
| S    | Supervisor only |
| N    | NetWare operating system only |

**Note:**  Most information about the object can be updated by the worksta-tion, although some properties of the object may be restricted to the super-visor or the NetWare operating system.

**Identifying objects**  Once you have an object name or an object ID, you can use this information to obtain additional information about the bindery ob-ject. The function called N_OBJECTNAME(), listed below, if passed a net-work object ID, returns the object's name. You can use this function along with the N_BINDLEVEL() function detailed earlier to determine the name of the user currently logged in at the workstation.

```
*************************************************************
*  Function:   N_ObjectName()
*    Purpose:  Returns object's name from a bindery object
*     Syntax:  cName  = N_ObjectName( nId )
* Arguments:   nId     - Bindery object id
*    Returns:  cName   - The object's name in the bindery
*
function N_ObjectName
PARAMETER nId
PRIVATE cBuffer,cRequest
PRIVATE cName

cBuffer  = SPACE(54)
cRequest = CHR(54)+Fox2Long(nId)
cName    = ""
IF Netware(227,cRequest,@cBuffer) == 0
   cName = CleanStr( SUBSTR(cBuffer,7) )
ENDIF
RETURN cName
*************************************************************
```

You can also determine an object's ID if you specify the object name and type. Here is a function called N_OBJECTID() that takes the name and type as parameters and returns the bindery object ID:

```
*************************************************************
*  Function:  N_ObjectId()
*   Purpose:  Returns the object ID for a given object
*    Syntax:  nIdCode = N_ObjectId( <cObject>,<nObjType> )
* Arguments:  cObject   - Object name
*             nObjType  - Type of object
*
*   Returns:  nIdCode   - Bindery id number
*
*     Notes:  Every object in the bindery has a unique
*             number to identify it. This function can be
*             used to determine the number for any object.
*
*************************************************************
function N_ObjectId
PARAMETERS cObject,nObjType
PRIVATE cBuffer,nId,cRequest
cBuffer  = SPACE(54)              && Set up Receive Buffer
nId      = 0
cRequest = CHR(53)+CHR(0)+CHR(nObjType)+;
           Lstring(cObject,48)

IF Netware(227, cRequest, @cBuffer) == 0
   nId = Long2Fox(SUBSTR(cBuffer,1,4))  && Extract id
ENDIF
RETURN nId
*************************************************************
```

**Determining user ID**   The N_BINDLEVEL() and N_OBJECTNAME() functions can be used in combination to produce a function, called N_WHOAMI(), that will return the ID of the user currently logged in.

```
*************************************************************
*  Function:  N_WhoAmI()
*   Purpose:  Get workstation's User ID
*    Syntax:  cUser = N_WhoAmI()
* Arguments:  <NONE>
*   Returns:  cUser - Object name for current connection
*
*     Notes:  This function is used to determine the
*             bindery name for the current connection.
*             You could use this function to determine
```

```
*              a user's ID code for logging purposes.
*
****************************************************************
function N_WhoAmI
PRIVATE nId,cUser
nId    = N_BindLevel("U")
cUser  = ""
IF not empty(nID)
   cUser = N_ObjectName(nId)
ENDIF
RETURN cUser
****************************************************************
```

## PROPERTIES

Each object may have any number of properties associated with it. The properties that are associated vary by object type. For example, a user ID object has a PASSWORD property, a GROUPS_I'M_IN property, and possibly an ACCOUNT_BALANCE property. Each property has the following four pieces of associated information:

▶ *Property Name*—a character string representing the name of the property. The name can be up to 15 uppercase characters.

▶ *Property Flag*—indicates whether this property is static or dynamic. Dynamic properties are temporary and will be removed when the network is brought down. Static properties remain with the object until they are specifically removed.

▶ *Item/Set Flag*—indicates whether a property is an item or a set. An item property has a single associated value; a PASSWORD property, for example, contains the encrypted password for a User ID object. A set property has multiple values; for example, a GROUP object has a property called GROUP_MEMBERS that lists the user objects belonging to the group.

▶ *Security*—indicates the other objects that have the ability to access this property. Each property has both a read security and a write security associated with it. This byte has the same format as the security byte on the object, although this one will not necessarily contain the same value.

Properties do not contain any data, but are merely the names of additional information attached to an object. This design allows for flexible object creation and definition. Table 8.2 lists some of the more common standard NetWare properties. You can add your own properties, as well. This list is likely to expand as more third-party products are developed for NetWare.

**Table 8.2: Standard NetWare Properties**

| Property Name | Type | Flag | Object(s) |
| --- | --- | --- | --- |
| ACCOUNT_BALANCE | Item | Static | Users |
| ACCOUNT_HOLDS | Item | Dynamic | Users |
| ACCOUNT_SERVERS | Set | Static | File server |
| ACCOUNT_LOCKOUT | Item | Static | File server |
| BLOCKS_READ | Item | Static | File server |
| BLOCKS_WRITTEN | Item | Static | File server |
| CONNECT_TIME | Item | Static | File server |
| DISK_STORAGE | Item | Static | File server |
| GROUP_MEMBERS | Set | Static | Group |
| GROUPS_I'M_IN | Set | Static | Users |
| IDENTIFICATION | Item | Static | Users, groups |
| LOGIN_CONTROL | Item | Static | Users |
| MANAGERS | Set | Static | Groups |
| NET_ADDRESS | Item | Dynamic | File server |
| NODE_CONTROL | Item | Static | User |
| OLD_PASSWORDS | Item | Static | User |
| OPERATORS | Set | Static | File server |
| PASSWORD | Item | Static | Users |
| Q_DIRECTORY | Item | Static | Any queue |
| Q_OPERATORS | Set | Static | Any queue |
| Q_SERVER | Set | Static | Any queue |
| Q_USERS | Set | Static | Any queue |
| REQUESTS_MADE | Item | Static | File server |
| SECURITY_EQUALS | Set | Static | User |
| USER_DEFAULTS | Item | Static | User |

**Accessing properties**   Once you know an object's name and type, you can use this information to determine the properties attached to that object. The function called N_PROPERTIES() listed below takes an object name, its type, and an array as parameters. It returns the count of the properties associated with this object. Be sure the array is passed by reference, because it will be updated to contain the property names.

```
****************************************************************
*  Function:  N_Properties()
*   Purpose:  Scans the bindery object for properties
*    Syntax:  nCount      = N_Properties(cObject,nType,;
*                                        aProperties )
* Arguments:  cObject     - Object to determine properties
*             nType       - Type of object being checked
*             aProperties - List of object's properties
*
*   Returns:  nCount      - Number of properties associated
*                           with this object
*
*     Notes:  This function is used to determine what
*             properties are associated with this object.
*             You can also use the N_PropVal() function to
*             determine the value of the properties.
*
****************************************************************

function N_Properties
PARAMETERS cObject, nType,aProperties
PRIVATE cBuffer,cRequest,nCount,cList
PRIVATE x,y,z

cBuffer      = SPACE(24)
cRequest     = CHR(60)+;
               CHR(0)+CHR(nType)+;
               Lstring(cObject,48)+;
               CHR(255)+CHR(255)+CHR(255)+CHR(255)+;
               Lstring("*",15)

nCount       = 0
cList        = ""

DO WHILE  Netware( 227, cRequest, @cBuffer) = 0
   nCount = nCount +1
   cList = cList +CleanStr(LEFT(cBuffer,16))+";"
   **
   ** replace sequence number with last one received
```

```
   **
   cRequest = STUFF(cRequest, 53, 4, SUBSTR(cBuffer,19,4))
ENDDO
IF nCount > 0
   DIMENSION aProperties[nCount]
   z  = 1
   FOR x = 1 TO nCount
      y = AT(";",cList,x)
      aProperties[x] = SUBSTR(cList, z, y - z)
      z = y + 1
   NEXT
ENDIF
RETURN nCount
*************************************************************
```

**Note:**   Keep in mind that the N_PROPERTIES() function returns only the properties; it does not return any values for those properties. The N_PROPVAL()
function, detailed in the section that follows, contains a function to determine
the value for any property. However, if passwords are encrypted, you will not
be able to determine an object's password through the bindery functions.

## PROPERTY VALUES

In addition to the properties themselves, the bindery also contains values for
the properties. The value may be an item such as a character string or a set of
object IDs. The property's item/set flag determines how the value is interpreted.
A property value string can be up to 128 characters and can contain multiple
strings, if needed, to represent the property. For set properties, 32 object IDs,
each one 4 characters long, can be stored in one string of 128 characters.

**Accessing property values**   The N_PROPVAL() function listed below accepts the following parameters: an object name; an object type; the property
name; a logical value indicating whether the returned value should be NULL-
stripped; and an array (passed by reference). The function returns the values
of the property passed to it.

If the property is a set property, then the array is updated and the count of
object IDs is returned.

If the property is an item property, then a string containing the information for that item is returned. Some of these item-property strings contain
structures holding multiple units of information. A good example is the AC-
COUNT_BALANCE property, which contains both the account balance and
the credit limit. The first 4 bytes of the string represent the account balance,

and the next 4 contain the credit limit. You will need to use the LONG2FOX() function from the BLNET library to convert this string into numeric values.

This function can be very handy for accessing the bindery when customizing your application.

```
*************************************************************
*  Function:  N_PropVal()
*   Purpose:  Return value of a specified property
*    Syntax:  xValue := N_PropVal( cObject,;
*                                  ntype,;
*                                  cProperty,;
*                                  lClean )
*
* Arguments:  cObject    - Object to be queried
*             nType      - Type of object being queried
*             cProperty  - Property value to extract
*             lClean     - Should the return value be
*                          NULL stripped?
*
*   Returns:  xValue     - Varies depending upon the
*                          object and property
*
*     Notes:  This function is used to determine the value
*             for a property from another object. For
*             example, you can use this function to
*             determine the full name of a bindery object.
*
*************************************************************

function N_PropVal
PARAMETERS cObject,nType,cProperty,lClean,aList
PRIVATE cBuffer,xReturn,nSegment,nPos,cName,nObjtype
PRIVATE cId,cRequest,cList,isList
PRIVATE x,y,z

cBuffer  = SPACE(13Ø)
xReturn  = ""
nSegment = 1
isList   = .F.

cRequest = CHR(61)+;
           CHR(Ø)+CHR(nType)+;
           Lstring(cObject,48)+;
           CHR(nSegment)+;
           Lstring(UPPER(cProperty),16)
```

```
IF type("lClean") <> "L"
   lClean = .T.
ENDIF

DO WHILE Netware(227, cRequest, @cBuffer) == Ø
   IF ASC(SUBSTR(cBuffer,13Ø,1)) >Ø
      IF nSegment == 1
         cList  = ""
         isList = .T.
         xReturn = Ø
      ENDIF
      nPos = 1

      DO WHILE nPos < 128
        cId = Long2Fox(SUBSTR(cBuffer,nPos,4))  && Read ID
        IF cId == Ø               && Check for end of segment
           EXIT
        ENDIF
        cName    = N_ObjectName(cId)    && Lookup Name & Type
        cList    = cList + cName+";"    && and put in Return Array
        xReturn  = xReturn +1
        nPos     = nPos + 4             && then point to next ID
      ENDDO
   ELSE
      IF nSegment == 1
         xReturn = ""
      ENDIF
      xReturn = xReturn + LEFT(cBuffer, 128)
   ENDIF
   nSegment = nSegment +1
   cRequest = STUFF(cRequest,53,1,CHR(nSegment))
ENDDO

DO CASE
CASE isList
   IF xReturn > Ø
      DIMENSION aList[xReturn]
      z  = 1
      FOR x = 1 TO xReturn
         y = AT(";",cList,x)
         aList[x] = SUBSTR(cList,z,y-z)
         z = y+1
      NEXT
   ENDIF
CASE lClean and type("xReturn")="C"
   xReturn = CleanStr(xReturn)
```

```
ENDCASE

RETURN (xReturn)
***********************************************************
```

# BINDERY OBJECT TYPES

The object type determines the behavior of the object. For example, a user object must have a PASSWORD property in order to log in to the server; a file-server object needs an OPERATORS property, and so on. The following sections describe the four most common object types.

### USER OBJECTS

A User ID object generally corresponds to a person using the network. The network administrator can grant rights to users individually or through their group membership. Users are generally clients of the network who request services, and they often have an associated network password.

The Supervisor is a unique user object that is automatically created by NetWare. Its object ID is always 1. The Supervisor User ID has access to many features of NetWare and can manipulate the bindery. For this reason, you should be very selective when allowing users to have Supervisor rights.

**User properties**  Each User ID object may contain any of the following properties:

▶ GROUPS_I'M_IN—a static set listing all groups of which this user is a member.

▶ IDENTIFICATION—a static item containing the user's full name.

▶ LOGIN_CONTROL—a static item that contains the log-in rules for this user, such as how long the password must be, whether unique passwords are required, and so on. The LOGIN_CONTROL property has the following structure:

| Byte | Size | Contents |
|------|------|----------|
| 1 | 3 | Account expiration date in YYMMDD format |
| 4 | 1 | 0=account active; 1=disabled |
| 5 | 3 | Password expiration date in YYMMDD format |
| 8 | 1 | Number of grace log-ins remaining |

| | | |
|---|---|---|
| 9 | 2 | Number of days between passwords |
| 11 | 1 | Grace log-in reset value |
| 12 | 1 | Minimum password length |
| 13 | 2 | Maximum concurrent connections |
| 15 | 42 | Bitmap of allowed log-in times; each group of 6 bytes contains 48 bits that represent half-slots of time |
| 57 | 6 | Last log-in date/time |
| 63 | 1 | Restriction flags |
| 64 | 1 | Not used |
| 65 | 4 | Maximum disk space allowed (in blocks) |
| 69 | 2 | Count of bad log-ins |
| 71 | 4 | Next log-in reset time |
| 75 | 1 | Bad log-in station address |

- NODE_CONTROL—a static item that indicates stations from which the user can log in.

- OLD_PASSWORD—a static item containing all prior passwords. This property exists only if unique passwords are required for this object. This item can usually be read only by the Supervisor or the network operating system.

- PASSWORD—a static item containing the encrypted password string.

- SECURITY_EQUALS—a static set that contains the list of objects to which this object is equivalent, in terms of security.

In addition, if accounting has been installed, each User ID object will also have the following properties that are used by the accounting functions:

- ACCOUNT_BALANCE—a static item consisting of account balance and credit limit. This property contains two 4-byte numbers. The first 4 bytes are the actual balance, and the second 4 bytes contain the credit limit.

- ACCOUNT_HOLDS—a dynamic item consisting of a string of network services with holds against this account. This is a list of up to 16 objects, each using 4 bytes for the object ID and another 4 bytes for the hold amount.

Figure 8.2 illustrates the structure of a user object on a server that has accounting installed.

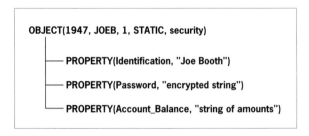

**OBJECT(1947, JOEB, 1, STATIC, security)**

├── **PROPERTY(Identification, "Joe Booth")**

├── **PROPERTY(Password, "encrypted string")**

└── **PROPERTY(Account_Balance, "string of amounts")**

**Figure 8.2: Example of a bindery user object**

**Functions for retrieving user information**    It is useful to be able to interpret the bindery's information for each user's properties and values. Using the functions described earlier in this chapter, we can create some additional functions to translate the user bindery information into a format that is usable by a Fox-Pro program.

Following are listings of a group of functions that will return information about the specified object name. The return value will vary depending upon the property. These functions and their return values are

| Function | Returns |
| --- | --- |
| N_FULLNAME() | Full name of the user |
| N_ACCTEXPIRE() | Date the account will expire |
| N_BALANCE() | Account balance |
| N_CREDLIMIT() | User's credit limit |

These functions and the following listings of code should give you the examples you need to help you extract whatever information your application might need from the user's bindery object.

```
*************************************************************
*  Function:  N_FullName()
*   Purpose:  Get the user's full name
*    Syntax:  <cFullName> = N_FullName( cUser )
*
* Arguments:  cUser        - User bindery name
*
*   Returns:  cFullName    - Full name of this user
*
```

```
*     Notes:  This function returns the user's
*             identification string, usually their name.
*
*
****************************************************************
function N_FullName
PARAMETER cUser
IF PARAMETERS() = Ø
   cUser = N_WhoAmI()
ENDIF
RETURN N_PropVal(cUser,1,"IDENTIFICATION",.T.)
****************************************************************


****************************************************************
*  Function:  N_AcctExpire()
*   Purpose:  Get the date this account expires
*    Syntax:  <dExpire> := N_AcctExpire( cUser )
*
* Arguments:  cUser      - User bindery name
*
*   Returns:  dExpire    - Expiration date of user's account
*
*     Notes:  This function returns the user's expiration
*             date, which can be used for scheduling purposes
*             to prevent future activities from being
*             scheduled past the user's access date.
*
*
****************************************************************
function N_AcctExpire
PARAMETER cUser
PRIVATE cString,yy,mm,dd
IF PARAMETERS() = Ø
   cUser = N_WhoAmI()
ENDIF
cString = N_PropVal(cUser,1,"LOGIN_CONTROL",.T.)
yy      = 19ØØ + ASC(SUBSTR(cString,1,1))
mm      = ASC(SUBSTR(cString,2,1))
dd      = ASC(SUBSTR(cString,3,1))
RETURN IIF(mm=Ø, CTOD("  /  /  "), CTOD(str(mm,2) + ;
                   "/" + STR(dd,2) + "/" + STR(yy,4)))


****************************************************************

*  Function:  N_Balance()
*   Purpose:  Get the current account balance for a user
```

```
*     Syntax:   <nBalance> = N_Balance( cUser )
*
* Arguments:   cUser      - User bindery name
*
*    Returns:  nBalance   - User's balance if accounting is
*                             installed
*
*     Notes:   This function returns the current balance for
*              the specified user. If accounting is not
*              installed, zero will be returned. You can use
*              this function to restrict certain program
*              operations to users with sufficient funds.
*
*
******************************************************************
function N_Balance
PARAMETER cUser
PRIVATE cAmt
IF PARAMETERS() = 0
   cUser = N_WhoAmI()
ENDIF
cAmt = N_PropVal(cUser,1,"ACCOUNT_BALANCE",.F.)
RETURN Long2Fox(SUBSTR(cAmt,1,4))
******************************************************************
******************************************************************

*   Function:  N_CredLimit()
*    Purpose:  Get the current credit limit for a user
*     Syntax:  <nCredLimit> = N_CredLimit( cUser )
*
* Arguments:   cUser      - User bindery name
*
*    Returns:  nBalance   - User's credit limit if accounting
*                             is installed
*
*     Notes:   This function returns the current credit limit
*              for the specified user. If accounting is not
*              installed, zero will be returned. You can use
*              this function to restrict certain program
*              operations to users with sufficient funds.
*
*
************************************************************
function N_CredLimit
PARAMETER cUser
PRIVATE cAmt
```

```
IF PARAMETERS() = Ø
   cUser = N_WhoAmI()
ENDIF
cAmt = N_PropVal(cUser,1,"ACCOUNT_BALANCE",.F.)
RETURN Long2Fox(SUBSTR(cAmt,5,4))
*************************************************************
```

## GROUP OBJECTS

A group is a collection of users who share similar rights to the network. Group membership (that is, the groups an object belongs to) is one of the properties of User ID objects. The network administrator can assign users to a group and then grant services to the group. Each member can access the services of the group, allowing easier maintenance.

> **Note:**  You can also use the group membership to control the behavior of your application. For example, you might limit access to the Payroll option on a menu to only those users who are members of the Payroll group. In our e-mail application at the end of this book, we allow mail to be sent to all members of a group by indicating the group's name.

**Group properties**    Each group object may contain any of the following properties:

- ▸ IDENTIFICATION—a static item usually containing the group's expanded name, such as "Finance Department"

- ▸ GROUP_MEMBERS—a static set containing a list of all user object IDs who are members of this group

- ▸ OBJ_SUPERVISORS—a static set containing a list of all user object IDs who are managers of this group

**FoxPro functions for groups**    There are several functions that are useful when working with group objects. The primary information about a group includes its name, its members, and its managers.

The N_MEMBERS() and N_MANAGERS() functions listed below can be used to return a list of User IDs that are either members or managers for the selected group. The functions take the group name and an array passed by reference, and return the number of users found.

```
*************************************************************
*  Function:  N_Members()
*   Purpose:  Get members of a group
*    Syntax:  <nCount> = N_Members( cObject,@ALIST )
```

```
*
* Arguments:  cGroup     - Group to test
*             aList      - List of users
*
*   Returns:  Number of users found within the group
*
*     Notes:  This function is used to determine the number
*             of members in a group. It also returns a
*             list of members.
*
*****************************************************************
function N_Members
PARAMETERS cGroup,aList
PRIVATE nCount
if PARAMETERS() < 2
   return 0
endif
nCount= N_PropVal(cGroup,2,"GROUP_MEMBERS",.F.,@ALIST)
RETURN nCount
*****************************************************************


*****************************************************************
*  Function:  N_Managers()
*   Purpose:  Get managers of a group
*    Syntax:  <nCount> = N_Managers( cObject,@ALIST )
*
* Arguments:  cGroup     - Group to test
*             aList      - List of managers
*
*   Returns:  Number of managers found within the group
*
*     Notes:  This function is used to determine the number
*             of managers in a group. It also returns a
*             list of managers.
*
*****************************************************************
function N_Managers
PARAMETERS cGroup,aList
PRIVATE nCount
if PARAMETERS() < 2
   return 0
endif
nCount= N_PropVal(cGroup,2,"OBJ_SUPERVISORS",.F.,@ALIST)
RETURN nCount
*****************************************************************
```

The final group functions, shown in the next two listings, are N_ISMEM-BER() and N_ISMANAGER(). These functions can be used to determine if a User ID is a member or a manager of the specified group. Both functions require the user object name and the name of the group. A logical value is returned indicating that the ID is either a member or a manager of the group.

```
****************************************************************
*   Function:  N_IsMember()
*    Purpose:  Check for group membership
*     Syntax:  <logical> = N_IsMember( cObject,cGroup )
*
* Arguments:  cObject   - Object to be tested
*             cGroup    - Group to test
*
*    Returns:  TRUE if object is a member, FALSE otherwise
*
*      Notes:  This function is used to see if an object is
*              a member of a group. It can be used to
*              restrict menu choices to only members of a
*              department.
*
****************************************************************
function N_IsMember
PARAMETERS cObject,cGroup
PRIVATE cRequest
cRequest = CHR(67)+;
         CHR(Ø)+CHR(1)+;
         Lstring(cObject,48)+;
         Lstring("GROUPS_I'M_IN",16)+;
         CHR(Ø)+CHR(2)+;
         Lstring(cGroup,48)

RETURN Netware(227,cRequest,"") == Ø
****************************************************************
****************************************************************
*   Function:  N_IsManager()
*    Purpose:  Check if user is manager of a group
*     Syntax:  <logical> = N_IsManager( cObject,cGroup )
*
* Arguments:  cObject   - Object to be tested
*             cGroup    - Group to test
*
*    Returns:  TRUE if object is a manager, FALSE otherwise
*
*      Notes:  This function is used to see if an object is
*              a manager of a group. It can be used to
```

```
*               restrict menu choices to only managers of a
*               department.
*
***************************************************************
function N_IsManager
PARAMETERS cObject,cGroup
PRIVATE cRequest
cRequest = CHR(67)+;
          CHR(Ø)+CHR(2)+;
          Lstring(cGroup,48)+;
          Lstring("OBJ_SUPERVISORS",16)+;
          CHR(Ø)+CHR(1)+;
          Lstring(cObject,48)

RETURN Netware(227,cRequest,"") == Ø
***************************************************************
```

The foregoing functions can be very handy when you need to determine if access to a special portion of a menu is allowed. For  example, the following code fragment allows only members in the Finance group to edit customer records, and allows only the group manager to issue credit memoranda. This simple example shows that by taking advantage of the Group objects in Net-Ware, you give your users one place to maintain security and user rights that can be used by many other applications, as well.

```
***************************************************************
*   Program:  FINMENU
*   Authors:  Joe Booth and Greg Lief
***************************************************************
PRIVATE cUser
cUser = N_WhoAmI()
DEFINE POPUP Finance AT 5,2Ø TO 11,4Ø

DEFINE BAR 1 OF Finance PROMPT "Browse Customer Files"
DEFINE BAR 2 OF Finance PROMPT "Enter Invoices"

IF N_IsMember(cUser,"FINANCE")
   DEFINE BAR 3 OF Finance PROMPT "Edit Customer Files"
ENDIF

IF N_IsManager(cUser,"FINANCE")
   DEFINE BAR 4 OF Finance PROMPT "Issue Credit Memos"
ENDIF

ON SELECTION POPUP Finance DO Choice ;
   IN FINMENU WITH PROMPT(),POPUP()
```

```
ACTIVATE POPUP Finance

PROCEDURE CHOICE
PARAMETERS cPrompt ,nOption
*
*   Process choices
*
*****************************************************************
```

**Checking membership**   We have also fashioned a general-purpose function called N_ISINSET() that indicates whether a particular object is within another object property set. Each object type has to be defined, so this function needs more parameters, but it can be used for many applications to determine allowable actions. N_ISINSET() accepts five parameters: the object name and type to check for membership, the object name and type for the object that owns the group, and the property name. It returns a logical value indicating whether the object is within the group.

```
*****************************************************************
*   Function:   N_IsInSet()
*    Purpose:   See if one object is within another's set
*               property
*     Syntax:   <logical> = N_IsInSet( cObject1,nType1,;
*                           cObject2,nType2,cProperty)
*
* Arguments:    cObject1  -Object to be tested for ownership
*               nType1    -Type of owner object
*               cObject2  -Object to be tested for membership
*               nType2    -Type of member object
*               cProperty -Set property to test
*
*    Returns:   TRUE if in group, FALSE otherwise
*
*      Notes:   This function is used to determine if one
*               object is a member of the specified property set
*               for another object. For example, you can
*               use this function to determine if a user
*               should be allowed to perform a menu option.
*
*****************************************************************
function N_IsInSet
PARAMETER cObject1,nType1,cObject2,nType2,cProperty
PRIVATE cRequest
cRequest = CHR(67)+;
```

```
                CHR(Ø)+CHR(nType1)+;
                Lstring(cObject1,48)+;
                Lstring(cProperty,16)+;
                CHR(Ø)+CHR(nType2)+;
                Lstring(cObject2,48)

RETURN Netware(227,cRequest,"") == Ø
******************************************************************
```

## PRINT QUEUE OBJECTS

A print queue is an object that offers printing services to network users. The print queue sets up a directory to hold the files to be printed until a printer is ready to service them. Each queue object may contain any of the following properties:

- ▸ Q_DIRECTORY—a static item containing the directory where files are stored until a printer can service the print request.

- ▸ Q_OPERATORS—a static set that lists the object IDs of queue operators. A queue operator can directly manipulate the print queue.

- ▸ Q_SERVERS—a static set listing the object IDs of servers that can service jobs in this queue.

- ▸ Q_USERS—a static set listing the object IDs of users or groups that can submit jobs into this queue.

**FoxPro functions for print queues**  There are several functions that are useful when working with print queues. The primary pieces of information about a print queue are its file storage directory, its operators, and its users.

We can use the functions we have developed thus far to add some functions to BINDERY.PRG, which accesses print queue information. These functions are shown in the following listing. By using our various functions, you could easily write, for instance, a program to allow the user to contact the appropriate operator to get special forms mounted on the printer.

```
******************************************************************
*  Function:  N_Qdir()
*   Purpose:  Get the name of the print queue's directory
*    Syntax:  <cDir> = N_Qdir( nQueueId )
*
* Arguments:  nQueueId  -Bindery object ID of queue
*
*   Returns:  cDir - Directory where files are stored
*
```

```
*     Notes:  This function is used to determine the name
*             of the directory where the print queues files
*             are stored until they are printed.
*
**************************************************************
function N_Qdir
PARAMETER nId
PRIVATE cDir
cDir = N_PropVal( nId,3,"Q_DIRECTORY",.T. )
RETURN cDir
**************************************************************


**************************************************************
*  Function:  N_QOperators()
*   Purpose:  Get a list of queue operators
*    Syntax:  <nCount> = N_QOperators( nQueueId,@aList )
*
* Arguments:  nQueueId  -Bindery object ID of queue
*             aList     -Array passed by reference
*
*   Returns:  nCount    -Number of queue operators
*
*     Notes:  This function is used to determine the User
*             IDs of the print queues operators.
*
**************************************************************
function N_QOperators
PARAMETER nId,aList
PRIVATE nCount
nCount = N_PropVal( nId,3,"Q_DIRECTORY",.T.,@ALIST )
RETURN nCount
**************************************************************
```

## FILE SERVER OBJECTS

The file server object is used to allow NetWare to control access to network resources and bindery rights. This object represents the computer that is being used as the file server.

**File server properties**    The file server object may contain any of the following properties:

▸ NET_ADDRESS—a dynamic item that contains the 12-byte Internet address of the file server

▸ OPERATORS—a static set that contains the IDs of objects authorized to operate the file console

Additionally, if accounting has been installed, the server object will have the following properties that are used by the accounting functions:

▸ ACCOUNT_SERVERS—a static set of all server object IDs that are allowed to charge a user for services

▸ ACCOUNT_LOCKOUT—a static item that lists the object IDs of locked-out accounts

▸ BLOCKS_READ—a static item that contains the amount to charge users for blocks read since they have logged on

▸ BLOCKS_WRITTEN—a static item that contains the amount to charge users for blocks written since they have logged on

▸ CONNECT_TIME—a static item that contains the amount the server will charge for connect time (from the time the object logged in until it logs out)

▸ DISK_STORAGE—a static item that contains the amount to charge users for disk storage

▸ REQUESTS_MADE—a static item that indicates what the system charges for requests made by a user

**FoxPro functions for file servers**     There are several functions that are useful when trying to get information from the file server. A lot of information is available, but some of it needs to be extracted from the property values. Some of the information from the file server may not be readable, depending upon the user's security level on the network.

Listed next are some sample FoxPro functions to read the information from the file server object:

```
**************************************************************
*  Function:  N_IsOperator( cUser, cServer )
*   Purpose:  See if the user has Operator rights to the
*             server
*    Syntax:  <logical> = N_IsOperator( cUser,cServer )
* Arguments:  cUser      - User Id to test
*             cServer    - Server to check
*
*   Returns:  TRUE if user has rights, FALSE otherwise
*
*     Notes:  This function is used to see if the User ID
*             has Operator rights on a server. You could
*             use this function to control access into
*             parts of your FoxPro application.
```

```
*
*
****************************************************************
function N_IsOperator
PARAMETERS cUser,cServer
PRIVATE x
X = PARAMETERS()
IF X < 1
   cUser = N_WhoAmI()
ENDIF
IF X < 2
   DIMENSION arr_(1)
   =N_ScanBindery(4,@arr_)
   cServer = arr_[1]
ENDIF
RETURN N_IsInSet( cServer,4,cUser,1,"OPERATORS" )
****************************************************************
****************************************************************
*   Function:   N_NetAddr()
*    Purpose:   Returns the file server's network address
*     Syntax:   <nAddr> := N_NetAddr()
* Arguments:    cServer
*
*    Returns:   zero or the specified server's network
*               address
*
****************************************************************
function N_NetAddr
PARAMETERS cServer
PRIVATE cString
IF PARAMETERS() < 1
   DIMENSION arr_(1)
   =N_ScanBindery(4,@arr_)
   cServer = arr_[1]
ENDIF
cString = N_PropVal(cServer,4,"NET_ADDRESS",.F.)
RETURN cString
****************************************************************
```

## OTHER OBJECT TYPES

Although the first four object types—user, group, print queue, and file server—
are the ones most commonly used, NetWare also supports many other object
types. Novell reserves object type numbers up to 65,536 for well-known object
types. Developers may use object types above that number for their applications,
if needed. If a common object type is needed, contact Novell to request that an
object type number be assigned for you.

# UPDATING THE BINDERY FILES

Since the bindery API is accessible directly from FoxPro, you can read and query the bindery, as well as update it.

> **Caution:** Although your application can add information to the bindery, it is best not to overload the bindery files. If the bindery is too large, network performance will deteriorate. If you need user-specific information, you should create a file in the user's mail directory.

Keep in mind that although the bindery can be updated from FoxPro, most bindery update rights are limited to the Supervisor. The functions in this chapter can be used to update bindery information, but NetWare will restrict most rights according to the internal security information. Unless you possess Supervisor rights, you will probably be able to update only your current object. If you have Supervisor rights, then you will be able to use these functions on almost any object in the bindery.

## BINDERY OBJECT FUNCTIONS

The following group of functions allows you to add, delete, and rename bindery objects. Once again, we stress that the bindery should remain small, so you should not allow your users to populate the bindery with information that could be stored elsewhere on the network.

**Adding an object to the bindery**   Here is a function called N_ADDOBJECT() that allows you to place an object into the bindery. It takes the object name and type as the first two required parameters. The next parameter is the Static/ Dynamic flag, which is either S (static) or D (dynamic); the default value is S. The next two parameters indicate the security and can be A (anyone), L (logged), O (object), S (supervisor), or N (NetWare); the default is O.

```
*****************************************************************
*   Function:   N_AddObject()
*    Purpose:   Adds an object into the bindery
*     Syntax:   <logical> = N_AddObject(cObject,;
*                                       nType,;
*                                       cFlag,;
*                                       cRead,;
*                                       cWrite )
* Arguments:    cObject    - Object to be added to the bindery
*               nType      - Type of object being added
*               cFlag      - Static/Dynamic
*               cRead      - Read security
```

```
*              cWrite     - Write security
*
*    Returns:  TRUE if added successfully, FALSE otherwise
*
*      Notes:  This function is used to add a new object into the
*              bindery. You must specify the object name, type,
*              flag, and security for any item added.
*
*********************************************************************
function N_AddObject
PARAMETERS cObject, nType, cFlag, cRead, cWrite
PRIVATE cRequest,nRead,nWrite

cRequest = chr(50)

IF PARAMETERS() < 4
   cFlag = "S"
ENDIF
IF PARAMETERS() < 5
   cRead = "O"
ENDIF
IF PARAMETERS() < 6
   cWrite = "O"
ENDIF
nWrite = AT(cWrite,"ALOSN")-1
nRead  = AT(cRead ,"ALOSN")-1

cRequest = cRequest + CHR(IIF(cFlag="D", 1, 0))+;
                      CHR((nWrite * 16) + nRead)+;
                      CHR(0)+CHR(nType) +;
                      Lstring(cObject,48)

RETURN Netware(227,cRequest,"") == 0
**********************************************************
```

**Removing an object from the bindery**   Here is a function called N_DEL-
OBJECT() that allows you to remove an object from the bindery. It takes the
object name and type as parameters and returns a logical value indicating
whether the object was removed.

```
**********************************************************
*   Function:  N_DelObject()
*   Purpose:  Removes an object from the bindery
*     Syntax:  <logical> = N_DelObject( cOject,nType )
*
* Arguments:  cObject    - Object to be remove from bindery
*             nType      - Type of object being removed
```

```
*
*    Returns:   TRUE if removed successfully, FALSE otherwise
*
*      Notes:   This function is used to remove a bindery
*               object. Keep in mind that NetWare's security
*               will probably restrict you from removing any
*               objects unless the ID has Supervisor rights.
*
****************************************************************
function N_DelObject
PARAMETERS cObject, nType
PRIVATE cRequest
cRequest = CHR(51)+;
           CHR(0)+CHR(nType)+;
           Lstring(cObject,48)
RETURN Netware(227,cRequest,"") == 0
****************************************************************
```

**Changing an object's name** This next function, called N_RENOBJECT(), allows you to change the name of an object. It accepts three parameters: the current object name and type, and the new name to assign to the object. It returns a logical value indicating whether the object name was changed.

Keep in mind that the functions to manipulate the bindery objects are subject to NetWare's bindery security. If your User ID does not have enough security, the function calls will return FALSE.

```
****************************************************************
*   Function:   N_RenObject()
*    Purpose:   Renames a bindery object
*     Syntax:   <logical> = N_RenObject( cOld,nType,cNew )
*
* Arguments:   cOld      - Original name of the object
*              nType     - Type of object being renamed
*              cNew      - New name of the bindery object
*
*    Returns:   TRUE if changed successfully, FALSE otherwise
*
*      Notes:   This function is used to rename an object
*               in the bindery.
*
****************************************************************
function N_RenObject
PARAMETERS cOld, nType, cNew
PRIVATE cRequest
cRequest = CHR(52)+;
           CHR(0)+CHR(nType)+;
```

```
            Lstring(cOld,48)+;
            Lstring(cNew,48)
RETURN Netware(227,cRequest,"") == 0
```

```
****************************************************************
```

## OBJECT PROPERTY FUNCTIONS

The following functions allow you to add and delete properties from bindery
objects. You can also use them to change the values of properties and add new
object IDs to set properties.

**Adding a property to an object**   The N_ADDPROPERTY() function listed
below adds the specified property to an object. It takes seven parameters and
returns a logical value indicating whether the property was added.

The required parameters are the current object name and type, followed by
the property you wish to add to the object. The fourth parameter is either S
(static) or D (dynamic) to indicate the duration of the property. The fifth parameter is either I (item) or S (set), indicating whether this is an item property
or a set of object IDs. The final two parameters indicate the security and can
be A (anyone), L (logged), O (object), S (supervisor), and N (NetWare); the
default is O.

```
******************************************************************
*   Function:  N_AddProperty()
*    Purpose:  Adds a property to a bindery object
*     Syntax:  <logical> = N_AddProperty( cObject,;
*                                         nType,;
*                                         cProperty,;
*                                         cFlag,;
*                                         cItemSet,;
*                                         cRead,;
*                                         cWrite )
*
* Arguments:  cObject   - Object to add the property to
*             nType     - Type of object
*             cProperty - Set property to add to object
*             cFlag     - Property flag, (S)tatic or (D)ynamic
*             cItemSet  - (I)tem or (S)et property
*             cRead     - Property read security
*             cWrite    - Property write security
*
*    Returns:  TRUE if added, FALSE otherwise
*
*      Notes:  This function is used to add a property to an
*              existing bindery object. For example, you can
```

```
*              use this function to add a fax number property
*              to a user object. Keep in mind this
*              function only adds the property; it does not
*              assign a value to it.
*
****************************************************************
function N_AddProperty
PARAMETERS cObject,nType,cProperty,cFlag,cItemSet,cRead,cWrite
PRIVATE cRequest,nRead,nWrite

cRequest = CHR(57)+;
           CHR(0)+CHR(nType)+;
           Lstring(cObject,48)

IF PARAMETERS() < 4
   cFlag = "S"
ENDIF
IF PARAMETERS() < 5
   cItemSet = "I"
ENDIF
IF PARAMETERS() < 6
   cRead = "O"
ENDIF
IF PARAMETERS() < 7
   cWrite = "O"
ENDIF
nWrite = AT(cWrite,"ALOSN")-1
nRead  = AT(cRead ,"ALOSN")-1

cRequest = cRequest +CHR(IIF(cFlag="D", 1, 0)+;
                     IIF(cItemSet="S",2,0))+;
                     CHR((nWrite*16)+nRead)+;
                     Lstring(UPPER(cProperty),16)

RETURN Netware(227,cRequest,"") == 0
****************************************************************
```

**Deleting a property from an object** The N_DELPROPERTY() function removes the specified property from an object. It accepts three parameters: the current object name and type, and the property that you wish to remove from the object. It returns a logical value indicating whether the property was removed.

```
****************************************************************
*  Function:  N_DelProperty()
*   Purpose:  Removes a property from a bindery object
*    Syntax:  <logical> = N_DelProperty( cObject,nType,;
*                                        cProperty )
```

```
*
* Arguments:  cObject   - Object to be updated
*             nType     - Type of object being updated
*             cProperty - Property to remove from object
*
*   Returns:  TRUE if removed, FALSE otherwise
*
*     Notes:  This function is used to remove a property
*             from a bindery object. For example, you can
*             use this function to remove the FAX_NUMBER
*             property from a user ID object
*
**************************************************************
function N_DelProperty
PARAMETERS cObject, nType, cProperty
PRIVATE cRequest

cRequest = CHR(58)+  ;
           CHR(0)+CHR(nType)+;
           Lstring(cObject,48)+;
           Lstring(UPPER(cProperty),16)

RETURN Netware(227,cRequest,"") == 0
**************************************************************
```

**Changing a property's value**    This next listing contains the N_CHGVALUE()
function, which allows you to change the value of a property. It accepts four
parameters: the current object name and type, the property you wish to change,
and the new value for the property. It returns a logical value indicating whether
the property's value was successfully changed.

> **Note:**   This function should be used only to change item properties. It does
> not check if the property is an item, but merely changes it; nor can it make
> an item larger than 128 characters.

```
**************************************************************
*   Function:  N_ChgValue()
*    Purpose:  Changes a property's value
*     Syntax:  <logical> = N_ChgValue( cObject,nType,;
*                              cProperty,xValue )
*
* Arguments:  cObject   - Object name to be updated
*             nType     - Type of object being updated
*             cProperty - Property to change
*             xValue    - New value for the property
*
```

```
*   Returns:   TRUE if property value was changed,
*              FALSE otherwise
*
*    Notes:    This function is used to change the value
*              for a given property. For example, after
*              adding a property called FAX_NUMBER to a
*              user object, you would use this function
*              to write in the person's fax number.
*
****************************************************************
function N_ChgValue
PARAMETERS cObject, nType, cProperty, xValue
PRIVATE cRequest

cRequest = CHR(62)+;
           CHR(0)+CHR(nType)+;
           Lstring(cObject,48)+;
           CHR(1)+CHR(255)+;
           Lstring(UPPER(cProperty),16)+;
           PADR(xValue,128,CHR(0))

RETURN Netware(227,cRequest,"")  == 0
****************************************************************
```

## WORKING WITH SET PROPERTIES

A set property contains a list of object IDs within that property. For example, each group has a set property called GROUP_MEMBERS that contains the object IDs for all users within the group. In this section, we will present functions to allow you to add and/or delete objects to and from set properties.

**Adding an object to a set**   The function called N_ADD2SET() listed below allows you to add more object IDs to a set property. It takes five parameters and returns a logical value indicating whether the object was added. The parameters are the current object name and type; followed by the object ID and type of the object you wish to add; and the property into which to add the object.

```
****************************************************************
*  Function:   N_Add2Set()
*  Purpose:    Adds an object to a set
*    Syntax:   <logical> = N_Add2Set( cOwner,nOwnType,;
*                              cObject,nType,cProperty )
*
* Arguments:   cOwner   - Bindery object that owns the set
*              nOwnType - Owner's object type
*              cObject  - Object to be added to owner set
```

```
*               nType     - Type of object being added
*               cProperty - Set property to add cObject to
*
*   Returns:  TRUE if added, FALSE otherwise
*
*     Notes:  This function is used to add an object to a
*             group owned by another object. For example,
*             you can use this function to place a user
*             bindery object into a group.
*
*************************************************************
function N_Add2Set
PARAMETERS cOwner, nOwnType, cObject, nType, cProperty
PRIVATE cRequest
cRequest = CHR(65)+;
          CHR(0)+CHR(nOwnType)+;
          Lstring(cOwner,48)+;
          Lstring(UPPER(cProperty),16)+;
          CHR(0)+CHR(nType)+;
          Lstring(cObject,48)

RETURN Netware(227,cRequest,"") == 0
*************************************************************
```

**Removing an object from a set**   The N_DELFROMSET() function allows
you to remove an object ID from a set property. N_DELFROMSET() accepts
five parameters: the current object name and type; object ID and type to be removed; and the property from which to remove the object. It returns a logical
value indicating whether the object was successfully removed.

```
*************************************************************
*   Function:  N_DelFromSet()
*    Purpose:  Removes an object from a set
*     Syntax:  <logical> = N_DelFromSet( cOwner,nOwnType,;
*                             cObject,nType,cProperty )
*
* Arguments:  cOwner    - Bindery object that owns the set
*             nOwnType  - Owner's object type
*             cObject   - Object to be removed to owner's
*                         set
*             nType     - Type of object being removed
*             cProperty - Set property to remove cObject
*                         from
*
*   Returns:  TRUE if removed, FALSE otherwise
*
```

```
*      Notes:  This function is used to remove an object
*              from a group owned by another object.
*
****************************************************************
function N_DelFromSet
PARAMETERS cOwner, nOwnType, cObject, nType, cProperty
PRIVATE cRequest
cRequest = CHR(66)+;
           CHR(0)+CHR(nOwnType)+;
           Lstring(cOwner,48)+;
           Lstring(UPPER(cProperty),16)+;
           CHR(0)+CHR(nType)+;
           Lstring(cObject,48)
RETURN Netware(227,cRequest,"") == 0
****************************************************************
```

# TECHNICAL OVERVIEW OF THE BINDERY

This section discusses the technical details of bindery files and record formats. (You may skip this section if this does not concern you; since the bindery is always open and always locked, it would be difficult for you to access the bindery at the record level, anyway.)

### BINDERY FILES

In Novell NetWare 2.*x* there are two files that contain the bindery information: NET$BIND.SYS and NET$BVAL.SYS. In NetWare 3.*x*, three files are used: NET$OBJ.SYS, NET$PROP.SYS, and NET$VAL.SYS. Table 8.3 shows which data is stored in these files.

**Table 8.3: Bindery File Contents**

| File Name | Contents |
| --- | --- |
| *NetWare 2.x:* | |
| NET$BIND.SYS | Objects and properties |
| NET$BVAL.SYS | Property values |
| *NetWare 3.x:* | |
| NET$OBJ.SYS | Objects |
| NET$PROP.SYS | Properties |
| NET$VAL.SYS | Property values |

These files are stored in the SYS:SYSTEM directory, with attributes set to Hidden and System. The most important thing to know about these files is that the NetWare operating system opens them and keeps them locked as long as the network is up and running. This makes bindery data extremely secure; the information in the bindery can be obtained only through a series of NetWare API calls. The bindery itself can be closed only by the Supervisor or a user with Supervisor rights. (Naturally, when the bindery is closed, the network is not tremendously useful!)

## BINDERY RECORD FORMATS

The structure for the bindery records is shown in Table 8.4.

**Table 8.4: Bindery Record Formats**

**Object Records Structure:**

| | |
|---|---|
| Object ID | 4 bytes |
| Object name | 1–48 bytes (first byte is name length) |
| Object type | 1 byte |
| Static/Dynamic flag | 1 byte (0 for Static and 1 for Dynamic) |
| Security flag | 1 byte |

**Property Records Structure:**

| | |
|---|---|
| Property name | 1–16 bytes (first byte is name length) |
| Static/Dynamic flag | Combined into 1 byte |
| Item /set flag | Bit 0 is set to 1 for a Dynamic property and 0 for a Static one. Bit 4 is set to 1 for a Set property and 0 for an Item property. |
| Security flag | 1 byte |

The security flag indicates who can read or write to this bindery object. It consists of two 4-bit fields placed into a single byte. Bits 1–4 are the write security, and bits 5–8 are the read security. Table 8.5 shows the security levels.

**Table 8.5: Bindery Security Levels**

| Level | Who | Explanation |
| --- | --- | --- |
| 0 | Anyone | Everyone, even users not yet logged in |
| 1 | Logged | Any object logged in to the server |
| 2 | Object | Only objects logged in with the same object name, type, and password |
| 3 | Supervisor | Supervisor, or objects with Supervisor rights |
| 4 | NetWare | Only the NetWare operating system |

# SUMMARY

In this chapter, we have explored NetWare's bindery and provided functions to allow your applications to access the bindery's information. We also discussed how the bindery is organized and how bindery records are stored within the bindery files. If you are looking for a secure environment for user information or simply want to take advantage of what NetWare offers, use the bindery. With the functions provided in this chapter, your application can access the bindery fairly easily. Many of these functions will be used in the e-mail programs at the end of this book.

# Printing and Network Print Queues

Printing with FoxPro

Accessing a network printer

Print queues

DOS printing

Printing from Windows

All together now: functions for printer management

# Chapter 9

O ne of the benefits that a network offers is the ability for workstations to share printers. Instead of having a laser printer for each computer, you can attach the printers to the file server and have the workstation send print jobs there for handling. In this chapter we will discuss how FoxPro can print to the network printer via print queues, and how to use the bindery functions from Chapter 8 to determine the queues that are available and check on the status of jobs in the print queue.

## PRINTING WITH FOXPRO

FoxPro includes a command called SET PRINTER, which has two forms. The first form

```
SET PRINTER ON | OFF
```

turns the printer either on or off. The second form

```
SET PRINTER TO
```

causes all subsequent output to be sent to the printer as well as to the screen. The second form specifies the destination of subsequent output. You can use SET PRINTER to print to a local printer (one attached to the workstation), a disk file, a communications port, or a network printer. Once you've specified the output destination, you then use the ON option to send output to the destination and the OFF option when you are done printing. The following listing shows an example of printing to the local printer attached to printer port LPT1:

```
set printer to LPT1:          && Specify where to print

? "This is on the screen."

set printer on               && Now we want to print

? "This will be on the printer!"
? "So will this..."

set printer off              && Now back to the screen

? "Back on the screen"
```

SET PRINTER ON is the command to send output to the printer. SET PRINTER OFF causes output to go to the screen. SET PRINTER TO is used to indicate the destination printer.

### TO THE LOCAL PRINTERS

Local printers may be attached to any of three parallel ports (LPT1, LPT2, and LPT3) or attached to one of two serial ports (COM1 and COM2). You may specify any of these five ports when you want to print to a local printer. On a network, it is possible that the local ports may be redirected to a network print queue.

### TO A FILE

You can also direct printed output into a disk file, using the SET PRINTER TO command followed by the disk file name. Printer output will overwrite the specified disk file if it already exists. To append the output to the existing disk file, specify the ADDITIVE keyword after the file name. For example,

```
SET PRINTER TO Report.txt          && Overwrites REPORT.TXT
SET PRINTER TO Log.txt ADDITIVE    && Appends data into LOG.TXT
```

### TO THE NETWORK PRINTER

A third form of the SET PRINTER TO command uses the \\SPOOLER option. The command SET PRINTER TO \\SPOOLER tells FoxPro to send the output to a network device. This causes printed output to be spooled to a temporary file. When a subsequent SET PRINTER TO command is issued (without any destination specified), the spooled temporary file is sent to the selected network printer.

**Network print command options**    The \\SPOOLER option is designed to work with most NetBIOS-compatible networks, including NetWare. In addition to the \\SPOOLER option, you can specify many of the options that are available to the network print commands, including the following:

\NB (No Banner)    This option tells NetWare not to add the usual banner page on the front of a print job to help identify its owner.

\B=<*banner*>    The \B option can be used to specify a banner name to appear on the front of your print jobs. The banner can be up to 12 characters and defaults to your network User ID.

\F=<*form_number*>    When a print queue is defined in NetWare, it can have up to 256 forms associated with it. A form is a set of printer characteristics including size, margins, and so forth. It allows the printer to print on many kinds of paper. NetWare assumes that the current form is form zero, although the operator can change this from the file console. If you specify the *form_number* with \F, then the job will not be printed until that form is mounted on the printer. The Supervisor can use the PRINTDEF program to define printer forms. Each form has a name, a form number, a number of lines per printed page, and a number of columns.

C=<*number of copies*>    The \C option allows you to specify the number of copies that should be made of the output when it is printed. The default value is 1, and the number can be from 1 to 255 copies.

\P=<*printer_number*>    The \P option designates which network printer number the output should be sent to. The network printers are numbered from 0 to the maximum number of server ports minus 1. The default printer is 0.

\S=*server_name*    You can use the \S option to designate the file server that should handle this print request. You can use the code example of N_START-CAP(), listed in the section, "Using CAPTURE," to determine the names of the available servers. The *server_name* is always expressed as a literal value, so it should not be enclosed in quotes. You can use the macro operator (&) to specify a variable *server_name*.

\Q=*queue_name*    The \Q option lets you designate the name of the destination print queue. You can use the code example of N_STARTCAP(), listed in the section, "Using CAPTURE," to determine the names of all available queues.

The *queue_name* is always expressed as a literal value, so it should not be enclosed in quotes. You can use the macro operator (&) to specify a variable *queue_name.*

## ACCESSING A NETWORK PRINTER

Although FoxPro can directly print on the network, you can gain more control over the process by interfacing with NetWare's CAPTURE interface. In this section, we will discuss how CAPTURE works and provide for you the FoxPro routines to access it.

When the network shell is loaded on a workstation, it redirects several of DOS's interrupts for its own use. One of these is the printer service interrupt (17H). When the workstation tries to print something, DOS gives control to the printer service interrupt and, therefore, to the network shell. The network shell can then pass the print request to a local printer or redirect it to the network.

NetWare provides a command called CAPTURE that instructs the shell to send print requests to the network. When CAPTURE is loaded, all data sent to the specified printer is sent to the network. The network operating system then takes the data and writes it into a file called the *capture file.* NetWare assigns the file to a *printer queue,* which is a bindery object that stores files and directs them to the specified printer. All subsequent printing is written to this capture file.

The application program can at some point direct the network to start printing the capture file on a printer. This can be done by *closing* the capture or by *flushing* the capture. A FLUSH command instructs the network to print the contents of the file, but does not release the printer capture. Closing the capture first flushes the file and then releases the printer capture. Once released, subsequent print requests will be handled by the local printer.

The capture system allows any application program to print on a network printer. Since the program turns the request over to DOS for processing, the program does not know where the information is printed. However, this presents a slight problem, because the application probably won't send the instruction to the network to print the capture file. (After all, the application thinks it is talking to a dumb printer, not a smart queue management system.)

CAPTURE solves the problem by allowing a timeout value to be specified. If no new data is received within the specified interval, the network assumes that the print request is complete and will start to print the capture file.

## USING CAPTURE

Although it is possible to load CAPTURE at the DOS prompt and then run your FoxPro application, doing so may present two problems: First, someone might forget to load CAPTURE and accidentally start printing on the local printer; and second, once CAPTURE is loaded, the captured printer port is no longer available for local printing. If you plan to use both a network and a local printer, loading CAPTURE before your program starts is not a viable solution. You can, however, use the FP_INT86() function from Chapter 7 to access the CAPTURE services from within the FoxPro application. If you want to print on a network, you can start CAPTURE before your print routine, and turn it off when your print routine is done. This allows the user to print locally from within your application.

**Starting a capture**   The function called N_STARTCAP(), listed below, starts a capture on the default local printer (usually LPT1). When we discuss capture flags later in the chapter, you will see how to designate which local printer is captured.

```
************************************************************
*    Program:   NETPRINT.PRG
*   Function:   N_STARTCAP()
*    Authors:   Joseph D. Booth and Greg Lief
*    Purpose:   To allow capture of local printers
*               from within a FoxPro program
*     Syntax:   <logical> = N_STARTCAP( [<nPrinter>] )
* Arguments:    nPrinter  - Optional print to capture
*    Returns:   TRUE is successful, FALSE otherwise
*
*      Notes:   This function is used to start a
*               capture to the specified printer.
*
************************************************************
function N_StartCap
PARAMETER nPrinter
DIMENSION aRegs(10)
PRIVATE is_ok
is_ok  = .F.
STORE Ø TO aRegs
IF PARAMETERS() = Ø
   aRegs(1) = 223 * 256        && DFh ØØh -Capture specific
   aRegs(4) = Ø
ELSE
   aRegs(1) = 223 * 256        && DFh Ø4h -Capture
   aRegs(4) = (nPrinter-1)*256 +4
```

```
ENDIF
IF FP_int86( 33, @aRegs )
   is_ok = (aRegs(1) % 256) = 0  && Extract low byte
ENDIF
RETURN is_ok
```

**Flushing the capture**    The function called N_FLUSHCAP(), listed below, flushes the current capture file to a network printer. It does not stop the capture, but merely asks the network to print the capture file and start another one. If the function is successful, it returns TRUE; if not, it returns FALSE.

```
************************************************************************
*   Program:   NETPRINT
*  Function:   N_FLUSHCAP()
*   Authors:   Joseph D. Booth and Greg Lief
*   Purpose:   To force the network to print the
*              current capture file.
*    Syntax:   <nJob> = N_FLUSHCAP( [<nPrinter>] )
*
* Arguments:   nPrinter  - Optional captured printer to flush
*
*   Returns:   Job number for print queue handling printing, or
*              zero if a problem occurs.
*
*     Notes:   This function is used to send a capture file to
*              the network printer. The capture will not be
*              stopped, and all subsequent output will be
*              redirected as well.
*
************************************************************************

function N_FlushCap
PARAMETER nPrinter
DIMENSION aRegs(10),arr_(12)
PRIVATE is_ok,nJob
is_ok  = .F.
nJob   = 0
STORE 0 TO aRegs
IF PARAMETERS() = 0
   aRegs(1) = 223 * 256      && DFh 03h -Flush default
   aRegs(4) = 3
ELSE
   aRegs(1) = 223 * 256      && DFh 07h -Flush specific
   aRegs(4) = (nPrinter-1)*256 +07
ENDIF
IF FP_int86( 33, @aRegs )
```

```
      is_ok =  (aRegs(1) % 256) = Ø  && Extract low byte
ENDIF
IF is_ok
   IF N_CapFlags(@arr)
      nJob = arr_(9)
   ENDIF
ENDIF
RETURN nJob
```

The N_FLUSHCAP() function can be called after each report if you are running several to the printer at once. If you want to return control to your user
after printing, you should probably use N_CLOSECAP(), discussed next, to
print the file and return control to the local printer.

**Closing the capture**    The function N_CLOSECAP(), listed next, closes the
current capture and returns control to the local printer. The function also requests that the network print the contents of the capture file.

```
********************************************************************
*    Program:   NETPRINT.PRG
*    Authors:   Joseph D. Booth and Greg Lief
*    Purpose:   To close the capture and return control
*               to the local printer
*     Syntax:   <nJob> = N_CLOSECAP( [<nPrinter>] )
*
* Arguments:   nPrinter  - Optional captured printer to close
*
*    Returns:   Job number for print queue handling printing, or
*               zero if a problem occurs.
*
*      Notes:   This function is used to close a capture being
*               run on a printer. The output will be set to the
*               network printer.
*
********************************************************************
function N_CloseCap
PARAMETERS nPrinter
DIMENSION aRegs(1Ø),arr_(12)
PRIVATE is_ok,nJob
is_ok  = .F.
nJob   = Ø
IF PARAMETERS() = Ø
   aRegs(1) = 223 * 256      && DFh Ø1h -Close default capture
   aRegs(4) = 1
ELSE
   aRegs(1) = 223 * 256      && DFh Ø5h -Close specific capture
```

```
   aRegs(4) = (nPrinter-1)*256 +5
ENDIF
IF FP_int86( 33, @aRegs )
   is_ok = (aRegs(1) % 256) = Ø  && Extract low byte
ENDIF
IF is_ok
   IF N_CapFlags(@arr_)
      nJob = arr_(9)
   ENDIF
ENDIF
RETURN nJob
```

Both N_FLUSHCAP() and N_CLOSECAP() place a job into the print queue and return a job number. This job number must be used later with the queue-management system, to determine information about the job. Be sure to save the job number to a variable if you want to be able to check on the job's status.

**Canceling the capture**    The function N_CANCELCAP(), listed in this section cancels the current capture and returns control to the local printer. Unlike N_CLOSECAP(), it does not request that the network print the contents of the capture file. The contents of the capture file are lost after N_CANCEL-CAP() is performed.

```
*******************************************************************
*    Program:   NETPRINT.PRG
*    Authors:   Joseph D. Booth and Greg Lief
*    Purpose:   To cancel the capture and return control
*               to the local printer.  The file is not printed.
*     Syntax:   <logical> = N_CANCELCAP( [<nPrinter>] )
*
* Arguments:    nPrinter  - Optional captured printer to cancel
*
*    Returns:   TRUE if canceled, FALSE otherwise
*
*      Notes:   This function is used to cancel a capture being
*               run on a printer. If the function returns TRUE,
*               no output will be sent to the network printer;
*               it will all be discarded.
*
*******************************************************************
function N_CancelCap
PARAMETERS nPrinter
DIMENSION aRegs(1Ø)
PRIVATE is_ok
is_ok  = .F.
IF PARAMETERS() = Ø
```

```
   aRegs(1)  = 223 * 256    && DFh Ø2h -Cancel default Capture
   aRegs(4)  = 2
ELSE
   aRegs(1) = 223 * 256    && DFh Ø6h -Cancel specific Capture
   aRegs(4) = (nPrinter-1)*256 +6
ENDIF
IF FP_int86( 33, @aRegs )
   is_ok =  (aRegs(1) % 256) = Ø  && Extract low byte
ENDIF
RETURN is_ok
```

## SETTING PRINTER FLAGS

The CAPTURE command operates on the default LPT*n*. This is usually LPT1, but it can be changed. In addition to capturing the printer, there are a number of flags that can be set to control the printing.

**Local Printers**    The local printer ports to be captured are referred to by number, starting with zero, as listed here:

| Printer | Number |
|---------|--------|
| LPT1    | 0      |
| LPT2    | 1      |
| LPT3    | 2      |

Serial ports (COM1, COM2, and so on) cannot be captured by the network, because these are two-way communications ports. The network operating system does not communicate to the port when it is capturing a file.

**Network Printers**    There can be five physical printers attached to a network file server. These are referred to by number, starting with zero; the first printer is 0, second printer is 1, and so on. Although you can specify which network printer to use, the network operating system still places your print requests into a print queue for servicing. It does not send data directly to a network printer from a workstation.

**Queue to Use**    You can specify the destination print queue for the capture file. The queue flag must contain the bindery ID of the destination print queue. Using the N_SCANBINDERY() function and the N_OBJECTID() functions from Chapter 8, you can print the capture file from any valid queue.

**Number of Copies**    You can specify the number of copies of your capture file to print, from 0 to 255. The default is 1.

**Print Form Names**    If you need to print on special paper, you can specify a print form number. If you specify a nonzero number, the network sends a message to the server instructing the operator to mount the form specified by that number. Until the print form is changed, only jobs matching the currently loaded form will print. You can also specify a form name for the convenience of the person operating the printer. Only the form number, however, determines whether the system can print.

**Banners**   A banner is a page that is printed at the front of your print job. This page usually contains your User ID and other information to identify the printouts. If the banner is not necessary, you can instruct the CAPTURE command to omit the banner page from the output, using the \NB option (and save a few trees).

**Job Number**   When a capture file is closed or flushed to the printer, the network assigns a job number to the request. This job number will be used by the queue functions, which are discussed later in this chapter.

### THE N_CAPFLAGS() FUNCTION

The following listing contains a function called N_CAPFLAGS() that is a GET/SET block for setting some of the common flags. It takes two arrays, one to get the current flags, and a second, optional array of parameters. If this second array is passed, then the appropriate flags are set to new values.

N_CAPFLAGS() returns an array containing the current settings. Table 9.1 lists the contents of the array:

**Table 9.1: N_CAPFLAGS() Array Structure**

| Element | Type | Contents |
|---------|---------|----------------------------------------------|
| 1 | Logical | Print banner pages |
| 2 | Char | Banner heading to use |
| 3 | Numeric | Local printer to capture |
| 4 | Numeric | Network printer to use |
| 5 | Numeric | Bindery ID of print queue |
| 6 | Numeric | Number of copies |
| 7 | Numeric | Form number to mount before printing |
| 8 | Char | Form name |
| 9 | Numeric | Job number |
| 10 | Numeric | Maximum lines per page; defaults to 66 |
| 11 | Numeric | Maximum characters per line; defaults to 132 |
| 12 | Numeric | Timeout value in seconds |

You can set any of the capture flags by updating the appropriate element in the array and passing a second array to N_CAPFLAGS(). The function updates the old array containing the original flags for the default capture. It also returns a logical value indicating whether or not the flags were updated.

Here is the N_CAPFLAGS() function code:

```
*********************************************************************
*    Program:   NETPRINT.PRG
*    Authors:   Joseph D. Booth and Greg Lief
*    Purpose:   To set the network capture flags
*     Syntax:   <logical> = N_CapFlags( aOldFlags [,<aNewFlags>] )
*
* Arguments:    aOldFlags - Current capture flags
*               aNewFlags - Optional array of new flags to set
*
*      Notes:   This function is used to set the capture flags
*               for the default printer. The array consists of
*               twelve elements as defined below:
*
*                1  Logical   Should banners be printed?
*                2  Char      Text of the banner
*                3  Numeric   Which local printer is captured?
*                4  Numeric   Which network printer is serving it?
*                5  Numeric   Bindery print queue object ID
*                6  Numeric   Number of copies to print
*                7  Numeric   Form number
*                8  Char      Name of the form to load in printer
*                9  Numeric   Job number
*               10  Numeric   Maximum lines down
*               11  Numeric   Maximum characters across
*               12  Numeric   Timeout value in seconds
*
*********************************************************************
function N_CapFlags
PARAMETERS aOldFlags,aNewFlags
DIMENSION aRegs(10)
PRIVATE is_ok,x,y,cReply

is_ok   = .F.
cReply  = SPACE(63)

aRegs(1)    = 184 * 256         && B8h 00h -Get Flags
aRegs(2)    = .F.
aRegs(3)    = 63
aRegs(9)    = cReply
```

```
IF FP_int86( 33, @aRegs )
    is_ok =  (aRegs(1) % 256)==0  && Extract low byte
    IF is_ok
        SET LIBRARY TO BLNET ADDITIVE
        cReply = aRegs(9)
        aOldFlags( 1) = ASC(SUBSTR(cReply,2,1))>127
        aOldFlags( 2) = CLEANSTR(SUBSTR(cReply,8,13))
        aOldFlags( 3) = ASC(SUBSTR(cReply,22,1))
        aOldFlags( 4) = ASC(SUBSTR(cReply,4,1))
        aOldFlags( 5) = LONG2FOX(SUBSTR(cReply,58,4))
        aOldFlags( 6) = ASC(SUBSTR(cReply,5,1))
        aOldFlags( 7) = ASC(SUBSTR(cReply,6,1))
        aOldFlags( 8) = CLEANSTR(SUBSTR(cReply,30,13))
        aOldFlags( 9) = INT2FOX(SUBSTR(cReply,62,2))
        aOldFlags(10) = INT2FOX(SUBSTR(cReply,26,2))
        aOldFlags(11) = INT2FOX(SUBSTR(cReply,28,2))
        aOldFlags(12) = INT2FOX(SUBSTR(cReply,23,2))
    ENDIF
ENDIF
IF PARAMETERS() = 2
    FOR x = 1 TO LEN(aNewFlags)
        DO CASE
        CASE x = 1
            IF aNewFlags(x) <> aOldFlags(x)
                IF aFlags(x)
                    y = ASC(SUBSTR(cReply,2,1)) +128
                ELSE
                    y = ASC(SUBSTR(cReply,2,1)) +128
                ENDIF
                cReply = STUFF(cReply,2,1,CHR(y))
            ENDIF
        CASE x = 2
            cReply =STUFF(cReply,8,13,PADR(aNewFlags(x),13,CHR(0)))
        CASE x = 3
            cReply =STUFF(cReply,22,1,CHR(aNewFlags(x)))
        CASE x = 4
            cReply =STUFF(cReply,4,1,CHR(aNewFlags(x)))
        CASE x = 5
            cReply =STUFF(cReply,58,4,FOX2LONG(aNewFlags(x)))
        CASE x = 6
            cReply =STUFF(cReply,5,1,CHR(aNewFlags(x)))
        CASE x = 7
            cReply =STUFF(cReply,6,1,CHR(aNewFlags(x)))
        CASE x = 8
            cReply =STUFF(cReply,31,13,PADR(aNewFlags(x),13,CHR(0)))
        CASE x = 10
```

```
          cReply =STUFF(cReply,26,2,FOX2INT(aNewFlags(x)))
      CASE x = 11
          cReply =STUFF(cReply,28,2,FOX2INT(aNewFlags(x)))
      CASE x = 12
          cReply =STUFF(cReply,23,2,FOX2INT(aNewFlags(x)))
      ENDCASE
    NEXT
    cReply     = SUBSTR(cReply,1,53)
    aRegs( 1) = 184 * 256  +1    && B8h 01h -Set Flags
    aRegs( 2) = .F.
    aRegs( 3) = 53
    aRegs( 9) = cReply

    IF FP_int86( 33, @aRegs )
        is_ok =  (aRegs(1) % 256) = 0   && Extract low byte
    ENDIF
ENDIF
RETURN is_ok
```

Using N_CAPFLAGS(), the following code changes to Printer 2 and requests three copies of a report:

```
DIMENSION aFlags(12)
DIMENSION aOld(12)

aFlags(2) = 2
aFlags(6) = 3

=N_CapFlags(@aOld,@aFlags)

=N_StartCap()
**
** Printing the report
**
=N_EndCap()
=N_CapFlags( @aOld,@aOld )        && Restore original flags
```

**Note:**   The P_START() function shown later in the chapter also provides an example of using the CAPTURE functions.

# PRINT QUEUES

The network does not allow a program direct access to the printers, but rather places all print requests into a directory. The network then prints the files from this directory one at a time; this process is known as *queuing*. The network provides services to manage the print queues, collectively called *queue manage-ment services* (QMS). These services allow you to control what jobs are printed and when, what forms must be mounted when printing, and so on.

### DETERMINING THE AVAILABLE PRINT QUEUES

In Chapter 8, we discussed a function called N_SCANBINDERY that returns a list of bindery objects available on the network. For your convenience, its syntax is repeated here:

> DIMENSION aQueues(1)
>
> =N_SCANBINDERY(3,@aQueues)

The function returns a list of queue names that are available for use.

You will also need the N_OBJECTID() function from Chapter 8, which gives you the bindery object ID number for a specified object and type. Print queues are object type 3, so the following syntax will return the bindery ID for a queue name:

> nId = N_OBJECTID( aQueues(x),3 )

All the QMS functions refer to a queue by its bindery ID number.

### LOCATING THE PRINT QUEUE

When either N_FLUSHCAP() or N_CLOSECAP() is called to print the capture file, a job number is assigned and returned. This job number is used in conjunction with the queue's bindery ID number to determine information about the print job. You can use the N_CAPFLAGS() function discussed earlier to determine the queue from which the job is being printed. Here is an example:

```
DIMENSION aFlags(12)
nJob      = N_FLUSHCAP( )
=N_CAPFLAGS(@aFlags)
nQueueId  = aFlags(5)
```

### GETTING A LIST OF JOBS IN A PRINT QUEUE

Once you know the queue ID, you can use the N_QJOBLIST() function shown below to return an array of jobs within that print queue. The function takes the queue's bindery ID number as a parameter, and returns an array of job descriptions for each queue job. The description consists of the job's position in the queue and a text string describing the job.

```
************************************************************
*   Program:  NETPRINT.PRG
*   Authors:  Joseph D. Booth and Greg Lief
```

```
*  Function:  N_QJOBLIST()
*   Purpose:  Get the list of jobs within the queue
*    Syntax:  <nCount> = N_QjobList(nQueue,@aJobs)
**********************************************************
function N_QJobList
PARAMETERS nQueue,aJobs
PRIVATE cReply,cRequest,cList,nCount,x,nJobs
cReply   = SPACE(506)                    && Reply buffer
cRequest = CHR(107)+FOX2LONG(nQueue)     && E3h 6Bh
IF NetWare( 243,cRequest,@cReply )  = 0
    nCount = INT2FOX(SUBSTR(cReply,1,2))
    cList  = SUBSTR(cReply,3)
    SET LIBRARY TO BLNET ADDITIVE
    DIMENSION aJobs(nCount)
    FOR x = 1 TO nCount
        nJob = LONG2FOX(SUBSTR(cList,(x-1)+1,4))
        IF nJob > 0
            cReply   = SPACE(258)
            cRequest = CHR(108)+FOX2LONG(nQueue)+;
                       FOX2INT(nJob)

            IF NetWare(243,cRequest,@cReply) = 0
                aJobs(x) = STR(ASC(SUBSTR(cReply,29,1)))+;
                       CleanStr(SUBSTR(cReply,57,50)) )
            ENDIF
        ENDIF
    NEXT
ENDIF
RETURN nCount
```

## CHANGING A JOB'S QUEUE POSITION

When your print job is placed into the queue, it is assigned the next queue position and waits its turn. You can request that the network change your position in the queue if you need to rush your job. The N_QPOSITION function shown next is a GET/SET function. If you pass it a position parameter, it attempts to change the job's position in the queue to the new position. The function returns the current position. If you need to determine the current position, just pass the queue ID number and the job number, and leave the third parameter blank.

```
**********************************************************
*   Program:  NETPRINT.PRG
*   Authors:  Joseph D. Booth and Greg Lief
*  Function:  N_QPOSITION()
*   Purpose:  Queries/changes a job's print position
```

```
*    Syntax:  <logical> = N_QPOSITION(nQueue,nJob,nPosition)
*******************************************************************
function N_QPOSITION
PARAMETERS nQueue,nJob,nPos
PRIVATE cReply,cRequest,nOld,pcount
pcount   = PARAMETERS()
cReply   = SPACE(258)
cRequest = CHR(108)+FOX2LONG(nQueue)+;
                     FOX2INT(nJob)
nOld     = 0
IF NetWare(243,cRequest,@cReply) == 0
    nOld = ASC(SUBSTR(cReply,29,1))
ENDIF
IF pcount = 3
    cReply   = SPACE(2)           && Reply buffer
    cRequest = CHR(110)+;         && E3h 6Eh
              FOX2LONG(nQueue)+;
              FOX2INT(nJob)+;
              CHR(nPos)
    =NetWare( 243,cRequest,@cReply )
ENDIF
RETURN nOld
```

## REMOVING A JOB FROM A QUEUE

If you need to cancel your print job, you can use the N_QREMOVE() function shown below. This function takes the queue ID and the job number as parameters. If the job can be successfully removed from the queue, a TRUE value is returned. If the job cannot be removed, the function returns FALSE. And if the job has already been printed, the function returns FALSE because print jobs are no longer present in the queue.

```
***********************************************************
*    Program:  NETPRINT.PRG
*    Authors:  Joseph D. Booth and Greg Lief
*    Function: N_QREMOVE()
*    Purpose:  Remove a job from the print queue
*    Syntax:   <logical> = N_QREMOVE(nQueue,nJob)
***********************************************************
function N_QREMOVE
PARAMETERS nQueue,nJob
PRIVATE cReply,cRequest,is_ok
cReply   = SPACE(2)           && Reply buffer
cRequest = CHR(106)+;
          FOX2LONG(nQueue)+;
          FOX2INT(nJob)
is_ok    = .F.
```

```
IF NetWare( 243,cRequest,@cReply ) = 0
    is_ok = .T.
ENDIF
RETURN is_ok
```

# DOS PRINTING

The DOS operating system also contains a print-queue program called PRINT-.EXE. This utility allows you to print files in the background while your application is running. You can use the FP_INT86() function from Chapter 6 to allow your FoxPro program access to the DOS utility. However, even with a function to access an interrupt, it is still necessary to find the appropriate interrupts. According to the trusty MS-DOS Programmer's Reference Manual, the DOS interrupts needed to handle the print queue are as follows:

| Hex | Decimal | Purpose |
|-----|---------|---------|
| 0100 | 256 | Find out if PRINT.EXE is installed |
| 0101 | 257 | Add a file to the printer queue |
| 0102 | 258 | Remove a file from the print queue |
| 0103 | 259 | Cancel all files in the print queue |

## CHECKING IF PRINT.EXE IS INSTALLED

The Q_INSTALLED() function listed below is used to check if the user has installed the DOS print queue (by typing PRINT at the DOS prompt). If the print queue has not been installed, then—obviously —FoxPro cannot use it.

```
*************************************************************
*    Program:  NETPRINT.PRG
*    Authors:  Joseph D. Booth and Greg Lief
*    Function: Q_installed()
*    Purpose:  To check installed state of PRINT.EXE
*    Returns:  lInstalled  - TRUE if installed, FALSE otherwise
*************************************************************
function Q_installed
* 100h - Get PRINT.EXE installed state
DIMENSION aRegs(10)
STORE 0 TO aRegs
aRegs(1) = 256
FP_int86(47,@aRegs)               && Execute multiplex interrupt
RETURN (aRegs(1)%256) =255        && AL is 255 if installed
```

If the PRINT utility is not installed, you might be able to install it for the user. If you are using the extended version of FoxPro, conventional memory is not being used, and PRINT can be safely installed by the FoxPro program. For example,

```
IF _DOS
   IF NOT Q_INSTALLED()
      RUN PRINT/D:PRN
   ENDIF
ENDIF
```

If you are running regular FoxPro for DOS, however, and not the extended version, then you should not run PRINT from within FoxPro, since it is installed as a TSR program and you cannot guarantee where it will be placed in memory.

### ADDING A FILE TO THE PRINT QUEUE

You can use the following Q_ADD() function to add a file to the DOS print queue. This function takes the file name as the parameter; it returns TRUE if the file was added to the print queue, or FALSE if not.

```
*****************************************************************
*    Program:  NETPRINT.PRG
*    Authors:  Joseph D. Booth and Greg Lief
*    Purpose:  To add a file to the print queue
*     Syntax:  Q_add( cFilename )
* Parameter:  cFilename
*    Returns:  lSuccess - TRUE if file added, FALSE otherwise
*****************************************************************
function Q_add
PARAMETERS cFilename
* 101h - Add a file to the queue
DIMENSION aRegs(10)
PRIVATE nAddr,nSize,hMem
STORE 0 to aRegs
aRegs(1) = 257
hMem     = BufAlloc(64)
nAddr    = BulLock(hMem)
aRegs(8) = CHR(0)+L2BIN(nAddr)    && Pass level/address
aRegs(4) = .T.                    && Tell interrupt we are
=FP_int86(47,@aRegs)              && using a string
=BufUnlock(hMem)
=BufFree(hMem)                    && Unallocate buffer
return (aRegs(10) % 2 ) = 0       && Check carry flag
```

**Note:** The BUFxxxx functions used in the QADD.PRG program are found in the BLNET library file.

## REMOVING A FILE FROM THE PRINT QUEUE

The Q_REMOVE() function, shown next, is used to remove a file from DOS's print queue. The function takes a file name as the parameter; it returns TRUE if the file was removed, or FALSE if not.

```
*************************************************************
*    Program:  NETPRINT.PRG
*    Authors:  Joseph D. Booth and Greg Lief
*    Purpose:  To remove a file from the print queue
*     Syntax:  Q_remove( cFilename )
* Parameter:  cFilename
*    Returns:  lSuccess - TRUE if removed, FALSE otherwise
*************************************************************
function Q_remove
PARAMETERS  cFilename
* 102h - Remove a file to the queue
DIMENSION aRegs(10)
STORE 0 TO aRegs
aRegs(1) = 258
aRegs(8) = cFilename         && File name
aRegs(4) = .T.               && Tell interrupt we
=FP_int86(47,@aRegs)         && are using a string
RETURN (aRegs(10) % 2) =0    && Check carry flag
```

## CANCELING ALL FILES IN THE PRINT QUEUE

You can also erase the entire print queue by using DOS interrupts, which is exactly what Q_CANCEL() does, as follows:

```
*************************************************************
*    Program:  NETPRINT.PRG
*    Authors:  Joseph D. Booth and Greg Lief
*    Purpose:  To cancel all jobs in the print queue
*     Syntax:  Q_cancel()
* Parameter:  NONE
*    Returns:  lSuccess - TRUE if all jobs were canceled
*                         FALSE otherwise
*************************************************************
function Q_cancel()
* 103h - Cancel all jobs in the print queue
DIMENSION aRegs(10)
STORE 0 TO aRegs
aRegs(1) = 259
RETURN FP_int86(47,@aRegs)       && Execute interrupt
```

## PRINTING FROM WINDOWS

FoxPro for Windows sends all local print requests to the Windows Print Manager. The Print Manager is a very efficient program that allows printing while the user continues running the application. If you are working in FoxPro for Windows, take advantage of its multitasking capability and use the Print Manager to handle all printing to local printers.

If, however, you are printing to a network printer from within Windows, you should disable Windows's Print Manager and let the network print queue handle the request. This will prevent timeouts and premature printing that can occur if Windows becomes very busy.

## ALL TOGETHER NOW: FUNCTIONS FOR PRINTER MANAGEMENT

Now that we have discussed the various printing options available to a workstation on a network, let's write some functions to handle printer management. Specifically, you'll want the user to be able to select where to print, to start and cancel the printing process, and to end printing. The functions to accomplish these tasks are as follows:

- ▸ P_WHERE() determines where the printing will take place—to a text file, a local printer, or a network printer. The function returns a logical TRUE if the user selects the print destination or FALSE if the Escape key is pressed.

- ▸ P_START() performs the necessary setup to start printing at the location specified by the user. This function's action will vary, depending upon what the user selects during the P_WHERE() function call.

- ▸ P_CANCEL() optionally cancels the printing and will cancel the job from the network print queue, if appropriate. You should call this function frequently while printing, to check if the Escape key has been pressed. When it has, then the user is given the option to cancel or continue. If cancel is selected, the function returns TRUE; otherwise, it returns FALSE.

- ▸ P_END() is called when the printing is completed. It cleans up the printing environment and prints the report at the selected destination.

In addition, to use these function, you need to create two public arrays to hold the names of the print queues and their bindery object numbers. The

following code fragment shows how to use the print functions to control your
application's printing needs:

```
**
** Using the printer functions
**
SET LIBRARY TO BLNET
SET PROCEDURE TO BINDERY

PUBLIC aQlist(1),aQnumbs(1)
y=N_ScanBindery(3,@aQlist)
DIMENSION aQnumbs[y]
FOR x = 1 TO y
   aQnumbs[x] = N_ObjectId(aQlist[x],3)
NEXT

SET PROCEDURE TO NETPRINT

IF P_Where()        && select where to print
   IF P_start()        && Able to start printing
       prt_cancel=.f.
       ON KEY LABEL ESC DO p_cancel()
       REPORT FORM <report> TO PRINT WHILE .NOT.prt_cancel
       ON KEY LABEL ESC
       =P_end()
   ENDIF
ENDIF
```

Following are the P_ printing functions.

```
*****************************************************
*    Program:  NETPRINT.PRG
*    Authors:  Joseph D. Booth and Greg Lief
*
*    Function:  P_Where()
*    Purpose:  Selects where to print a report
*    Returns:  TRUE if printer select,
*              FALSE if the escape key pressed
*****************************************************
function P_Where
PUBLIC prt_where,prt_file,prt_cancel
PRIVATE x,clist
FOR x = 1 to LEN(aQlist)-1
     cList = cList + aQlist[x]+";"
NEXT
cList      = cList+aQlist( LEN(aQlist) )
x          = Ø
```

```
prt_cancel = .F.
@ 5,5 GET x FUNCTION '^ Local Printer;Text File;"+cList
READ
DO CASE
CASE x = 1
   prt_where = "L"
   IF Q_INSTALLED()
       prt_file = SYS(3)
   ELSE
       prt_file = "LPT1:"
   ENDIF
CASE x = 2
   prt_where = "T"
   prt_file  = SPACE(12)
   @ 7,15 GET prt_file PICTURE "!!!!!!!!!!!!!" ;
           VALID !EMPTY(prt_file)
   READ
   IF LASTKEY() = 27
       prt_where = ""
   ENDIF
CASE x > 2
   Prt_Where = "N"
   =N_CAPFLAGS(@aOld)
   aOld(5) = aQnumbs(x-2)
   =N_CAPFLAGS(@aOld,@aOld)
   prt_file = "LPT1:"

ENDCASE
RETURN x > 0
*******************************************************
*  Function:  P_Start()
*   Purpose:  Sets up the environment to print
*******************************************************
function P_Start
ON ERROR OK = .F.
OK = .T.
SET PRINT TO &PRT_FILE
SET PRINTER ON
SET CONSOLE OFF
RETURN OK
*******************************************************
*  Function:  P_Cancel()
*   Purpose:  Check to see if ESCAPE was pressed
*******************************************************
function P_Cancel
Prt_Cancel = .T.
```

```
RETURN
*******************************************************
*   Function:  P_End()
*    Purpose:  Finishes the report and prints it
*******************************************************

function P_End
SET PRINTER OFF
SET PRINTER TO
SET CONSOLE ON
DO CASE
CASE prt_Where = "L"
   IF NOT prt_cancel
       IF Q_INSTALLED()
          =Q_ADD(prt_file)
        ENDIF
   ENDIF
CASE Prt_Where = "N"
   IF NOT prt_cancel
       =N_CLOSECAP()
   ELSE
       =N_CANCELCAP()
   ENDIF
ENDCASE
RETURN ""
```

# SUMMARY

After reading this chapter, you should be able to give your user the option of printing just about anywhere on the network. By using the print queue information from the bindery, we can use these routines on any NetWare configuration that has printers.

# Messaging Between Workstations

Broadcast messages

Message Handling Service (MHS)

NetWare semaphores

# Chapter 100

N etWare provides a wide variety of ways for workstations and programs to communicate. FoxPro can easily take advantage of these services through NetWare's API. In this chapter we will discuss the services available and provide FoxPro code to access them.

## BROADCAST MESSAGES

*Broadcast messages* are one-line messages that are limited to 55 characters. They should be used for short, quick messages, such as "Please turn on the laser printer." Users can control whether or not their workstations can receive broadcast messages. There are two kinds of broadcast messages: server broadcasts, and broadcast messages that come from other users. The way the shell processes those messages is determined by the broadcast mode.

In this section, we will provide the FoxPro code to control the user's broadcast message mode, and to send broadcast messages. Later we will discuss message handling and semaphore services as well, although these require a little more programming work.

### SETTING THE BROADCAST MODE

The *broadcast mode* determines which messages get displayed at the workstation and which ones get discarded. A workstation can have one of four valid broadcast modes:

▶ **0**    The file server stores both user and server messages sent to this workstation. The shell software retrieves and displays the message. This is the normal broadcast mode.

▶ **1**  The shell software displays server messages sent to this workstation, but discards user messages.

▶ **2**  The file server stores server messages sent to this workstation and discards user messages. The shell software does not display messages automatically.

▶ **3**  The file server stores both server and user messages sent to this workstation, but the shell software does not display either type of message. The workstation must ask the file server for any messages.

The FoxPro N_MSGMODE() function, listed below, allows you to set a new broadcast mode for a workstation. The function returns the original mode (prior to your change).

```
**********************************************************
*   Program:    MESSAGES.PRG
*   Authors:    Joseph D. Booth and Greg Lief
*   Function:   N_MSGMODE()
*   Purpose:    Set the workstation's broadcast mode
*   Returns:    nOldMode - prior broadcast mode setting
**********************************************************

function N_MSGMODE()
PARAMETERS  nMode
DIMENSION aRegs(10)
STORE Ø TO aRegs

IF PARAMETERS() = Ø
   nMode = Ø
ENDIF

aRegs(1)   = 222 * 256
aRegs(4)   = nMode

FP_INT86( 33, @aRegs )
RETURN  aRegs(1) % 256
```

### SENDING A BROADCAST MESSAGE

You can use the N_SENDMSG() function, listed next, to send a message to another workstation. This function takes the text of the message as the first parameter, and the workstation number as the second parameter. If the message was sent, the function returns a logical value indicating TRUE; otherwise it returns FALSE.

```
************************************************************
*    Program:  MESSAGES.PRG
*    Authors:  Joseph D. Booth and Greg Lief
*   Function:  N_SendMsg()
*    Purpose:  Sends a message to another workstation
*     Syntax:  <logical> := N_SendMsg( cMessage,nStation )
************************************************************
function N_SendMsg
PARAMETERS cMessage, nStation
PRIVATE cReply,cRequest,is_ok
cReply   = SPACE(2)              && Reply buffer
cRequest = CHR(0)+;
           CHR(1)+;
           CHR(nStation)+;
           CHR(LEN(cMessage))+;
           cMessage
is_ok    = .F.
IF NetWare( 225,cRequest,@cReply )  = 0
   is_ok = (ASC(SUBSTR(cReply,2,1)) = 0)
ENDIF
RETURN is_ok
```

## LOCATING A USER

When sending a broadcast message, you need to know the user's workstation.
The N_FINDSTAT() function, listed below, fills an array with the station numbers and returns a count of stations onto which the user is logged. This function expects the User ID as the first parameter, and an array of stations as the second. This function allows you to send a message to all workstations onto which a particular user is logged.

```
************************************************************
*    Program:  MESSAGES.PRG
*    Authors:  Joseph D. Booth and Greg Lief
*   Function:  N_FindStat()
*    Purpose:  Get a list of stations for a user
*     Syntax:  <nCount> = N_FindStat( cUser,@aList )
************************************************************
function N_FindStat
PARAMETERS cUser, aStations
PRIVATE cReply,cRequest,nCount,x
cReply   = SPACE(103)            && Reply buffer
cRequest = CHR(21)+;
           FOX2INT(1)+;
           LSTRING(cUser,47)
nCount   = 0
IF NetWare( 227,cRequest,@cReply )  = 0
```

```
      nCount = ASC(SUBSTR(cReply,1,1))
      If nCount > 0
         DIMENSION aStations(nCount)
         FOR x = 1 TO nCount
            aStations(x) = ASC(SUBSTR(cReply,x+1,1))
         NEXT
      ENDIF
   ENDIF
ENDIF
RETURN nCount
```

## GETTING A BROADCAST MESSAGE

When a workstation has its broadcast mode set to a number other than zero (see "Setting the Broadcast Mode," earlier), messages will not be automatically displayed by the shell software. In this case, it is necessary to check for messages and have your application take care of displaying them. In the following listing, a function called N_GETMSG() returns the text of any pending messages. Keep in mind that new messages will overwrite older ones, so this function should be called frequently to ensure that messages are received.

```
**********************************************************
*   Program:  MESSAGES.PRG
*   Authors:  Joseph D. Booth and Greg Lief
*   Function: N_GetMsg()
*   Purpose:  Get the next pending message
*    Syntax:  <cMessage> = N_GetMsg()
**********************************************************
function N_GetMsg()
PRIVATE cReply,cRequest,cMessage
cReply   = SPACE(58)          && Reply buffer
cRequest = CHR(1)             && E1h 01h - Get message
cMessage = ""
IF NetWare( 225,cRequest,@cReply )  == 0
   cMessage = SUBSTR(cReply,2)
ENDIF
RETURN cMessage
```

## SENDING MESSAGES TO THE CONSOLE

You can instruct the workstation to send a message to be broadcast on the file server console. The function called N_CONSOLE(), listed below, can be used to send the message. It expects the message text as a parameter, and returns TRUE or FALSE, depending upon whether the message was sent. Keep in mind that NetWare will not confirm whether the message has been received, so a TRUE return does not guarantee that someone actually read the message.

This function can fail if the server's message queue is already filled or if an I/O error occurs. When the broadcast message is received, it will appear on the server, after the server's normal colon prompt.

```
**********************************************************
*    Program:   MESSAGES.PRG
*    Authors:   Joseph D. Booth and Greg Lief
*   Function:   N_Console()
*    Purpose:   Sends a message to the file server console
*     Syntax:   <logical> = N_Console( cMessage )
**********************************************************
function N_Console
PARAMETER  cMsg
PRIVATE cReply,cRequest,is_ok
cReply   = SPACE(2)            && Reply buffer
cRequest = CHR(Ø9)+ ;
            CHR(LEN(cMsg))+;
            cMsg
is_ok    = .F.
IF NetWare( 225,cRequest,@cReply ) == Ø
   is_ok = .T.
ENDIF
RETURN is_ok
```

# MESSAGE HANDLING SERVICE (MHS)

NetWare has a service called Message Handling Service (MHS) that provides messaging and directory services to any workstation attached to the network. Many third-party programs, particularly e-mail programs, interface with MHS when running on NetWare.

To submit a message to MHS, create a text file with appropriate headers and allow MHS to access the file. MHS then determines how to the get the message into an application that the destination user can access. In addition to message delivery services, the MHS also provide a directory of users, groups, and applications that can communicate with the MHS server.

This section provides some functions that allow you to work with the MHS services if they are installed on the network. (Although registered NetWare users can get MHS directly from Novell, it is not always installed on every NetWare server.)

### GETTING MHS USER LIST

If MHS is installed, it maintains a list of users who are able to receive messages. You can use the following MHS_ULIST() function to get a list of user names. The function needs an array name passed by reference as a parameter, and it returns the number of users found.

```
***********************************************************
*    Program:   MESSAGES.PRG
*    Authors:   Joseph D. Booth and Greg Lief
*    Function:  MHS_List()
*    Purpose:   Get list of MHS users
*     Syntax:   <nCount> = MHS_LIST( aUsers )
***********************************************************
function MHS_List
PARAMETERS aUsers
PRIVATE nHand,ulist,nCount,cBuf
***********************************************************
*    NETDIR.TAB is a file that contains the MHS
*    users. It is created and maintained by NetWare.
***********************************************************
nHand  = FOPEN("\MHS\MAIL\PUBLIC\NETDIR.TAB",10)
nCount = 0
ulist  = ""

IF nHand >= 0
   cBuf = FREAD(nHand,128)
   DO WHILE NOT EMPTY(cBuf)
      x    = ASC(SUBSTR(cBuf,1,1))
      IF x = 2
          ulist = ulist +SUBSTR(cBuf,2,9)
      ENDIF
      cBuf = FREAD(nHand,128)
   ENDDO
   =FCLOSE(nHand)
   nCount = LEN(ulist)/8
   DIMENSION aUsers( nCount )
   FOR x = 1 TO nCount
       aUsers(x) = SUBSTR(ulist,(x-1)*8+1,8)
   NEXT
ENDIF
RETURN nCount
```

### MHS HOSTS, GATEWAYS, AND WORKGROUPS

The MHS services can communicate with other networks using various *message transport standards*. MHS always determines the proper method for transporting the message to its destination, which can be another network, CompuServe, or another on-line service. The MHS_Hosts() function, listed below, returns a list of known gateways and hosts with which this MHS system can communicate.

The function needs an array name passed by reference as a parameter, and it returns the number of hosts found.

```
**********************************************************
*    Program:   MESSAGES.PRG
*    Authors:   Joseph D. Booth and Greg Lief
*   Function:   MHS_Hosts()
*    Purpose:   Get list of MHS hosts
*     Syntax:   <nCount> = MHS_HOSTS( aHosts )
**********************************************************
function MHS_HOSTS
PARAMETERS aHosts
PRIVATE nHand,hlist,nCount,cBuf
nHand  = FOPEN("\MHS\MAIL\PUBLIC\NETDIR.TAB",10)
nCount = 0
hList  = ""

IF nHand >= 0
   cBuf = FREAD(nHand,128)
   DO WHILE NOT EMPTY(cBuf)
       x    = ASC(SUBSTR(cBuf,1,1))
       IF x = 4
          hlist = hlist +SUBSTR(cBuf,2,9)
       ENDIF
       cBuf = FREAD(nHand,128)
   ENDDO
   =FCLOSE(nHand)
   nCount = LEN(hlist)/8
   DIMENSION aHosts( nCount )
   FOR x = 1 TO nCount
       aHosts(x) = SUBSTR(hlist,(x-1)*8+1,8)
   NEXT
ENDIF
RETURN nCount
```

## SENDING A MESSAGE TO MHS

To send a message to another user via MHS, you format a text file that contains the user's name and destination, your name, the date, an optional subject, and finally the message itself. Table 10.1 shows the contents of the text file.

The MHS_SEND() function, listed below, takes three parameters—the destination, the subject, and the actual text file—and formats a text file into the MHS format. It then copies this text file into an MHS directory, from which the MHS load module delivers it to its destination. MHS provides a basic transport mechanism that is accessible from within your FoxPro application.

**Table 10.1: MHS Message File**

| Line | Contents |
|------|----------|
| SMF-70 | Standard header and version number. Version numbers can be 64 (for MHS 1.1), 70 (for MHS 1.5), and 71 (for MHS 2.0, which is not available as of this writing) |
| TO: *users* | A comma-separated list of user names. Each user has an ID code; followed by an ampersand; followed by a host, gateway, or workgroup |
| FROM: *user* | The user sending the message, in the form of User ID, followed by an ampersand, and then the host name |
| DATE: *dd-mmm-yy* | The date the message was sent |
| SUBJECT: *cSubj* | Optional subject text |
| Blank line | A blank line |
| *text* | The text of the message, up to 64,000 bytes |

If MHS is installed on your network and you want a fast way to send messages to a disparate group of users, MHS may provide the solution.

```
**********************************************************
*   Program:   MESSAGES.PRG
*   Authors:   Joseph D. Booth and Greg Lief
*   Function:  MHS_Send()
*   Purpose:   Send a message to an MHS user
*    Syntax:   <logical> = MHS_SEND( cTo,cFrom,cSubj,cMsg)
**********************************************************
function MHS_SEND
PARAMETERS cTo,cFrom,cSubj,cMsg
PRIVATE nHand,cHost,cDate,is_ok
is_ok  = .F.
cHost  = MHSGetHost()
nHand  = FCREATE("\MHS\MAIL\SND\"+SYS(3) )
cDate  = DMY( DATE() )
IF nHand >= Ø
   =FPUTS(nHand,"SFM-7Ø")
   =FPUTS(nHand,"To: "+cTo)
   =FPUTS(nHand,"From: "+cFrom+"@"+cHost)
   =FPUTS(nHand,"Date: "+cDate)
   IF !EMPTY(cSubj)
      =FPUTS(nHand,"Subject: "+cSubj)
   ENDIF
```

```
   =FPUTS(nHand," ")
   =FPUTS(nHand,cMsg)
   =FCLOSE(nHand)
   is_ok = .T.
ENDIF
RETURN is_ok

function MHSGetHost
PRIVATE nHand,hlist,cBuf,cHost
nHand  = FOPEN("\MHS\MAIL\PUBLIC\NETDIR.TAB",10)
cHost  = ""

IF nHand >= 0
   cBuf = FREAD(nHand,128)
   DO WHILE NOT EMPTY(cBuf)
       x    = ASC(SUBSTR(cBuf,1,1))
       IF x = 0
          cHost = SUBSTR(cBuf,2,9)
          EXIT
       ENDIF
       cBuf = FREAD(nHand,128)
   ENDDO
   =FCLOSE(nHand)
ENDIF
RETURN cHost
```

# NetWare semaphores

The word *semaphore* comes from two Greek words: *sema*, which means a sign, and *pherein*, which means to bear. In computer parlance, a semaphore is a sign between two processes that can be used to indicate how those processes should operate. (For example, a traffic light is a sign between two cars. By intrepreting the light's color, each car's driver knows whether to go or stop, assuming both cars agree on the meaning of the colors.) Semaphores can be used to bridge the gap between FoxPro's file and record-locking abilities, and provide full control over network resources. When all programs agree on the use of the semaphore, it can be a very powerful tool for the network programmer.

> **Note:** The primary requirement when using semaphores is consistency. Semaphores only work among programs that agree to use the same semaphore names and values. You can hardly expect a CA-Clipper program to abide by the rules you've set up for printer access, although if you could

determine the semaphores the CA-Clipper program used, you can easily have your FoxPro program respect them.

NetWare provides semaphore services that you can use to control the behavior of your FoxPro program. As long as the programs agree on the user of the semaphore, any kind of control over network files and resources can be achieved. You can access semaphores from other languages as well, so a FoxPro application and a CA-Clipper program could use the semaphore system to control resources amongst themselves.

The following sections describe the five network services that deal with semaphores.

### OPENING A SEMAPHORE

To use the semaphore system, you must first open the semaphore by specifying a name and an initial maximum value. If the semaphore name does not exist, NetWare creates one and assigns the initial maximum value to it. If the semaphore already exists, NetWare opens it and ignores the initial value. Semaphore names may be from 1 to 127 characters long. The maximum value must be positive and cannot be greater than 127 (future versions of NetWare may increase this number). Once a semaphore is created, it is given a number known as a *handle*. This handle is used in any other semaphore services that refer to the semaphore.

The function called N_OPENSEM, listed below, is used to open a network semaphore. It expects two parameters: the semaphore name, and the initial maximum value to assign if the semaphore does not exist. It returns a numeric handle that is passed to the other semaphore functions. Be sure to save this numeric handle, because other functions will need to refer to it.

```
***********************************************************
*   Program:  MESSAGES.PRG
*   Authors:  Joseph D. Booth and Greg Lief
*   Function: N_OpenSem()
*   Purpose:  Open a semaphore and assign a value to it
*   Returns:  nHandle
***********************************************************
function N_OpenSem
PARAMETER cLabel,nInitial
PRIVATE nSize,nHandle,nReturn
DIMENSION aRegs(10)
STORE 0 TO aRegs
nSize   = len(cLabel)
nHandle = 0
```

```
aRegs(1) = 197 * 256         && Set AH to nService
aRegs(8) = chr(nSize)+cLabel  && Request packet
aRegs(3) = nInitial          && Initial maximum
aRegs(4) = .T.               && Using a string

IF FP_int86( 33, @aRegs )
   nReturn =  aRegs(1) % 256     && Extract low byte
   IF nReturn = Ø
      nHandle = BIN2L( I2BIN( aRegs(3) ) +;
                I2BIN( aRegs(4) ) )
   ENDIF
ENDIF
RETURN nHandle
```

## EXAMINING A SEMAPHORE

You can examine the current value of a semaphore without making any
changes to it. If the value is greater than zero, there are still semaphore slots
available. If the value is less than zero, the number indicates how many users
are currently in the queue waiting for this semaphore.

The N_EXAMSEM() function, listed next, takes as a parameter the handle
returned from N_OPENSEM(). It returns the semaphore's value, or –99 if an
error occurs.

```
**********************************************************
*    Program:  MESSAGES.PRG
*    Authors:  Joseph D. Booth and Greg Lief
*    Function: N_ExamSem()
*    Purpose:  Examines a semaphore handle and returns
*              the semaphore value
*     Syntax:  nValue = N_ExamSem( nHandle )
**********************************************************
function N_ExamSem
PARAMETER nHandle
PRIVATE nValue,nReturn
DIMENSION aRegs(1Ø)
STORE Ø TO aRegs
nValue     = -99

aRegs(1) = 197 * 256 +1      && Set AH to C5h, Ø1h
aRegs(3) = BIN2I(SUBSTR(l2BIN(nHandle),1,2))
aRegs(4) = BIN2I(SUBSTR(l2BIN(nHandle),3,2))

IF FP_int86( 33, @aRegs )
   nReturn =  aRegs(1) % 256  && Extract low byte
   IF nReturn = Ø
```

```
        nValue = aRegs(3) % 256
    ENDIF
ENDIF
RETURN nValue
```

### CLOSING A SEMAPHORE

Once you've finished using a semaphore, be sure to close it. The following N_CLOSESEM() function expects the semaphore handle from N_OPEN-SEM(), and returns a logical value indicating whether the semaphore has been closed. This function decrements by one the count of the number of users who are using this semaphore. If the count equals zero as a result of the close semaphore call, then the semaphore is deleted.

```
*******************************************************
*    Program:  MESSAGES.PRG
*    Authors:  Joseph D. Booth and Greg Lief
*    Function: N_CloseSem()
*    Purpose:  Closes a semaphore handle
*      Syntax: logical = N_CloseSem( nHandle )
*******************************************************
function N_CloseSem
PARAMETERS  nHandle
PRIVATE is_ok
DIMENSION aRegs(10)
STORE Ø TO aRegs
aRegs(1) = 197 * 256 +4          && Service C5h, Ø4h
aRegs(3) = BIN2I(SUBSTR(l2BIN(nHandle),1,2))
aRegs(4) = BIN2I(SUBSTR(l2BIN(nHandle),3,2))
IF FP_int86( 33, @aRegs )
   is_ok  =  (aRegs(1) % 256) = Ø
ENDIF
RETURN is_ok
```

### USING A SEMAPHORE

There are two services used to manage the semaphore counts. When you want to access a semaphore-controlled resource, you begin by waiting for that semaphore. If the semaphore is not fully used, you are immediately allowed access, and the count of available slots decreases by one. If the semaphore is not available for use, the count still decreases. The function waits a specified amount of time for the semaphore to become available. If that interval passes and the semaphore is not free, the count is then increased by one and access is denied.

**Note:**  Once you've finished using the network resource, signal the semaphore that you are done. Signaling the semaphore increases the number of open semaphore slots by one, which allows other users access to the resource.

The following code contains two functions. The first, N_WAITSEM(), is used to check for access to a semaphore. It expects the semaphore handle and an optional number of seconds to wait. If the semaphore is available, TRUE is returned and the program will continue. If FALSE is returned, the semaphore has no open slots, and the program should inform the user that the resource is not available.

The second function, N_SIGNALSEM(), is used to inform the semaphore that you've finished using the resource. It increases the number of open semaphore slots. This function expects the handle from N_OPENSEM().

```
************************************************************
*    Program:  MESSAGES.PRG
*    Authors:  Joseph D. Booth and Greg Lief
*    Function: N_WaitSem()
*    Purpose:  Wait for semaphore resource
*     Syntax:  logical = N_WaitSem( nHandle,nTimeOut )
************************************************************
function N_WaitSem
PARAMETER nHandle,nTimeOut
PRIVATE is_ok
DIMENSION aRegs(10)
STORE Ø TO aRegs
is_ok = .F.

aRegs(1) = 197 * 256 +2        && Service C5h, Ø2h
aRegs(3) = BIN2I(SUBSTR(I2BIN(nHandle),1,2))
aRegs(4) = BIN2I(SUBSTR(I2BIN(nHandle),3,2))
aRegs(7) = nTimeOut * 18       && In clock ticks
IF FP_int86( 33, @aRegs )
   is_ok  = (aRegs(1) % 256) = Ø
ENDIF
RETURN isok
************************************************************
*  Function: N_SignalSem()
*   Purpose: Signal semaphore that we are done
*    Syntax: logical = N_SignalSem( nHandle )
************************************************************
function N_SignalSem
PARAMETER nHandle
PRIVATE is_ok
DIMENSION aRegs(10)
is_ok  = .F.
```

```
aRegs(1) = 197 * 256 +3          && Service C5h, 02h
aRegs(3) = BIN2I(SUBSTR(l2BIN(nHandle),1,2))
aRegs(4) = BIN2I(SUBSTR(l2BIN(nHandle),3,2))

IF FP_int86( 33, @aRegs )
   is_ok  =  (aRegs(1) % 256) == 0
ENDIF
RETURN is_ok
```

## A SEMAPHORE EXAMPLE

In this section, we will look at an example in which semaphores are used to handle network problems. This example will provide a foundation for your own ideas about possible uses for a signal system between two applications.

**Limiting the number of users** The semaphore system can be used to restrict the number of users who can simultaneously run your application. If your application is licensed to a maximum of three simultaneous users, for instance, you might want the program to detect a fourth user's attempts to access the program. This user would then be denied access to the program until another user finished.

The following example contains a function called USE_APP() that returns a logical value indicating whether the maximum number of users has been exceeded. Your program can then determine the appropriate course of action.

```
***********************************************************
*    Program:  MESSAGES.PRG
*    Authors:  Joseph D. Booth and Greg Lief
*    Function:  Use_App()
*    Purpose:  Check that the application's maximum number
*              of users has not been exceeded
*      Syntax:  logical = Use_App( nMaximum )
***********************************************************

function Use_App
PARAMETERS nMaxUsers
PUBLIC nSemHandle
nSemHandle = N_OpenSem( "LEDGER.EXE" ,nMaxUsers )
RETURN N_WaitSem(nSemHandle,1)

function Close_App()
RETURN n_CloseSem(nSemHandle)
```

The USE_APP() function should be placed at the beginning of the code, as shown here:

```
IF Use_App( 3 )     && Allow up to three users
   **
   ** Call your program
   **
   Close_App()      && Close the semaphores
ELSE
   WAIT "Too many users!"  WINDOW TIMEOUT 60
ENDIF
```

Once the program is finished, be sure to call the CLOSE_APP() function to close the semaphore and allow another user to access your program. Place the call to CLOSE_APP() into your program's exit procedure and, optionally, into its error-handling routine.

## SUMMARY

NetWare provides many ways for workstations and applications to communicate. This chapter has provided the necessary tools to allow your programs to talk amongst themselves and to allow your users to communicate between their workstations.

# System Information

Making contact with a file server

Obtaining workstation information

Determining the network shell
version

File server information

Console operations

The network operating system maintains substantial information about the network and the workstations connected to it. This information can be used for a wide variety of purposes. For example, you might restrict your application to run only on a specific server, or have it confirm that a particular drive letter is a valid network drive.

In this chapter, we discuss how a workstation makes its connection to the network, and what information is available from the workstation. We also examine the type of information available from the file server and provide the FoxPro code to access this information.

## MAKING CONTACT WITH A FILE SERVER

When a user attempts to make contact with a network server, two programs are loaded into memory. The first program, usually IPX, handles communications between the network cards and the cabling. IPX does not understand the network but serves merely as a transport mechanism. The second program, usually called NETX, is the network shell. This program is responsible for receiving DOS requests and either delegating them to DOS for handling or routing them to the network.

The network shell program does not communicate directly with the file server, but rather uses IPX to handle the messaging. When the shell program (NETX) starts, the workstation requests a connection with the nearest server. It places the server name into a table and sends a request for connection to the IPX program, which passes the request to the file server. If a connection is granted, the server returns a connection number.

The version of NetWare you are using, along with the user's purchased license, determine the maximum number of connections a file server may have. NetWare 2.*x* allows up to 100 connections; NetWare 386 allows 250. On newer versions of NetWare, this number will undoubtedly be increased.

## LOGGING IN

Once a user has gained a connection to a server, the user must log in as a valid user of that server, supplying a valid object name and password. The N_LOGIN() function listed below takes a User ID and a password. It returns TRUE if the log-in was successful, or FALSE if not.

> **Note:** The N_LOGIN() function only works if you are using unencrypted passwords on the network. If password are encrypted, this API will not work.

```
***********************************************************
*   Program:  SYSINFO.PRG
*   Authors:  Joseph D. Booth and Greg Lief
*   Function: N_Login()
*   Purpose:  Attempt to log in to a server
*     Syntax: <logical> = N_Login(cUser,cPassword)
***********************************************************
function N_login
PARAMETERS cUser,cPassword
PRIVATE cRequest,cReply
cRequest   = CHR(14)+;
             FOX2LONG(1)+;
             LSTRING(UPPER(cUser),48)
IF LEN(TRIM(cPassword)) > 0
   cRequest = cRequest +LSTRING(UPPER(cPassword),16)
ENDIF
cReply     = SPACE(2)
return ( NetWare( 227, cRequest, @cReply ) = 0 )
```

## LOGGING OUT

Log-out from the server is accomplished using the N_LOGOUT() function listed below. If the user successfully logs out from the server, the function returns TRUE. Logging out does not disconnect the user from the server. However, some networks might be configured to disconnect a workstation if it does not log in within a certain period of time.

```
***********************************************************
*   Program:  SYSINFO.PRG
*   Authors:  Joseph D. Booth and Greg Lief
*   Function: N_Logout()
```

```
*   Purpose:  Attempt to log out from the server
*     Syntax:  <logical> = N_Logout()
************************************************************
function N_Logout
PRIVATE is_gone
DIMENSION aRegs(10)
STORE 0 TO aRegs
aRegs[1] = 215 * 256
is_gone = FP_int86(33,@aRegs)
RETURN is_gone
```

# OBTAINING WORKSTATION INFORMATION

Once connected and logged in to a server, the user can obtain connection information, such as bindery and drive-mapping settings. The N_CONINFO() function listed below determines the ID and log-in time of any connection on the workstation. The N_CONINFO() function takes the User ID as the first parameter, and updates the second parameter (an array) with the user's connection information.

| Element | Type | Contents |
|---|---|---|
| 1 | Num | Connection's bindery ID |
| 2 | Num | Connection's object type |
| 3 | Char | Object name |
| 4 | Date | Last log-in date |
| 5 | Char | Last log-in time |

```
************************************************************
*   Program:  SYSINFO.PRG
*   Authors:  Joseph D. Booth and Greg Lief
*  Function:  N_ConInfo()
*   Purpose:  Get array of connection information
*     Syntax:  <logical> = N_ConInfo(cUser,@aInfo)
************************************************************
function N_ConInfo
PARAMETERS cUser,aInfo
PRIVATE cRequest,cReply,dLogDate,cLogTime,is_ok
DIMENSION aRegs(10),aWhere(1)
STORE 0 TO aRegs
is_ok = .F.
IF N_FINDSTAT(cUser,@aWhere) > 0
   cRequest = CHR(22)+CHR( aWhere(1) )
   cReply   = SPACE(63)
```

```
    IF NetWare(227,cRequest,@cReply) = 0
       DIMENSION aInfo(5)
       aInfo(1) = LONG2FOX(SUBSTR(cReply,1,4)) )
       aInfo(2) = INT2FOX(SUBSTR(cReply,5,2)) )
       aInfo(3) = CLEANSTR(SUBSTR(cReply,7,48)) )
       dLogDate = CTOD( STR(ASC(SUBSTR(cReply,56,1)),2)+"/"+;
                        STR(ASC(SUBSTR(cReply,57,1)),2)+"/"+;
                        STR(ASC(SUBSTR(cReply,55,1)),2) )
       aInfo(4) = dLogDate
       cLogTime = STR(ASC(SUBSTR(cReply,58,1)),2)+":"+;
                  STR(ASC(SUBSTR(cReply,59,1)),2)+":"+;
                  STR(ASC(SUBSTR(cReply,60,1)),2)
       aInfo(5) = cLogTime
       is_ok = .T.
    ENDIF
ENDIF
RETURN is_ok

function N_FindStat
PARAMETERS cUser, aStations
PRIVATE cReply,cRequest,nCount,x
cReply   = SPACE(103)            && Reply buffer
cRequest = CHR(21)+;
           FOX2INT(1)+;
           LSTRING(cUser,47)
nCount   = 0
IF NetWare( 227,cRequest,@cReply ) = 0
   nCount = ASC(SUBSTR(cReply,1,1))
   DIMENSION aStations(nCount)
   FOR x = 1 TO nCount
      aStations(x) = ASC(SUBSTR(cReply,x+1,1))
   NEXT
ENDIF
RETURN nCount
```

## DETERMINING THE NETWORK SHELL VERSION

You can also ask the shell software to identify itself. The following N_SHELL-VER() function returns a character string that represents the current shell version:

```
************************************************************
*   Program:  SYSINFO.PRG
*   Authors:  Joseph D. Booth and Greg Lief
*   Function: N_ShellVer()
*   Purpose:  Retrieves network shell information
*    Syntax:  cVersion = N_ShellVer()
```

```
*******************************************************
function N_ShellVer
PRIVATE x,cVersion
DIMENSION aRegs[10]
STORE 0 TO aRegs
cVersion = ""
aRegs(1)  = 234 * 256
IF FP_int86(33,@aRegs)
   IF aRegs(1) >= 0
      cVersion = ALLTRIM(STR(INT(aRegs(2)/256)))+"."+;
                  ALLTRIM(STR(INT(aRegs(2)%256)))+;
                  CHR(65+(aRegs(3)%256))
      IF SUBSTR(cVersion,1,1)>="3"
         x = aRegs(3)/256
         IF x > 0
             cVersion = cVersion + IIF(x=1,"e","x")
         ENDIF
      ENDIF
   ENDIF
ENDIF
RETURN cVersion
```

# FILE SERVER INFORMATION

The file server itself maintains a large amount of information about the network, although much of this is available only to the Supervisor or an equivalent user. This section contains a sampling of some of the information available from the file server to a user with Supervisor privileges.

## CHECKING CONSOLE PRIVILEGES

In order to perform some processes on the file server, the user must have *console privileges*. Almost all options that can be performed at the file server console can also be done through the NetWare API if the user has sufficient security and privileges. Here is the N_CONSPRIV() function, which returns TRUE if the user has console privileges and FALSE if not.

```
*******************************************************
*    Program:   SYSINFO.PRG
*    Authors:   Joseph D. Booth and Greg Lief
*    Function:  N_ConsPriv()
*    Purpose:   Determines if user has console privileges
*     Syntax:   <logical> = N_ConsPriv()
*******************************************************
function N_ConsPriv()
PRIVATE cReply,cRequest,is_ok
```

```
is_ok = .F.
cReply  = SPACE(2)
cRequest = CHR(200)
IF NetWare(227,cRequest,@cReply) = 0
   is_ok = .T.
ENDIF
RETURN is_ok
```

### DETERMINING THE CURRENT LOG-IN STATUS

You can enable or disable log-in capabilities on a server. When the log-in is disabled, no additional users can log in to the server, although current users are not affected. The following N_SERVLOGIN() function is a GET/SET function that allows you to get the current status of log-ins (TRUE if allowed, FALSE if not). You can also pass a parameter to determine whether additional log-ins are allowed. If the optional parameter is set to TRUE, then additional log-ins will be permitted; if FALSE, no other users will be able to log in to the server.

```
***********************************************************
*   Program:  SYSINFO.PRG
*   Authors:  Joseph D. Booth and Greg Lief
*   Function: N_ServLogin()
*   Purpose:  GET/SET block for server log-ins allowed
*     Syntax: <logical> = N_ServLogin( [lSetting] )
***********************************************************
function N_ServLogin
PARAMETER lSetting
PRIVATE is_allowed,cReply,pcount
pcount      = PARAMETERS()
is_allowed = .T.
cReply      = space(1)
IF NetWare(227,CHR(205),@cReply) = 0
   is_allowed =  ASC(cRep)<>0
   IF pcount > 0
      cReply = SPACE(2)
      =NetWare( 227, CHR(IIF(lSetting,204,203)),@cReply )
   ENDIF
ENDIF
RETURN is_allowed
```

### RETRIEVING THE SERVER DATE AND TIME

You can also get the file server's date and time from within your FoxPro application. This next function, FSDATETIME(), fills a two-element array. The first element is the date from the file server, and the second is the time. If there is a problem with the connection or the server, then the function returns FALSE.

```
**********************************************************
*    Program:   SYSINFO.PRG
*    Authors:   Joseph D. Booth and Greg Lief
*    Function:  FsDateTime()
*    Purpose:   Get the file server date and time
*     Syntax:   <array> = FSDateTime()
**********************************************************
function FsDateTime(aInfo)
DIMENSION aRegs(10)
PRIVATE cReply,dDate,cTime,is_ok
STORE 0 TO aRegs
is_ok      = .F.
cReply     = space(7)
aRegs(1)   = 231 * 256
aRegs(8)   = cReply
aRegs(4)   = .T.
IF FP_int86( 33, @aRegs )
   dDate  = CTOD( STR(ASC(SUBSTR(aRegs(8),2,1)),2)+"/"+;
                 STR(ASC(SUBSTR(aRegs(8),3,1)),2)+"/"+;
                 STR(ASC(SUBSTR(aRegs(8),1,1)),2) )
   cTime  =   STR(ASC(SUBSTR(aRegs(8),4,1)),2)+":"+;
              STR(ASC(SUBSTR(aRegs(8),5,1)),2)+":"+;
              STR(ASC(SUBSTR(aRegs(8),6,1)),2)
   aInfo(1) = dDate
   aInfo(2) = cTime
   is_ok      = .T.
ENDIF
RETURN is_ok
```

## RETRIEVING NETWORK INSTALLATION INFORMATION

One tidbit of information buried in the file server is the name of the NetWare distributor for the server, along with the version number and revision date, and the copyright notice. You can obtain this information by using the N_WHOBLAME() function listed below. The function returns an array with four elements, having the following structure:

| Element | Type | Contents |
|---------|------|----------|
| 1 | Char | Name of company that installed network |
| 2 | Char | NetWare version and revision |
| 3 | Date | NetWare revision date |
| 4 | Char | NetWare copyright notice |

```
***********************************************************
*   Program:  SYSINFO.PRG
*   Authors:  Joseph D. Booth and Greg Lief
*  Function:  N_WhoBlame()
*   Purpose:  Get the file server installation array
*    Syntax:  N_WhoBlame( @array )
***********************************************************
function N_WhoBlame
PARAMETERS aInfo
PRIVATE cRequest,cReply,x,jj,is_ok
cRequest = CHR(201)
cReply   = SPACE(512)
is_ok    = .F.

IF NetWare( 227, cRequest, @cReply ) = 0
   DIMENSION aInfo(4)
   FOR jj = 1 TO 4
      x          = AT(CHR(0),cReply)
      IF x > 0
         IF jj = 3
            aInfo[jj] = CTOD(SUBSTR(cReply,1,x-1))
         ELSE
            aInfo[jj] = SUBSTR(cReply,1,x-1)
         ENDIF
         cReply     = SUBSTR(cReply,x+1)
      ENDIF
   NEXT
   is_ok = .T.
ENDIF
RETURN is_ok
```

## GETTING MISCELLANEOUS SERVER INFORMATION

There is a NetWare API that returns miscellaneous information about the server, such as its name, the NetWare version, number of connections, and so on. This function, called N_MISCINFO(), fills an array of miscellaneous server information. If no server is found, FALSE is returned. The contents of the returned array are as follows:

| Element | Type | Contents |
|---------|------|----------|
| 1 | Char | File server name |
| 2 | Num | NetWare major version number |
| 3 | Num | NetWare minor version number |
| 4 | Num | Maximum connections allowed |

| 5 | Num | Connections currently in use |
| 6 | Num | Maximum connected volumes |
| 7 | Num | OS revision number |
| 8 | Num | SFT level |
| 9 | Num | TTS level |
| 10 | Num | Peak connections used |
| 11 | Num | Accounting version number |
| 12 | Num | VAP version number |
| 13 | Num | Queuing version number |
| 14 | Num | Print server version number |
| 15 | Num | Virtual console version number |
| 16 | Num | Security restrictions level |
| 17 | Num | Internetwork bridge version number |

The SYSINFO.PRG program listed below contains the source to the N_MISCINFO() function:

```
******************************************************************
*    Program:  SYSINFO.PRG
*    Authors:  Joseph D. Booth and Greg Lief
*    Function: N_MiscInfo()
*    Purpose:  Get an array of miscellaneous server information
*    Syntax:   N_MiscInfo(@array)
******************************************************************
function MiscInfo(aInfo)
PRIVATE cRequest,cReply,is_ok
cRequest = CHR(17)
cReply   = SPACE(130)
is_ok    = .F.

IF NetWare( 227, cRequest, @cReply ) = 0
   DIMENSION aInfo(17)
   SET LIBRARY TO BLNET ADDITIVE
   aInfo[ 1] = CLEANSTR(SUBSTR(cReply,1,48))
   aInfo[ 2] = ASC(SUBSTR(cReply,49,1))
   aInfo[ 3] = ASC(SUBSTR(cReply,50,1))
   aInfo[ 4] = INT2FOX(SUBSTR(cReply,51,2))
   aInfo[ 5] = INT2FOX(SUBSTR(cReply,53,2))
   aInfo[ 6] = INT2FOX(SUBSTR(cReply,55,2))
```

```
    aInfo[ 7] = ASC(SUBSTR(cReply,57,1))
    aInfo[ 8] = ASC(SUBSTR(cReply,58,1))
    aInfo[ 9] = ASC(SUBSTR(cReply,59,1))
    aInfo[10] = INT2FOX(SUBSTR(cReply,60,2))
    aInfo[11] = ASC(SUBSTR(cReply,62,1))
    aInfo[12] = ASC(SUBSTR(cReply,63,1))
    aInfo[13] = ASC(SUBSTR(cReply,64,1))
    aInfo[14] = ASC(SUBSTR(cReply,65,1))
    aInfo[15] = ASC(SUBSTR(cReply,66,1))
    aInfo[16] = ASC(SUBSTR(cReply,67,1))
    aInfo[17] = ASC(SUBSTR(cReply,68,1))
    is_ok     = .T.
ENDIF
RETURN is_ok
```

## Console operations

If your User ID has console privileges and Supervisor rights, you can perform some console tasks from within your FoxPro application. Normally these tasks would be performed from the file server's keyboard, but you can do them from within your program if need be. Use discretion when experimenting with bringing the server down or clearing someone's connection.

### BRINGING DOWN THE FILE SERVER

The N_DOWN function brings the server down. Normally, the server will not be brought down if there are files currently open on it. However, you can pass a TRUE to the N_DOWN() function to bring the server down regardless of the presence of open files.

```
******************************************************************
*    Program:  SYSINFO.PRG
*    Authors:  Joseph D. Booth and Greg Lief
*    Function: N_Down()
*    Purpose:  Brings down the file server
*     Syntax:  N_Down( lForceDown )
******************************************************************
function Down
PARAMETER lForceDown
PRIVATE cRequest,cReply

cRequest = CHR(211)+IIF(lForceDown,1,0)
cReply   = SPACE(2)

return NetWare(227,cRequest,@cReply)
```

## CLEARING A CONNECTION

There may be times when a connection gets hung on the server. Using the N_CLEARCON() function listed below, you can clear a workstation's connection to the server. If the workstation needs to log back on to the server, the user will need to reconnect with the workstation and log on again. If the connection exists and was cleared, the function returns TRUE. If a problem occurs (most likely when the user does not have console privileges), FALSE is returned.

```
******************************************************************
*    Program:  SYSINFO.PRG
*    Authors:  Joseph D. Booth and Greg Lief
*    Function: N_ClearCon()
*    Purpose:  Clear an individual connection
*     Syntax:  N_ClearCon( nConnect )
******************************************************************
function N_ClearCon
PARAMETER nConnect
PRIVATE cRequest,cReply

cRequest = CHR(210)+CHR(nConnect)
cReply   = SPACE(2)

return NetWare(227,cRequest,@cReply)
```

## SETTING THE SERVER DATE AND TIME

You can set the server's date and time from within your FoxPro program, using the N_SETDATE() function. N_SETDATE() takes two parameters: the date and the time to which you want the file server set. If the date and time were changed, TRUE is returned. If a problem occurred (such as insufficient security or a bad connection), the function returns FALSE.

```
******************************************************************
*    Program:  SYSINFO.PRG
*    Authors:  Joseph D. Booth and Greg Lief
*    Function: N_SetDate()
*    Purpose:  Sets the server's date and time
*     Syntax:  N_SetDate( dDate,cTime )
******************************************************************
function N_SetDate
PARAMETERS dDate,cTime
PRIVATE cRequest,cReply

cRequest = CHR(202)+;
           CHR(YEAR(dDate)-1900)+;
```

```
                  CHR(MONTH(dDate))+;
                  CHR(DAY(dDate))+;
                  CHR(VAL(SUBSTR(cTime,1,2)))+;
                  CHR(VAL(SUBSTR(cTime,4,2)))+;
                  CHR(VAL(SUBSTR(cTime,7,2)))
      cReply   = SPACE(2)

      return NetWare(227,cRequest,@cReply)
```

## SUMMARY

In this chapter, we touched upon some of the information available, and how to obtain it, from the workstation and the file server. This data can be used for a variety of purposes, depending upon the needs of your application. Additional network information is listed in Appendix A.

# EMAIL Program
# User Reference

WHAT IS E-MAIL?

EMAIL PROGRAM MODULES

EMAIL AND THE NETWORK

THE EMAIL PROGRAM MENU

USING THE MAIL SYSTEM

I n this chapter you'll examine a sample application that can be written in FoxPro for a network environment. (Chapter 13 provides the complete source code and the data structures for the EMAIL program, which runs under both Windows and DOS.) The program uses many of the functions and much of the information found in this book.

## WHAT IS E-MAIL?

Electronic mail (e-mail) is part of a new category of software called *groupware.* Groupware is software that helps members of a group to communicate and work as a team. Think of e-mail as electronic Post-it notes. It allows you to send a message or letter via computer to another user or group of users.

The mail program, EMAIL, included in this book is designed to provide basic mail services on a Novell network. Because this program is a FoxPro-based system, it provides the added benefit of permitting other FoxPro applications to send mail to network users. For example, many companies run reports during the nighttime hours. With these reports programmed in FoxPro, summarized versions can be sent to various network users via the e-mail system. When the users arrive the next morning, they can just check their e-mail to view the reports.

By incorporating the SENDMAIL component into your error-handling program, you can ensure that critical errors requiring intervention will be directed to the network administrator or to another user capable of fixing the problem.

# EMAIL program modules

There are three main components to our e-mail system. These modules probably reflect how you handle your traditional mail: You check to see if you have any unopened mail; if you do, you read and perhaps respond to it; and you send mail to other individuals or groups. This section briefly covers the three EMAIL modules: CHKMAIL, SENDMAIL, and READMAIL.

### CHECKING YOUR MAIL: CHKMAIL

The CHKMAIL module checks to see if any mail has been sent to your User ID. Generally, this program is called in the system start-up file—either AUTO-EXEC.BAT or the log-in script. If any unread mail is found, a message is displayed so that you can choose whether to read the mail. The DOS ErrorLevel command is set, also, so you can have a batch file call the mail program directly if mail is found.

### SENDING MAIL: SENDMAIL

The SENDMAIL module allows you to send mail to another user or a group of network users. It requires you to specify the user name and a brief subject, along with the actual mail text. This information is recorded in the central mail repository file (called POSTBOX) until the addressee of the mail next accesses the mail system.

### READING YOUR MAIL: READMAIL

The READMAIL module allows you to read any mail you have received. It displays a list of current mail and lets you scroll through your mail messages. You can forward, reply to, or discard any message. The READMAIL program handles all these functions.

# EMAIL and the network

Now that we have briefly described what the EMAIL program components do, let's explore them in more detail to see how the system works and how it will interface with the network.

Figure 12.1 shows how the mail system is organized on the network. The file called POSTBOX is the central repository for all mail in the system. Each record in this file represents one item of mail that is addressed to either a single user or a group of users. In addition to the POSTBOX central mail file, each user has a personal file called MAILBOX. This file contains any mail sent to the user as an individual or as a member of a group.

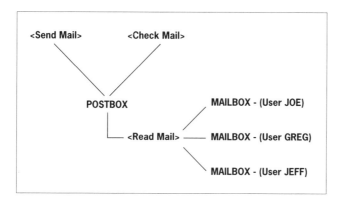

**Figure 12.1: EMAIL file structure**

## EMAIL'S DIRECTORY STRUCTURE

The mail program places POSTBOX in the F:\MAIL directory (you can change this name in the source code, if you like). This directory should be set up so that all network users have read/write access to it. Within this directory, each user has a subdirectory that has the user's bindery ID as a name. Each user has read/write access to only his or her own directory; this allows the network to enforce security and protect the privacy of all individuals' mail.

# THE EMAIL PROGRAM MENU

The EMAIL program has a main menu with five options, as shown in Figure 12.2. From this main menu, the user can read or send mail, discard old mail, update system colors and directories, and *pack* the file (that is, remove deleted mail). The user selects a menu option by highlighting it and pressing the Enter key.

Each of the main menu options is described in the following sections.

## READING MAIL

When you select the Read menu option, the program checks to see if any mail has been sent to you. If you don't have any mail, you'll see a message to this effect and you are returned to the main menu. If mail is found, the screen in Figure 12.3 is displayed.

In the Read Mail screen, options at the left side of the screen allow you to examine your mail. You can scroll up and down through your mail messages. The mail is sorted so that the newest messages are at the top of the list and the oldest are at the bottom. Unread mail is shown in a color different from mail

**Figure 12.2: The EMAIL main menu**

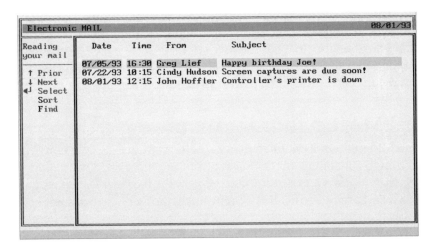

**Figure 12.3: The Read Mail screen**

you've already read. Once you've positioned the highlight bar on the mail you want to read, you can press Enter to read the message. The mail will be displayed as shown in Figure 12.4.

**Sorting mail**    You can also change the sort order of the mail in your MAILBOX file. This change is "sticky," meaning that the new order will be used until you change it to something different. If you press **S** to select the Sort option, a check

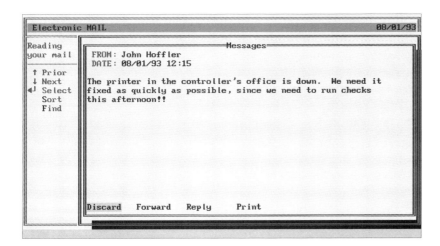

**Figure 12.4: Reading a message**

box will appear under each column. You would then enter **Y** in the checkbox for the column you wish to sort on. Your MAILBOX file contents are then sorted and redisplayed in the specified order.

**Finding mail**    You can use the Find option to scan the subject and/or sender fields of your mail messages for a particular keyword. This feature does not check the mail text, but only the subject information or sender's name. If mail that contains the keyword is found, the highlight bar will be positioned on that mail item. If the keyword is not found, you will receive an error message and the highlight bar will stay in its original position.

**Responding to mail**    When a mail message is displayed on the screen, you may discard it, forward it to another user, send a reply, or print it. (These options appear on the left side of the screen.)

**Discarding the message**    Press **D**, and the message currently displayed is marked for deletion. Try to get in the habit of deleting mail you don't need, rather than letting it accumulate in your MAILBOX file. If you marked a message for deletion but haven't packed the file (that is, physically removed the deleted records), you can still recall the message and its text. Once you've packed the file, however, the message is gone forever.

**Forwarding the message**    Press **F** when you want the message currently displayed to be forwarded to another user and then deleted from your MAILBOX file. You will be prompted for the recipient's User ID. If you don't know the user's network ID, press the F4 key to get a list from which you can select a person or group.

**Replying to the message**    Press **R** to reply to a message, and the Send Mail screen will appear. The To: field will automatically contain the User ID of the person who sent you the message in question. In addition, the text of the original message will be copied into the editing area of the Read Mail screen. This way, you can quote text and questions from the original message. Once you've written your reply, press Enter to send the mail to the requested user.

**Printing the message**    Press **P** to print the message currently displayed. A list box of available printers will be displayed, and you may select any printer, the screen, or a text file as the output destination. The mail will be formatted and printed accordingly.

### SENDING MAIL

If you choose Send on the menu to send mail to another user, the window shown in Figure 12.5 is displayed. You can then specify the user or group name to whom you want the message sent. Press F4 to display a list of Users and Group IDs for selection.

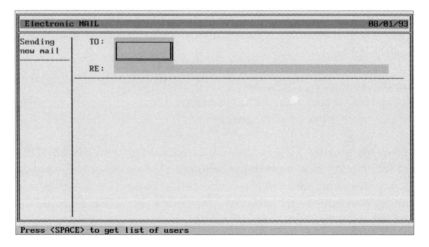

**Figure 12.5: Sending a message**

Once you specify the mail recipient, you can enter the Subject and the actual text of the mail message. When done, look over your message; if it looks OK, just press Enter to send it on its way.

### ERASING MAIL

Since mail tends to accumulate, you need an option on the menu that lets you mark messages for deletion. This is the function of the Erase option. When you select Erase, a list of all recent messages is displayed. To discard or save a message, press the Spacebar to toggle the setting (to either Discard or Save). When you have marked all the messages you want to delete, return to the main menu by pressing the Escape key. From there, select Pack/Index (explained in a later section) to remove the deleted mail permanently.

Figure 12.6 shows the screen for marking mail to be erased.

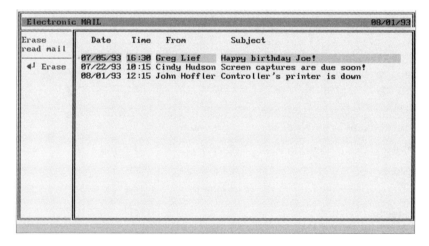

**Figure 12.6: Erasing a mail message**

### CONFIGURING THE MAIL SYSTEM

The mail system's screen colors and display formats, as well as the location of the POSTBOX central mail directory, are all configurable. Selecting **O** from the main menu displays the screen shown in Figure 12.7. You may change the settings as required to designate your configuration, and press Enter when done. If you press Escape, the original (default) options will be restored.

You can change the colors of various elements of the mail system using the normal FoxPro color syntax. Each element's color designation consists of a foreground setting, the slash character, and a background setting. The following

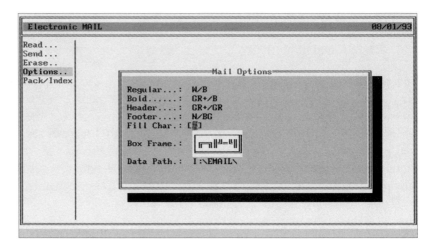

**Figure 12.7: EMAIL configuration options**

chart shows the colors you can use. Only the colors in the left column can be used for the background setting; the colors in either column can be used for the foreground.

| Background or Foreground | | Foreground Only | |
|---|---|---|---|
| **Color** | **Setting** | **Color** | **Setting** |
| Black | N | Gray | N+ |
| Blue | B | Bright Blue | B+ |
| Green | G | Bright Green | G+ |
| Cyan | BG | Bright Cyan | BG+ |
| Red | R | Bright Red | R+ |
| Magenta | RB | Bright Magenta | RB+ |
| Brown | GR | Yellow | GR+ |
| White | W | Bright White | W+ |

In addition to setting the colors of the main screen, you can also change its background fill character and the frame style. And you can set the data path for the POSTBOX central mailbox. When entering a path name, be sure to use a slash as the last character.

### THE PACK/INDEX OPTION

Use this option on the menu to remove all records that are marked for deletion from your personal MAILBOX file. You should pack the file periodically to keep its size to a minimum.

> **Note:** Once the MAILBOX file is packed, there is no way to restore any deleted messages.

Selecting the Pack/Index option also re-indexes the MAILBOX file. Should the index files become corrupted, you can run this option to re-create them. Because the MAILBOX file will typically be small, the pack and index operations are performed together to keep the files up-to-date.

## USING THE MAIL SYSTEM

One of the benefits of a FoxPro-based mail system is that it allows your other FoxPro applications to send mail to the appropriate user if some condition occurs. For example, consider a company that runs several reports each night. These reports update a log indicating the start and end time for each report. As each report starts to print, it erases the end time and records a new start time. The next morning, the log can be examined to verify that all the reports were run satisfactorily.

Here is the log file's structure:

| Field | Type | Size |
|-------|------|------|
| RPT_NAME | Char | 25 |
| STARTED | Date | 8 |
| S_TIME | Char | 5 |
| ENDED | Date | 8 |
| E_TIME | Char | 5 |

Instead of manually checking the report completion log, however, you can easily automate this process. The CHECKLOG program listed below reads the log file. If a report has not run completely, a message to that effect is sent via e-mail to Betty, who is in charge of report distribution.

```
***********************************************************
*   Program:  CheckLog
*   Authors:  Joseph D. Booth and Greg Lief
*   Purpose:  A sample FoxPro program to send messages
*             via the e-mail system
```

```
************************************************************
function CheckLog()
PRIVATE cFailed = ""
PRIVATE cText,x
USE rpt_log SHARE IN 0
IF NOT NETERR()
   GO TOP
   DO WHILE NOT EOF()
      IF EMPTY(RPT_LOG.ended)
         cFailed = cFailed +RPT_LOG.rpt_name
      ENDIF
      SKIP +1
   ENDDO
   USE
   IF NOT EMPTY(cFailed)
      cText = "The following reports did not "+;
              "finish running last night."+CHR(13)+CHR(10)
      FOR x = 1 TO LEN(cFailed) STEP 25
          cText = cText +TRIM(substr(cFailed,(x-1)*25+1,25))+","
      NEXT
      =SendMail("BETTY","Some Reports Failed",cText)
   ENDIF
ENDIF
RETURN ""
```

# Summary

The EMAIL program is an example of the type of FoxPro application that can be run on a network. Chapter 13 provides the complete source code for this mail system. Experiment with the code—it will provide you with some idea of the power available by combining FoxPro and NetWare.

# EMAIL Program Source Code

I n this chapter we present the source code for the EMAIL application discussed in Chapter 12. The EMAIL application can be used directly in your FoxPro programs, and it also demonstrates some of the networking functions we've discussed in the book.

**Note:** In order to successfully run the EMAIL application, be sure the BLNET library file and the NETPRINT, BINDERY, and MESSAGES procedure files are available. The program uses a number of functions from within these libraries.

## DATABASE STRUCTURES

The EMAIL application requires two databases. The first one, POSTBOX, is a central repository for all messages. It must be stored in a directory that all users can read from and write to. POSTBOX has the following structure:

| Field | Type | Size | Contents |
|---|---|---|---|
| FOR_USER | Number | 12 | User's bindery ID |
| BEEN_READ | Character | 1 | Y if already read, N otherwise |
| DATE_SENT | Date | 8 | Date mail was sent |
| TIME_SENT | Character | 5 | Time mail was sent |
| FROM_USER | Character | 15 | User who sent the mail |
| SUBJECT | Character | 55 | Brief description of mail |
| MESSAGE | Memo | 10 | Actual mail contents |

The second database is called MAILBOX; each user has his or her own MAILBOX. Its structure is as follows:

| Field | Type | Size | Contents |
|---|---|---|---|
| READ | Logical | 1 | Y if already read, N otherwise |
| DATE | Date | 8 | Date mail was sent |
| TIME | Character | 5 | Time mail was sent |
| SENDER | Character | 15 | User who sent the mail |
| SUBJECT | Character | 55 | Brief description of mail |
| MESSAGE | Memo | 10 | Actual mail contents |

The EMAIL program creates any missing files and the index files, as well. The index file keys are

```
PostBox - been_read+STR(for_user,12)
MailBox - DTOS(date)+time DESCENDING
```

# INITIALIZATION

The program begins by initializing the environment and the various memory variables needed. It also opens the databases that are needed. If the databases do not exist, the program creates them.

**Note:** The variable cPath contains the path name where the mailbox files are located. Be sure to change this to a directory that exists on your network.

```
****************************************************************
*  Program:  EMAIL
*  Authors:  Joseph D. Booth and Greg Lief
*  Purpose:  An e-mail application to demonstrate the functions
*            and techniques included in Network Programming
*            with FoxPro published by Ziff-Davis Press.
*
****************************************************************

SET SAFETY OFF
SET TALK OFF
SET SCOREBOARD OFF
SET STATUS OFF

PUBLIC userlist(1)                  && List of network users
PUBLIC whoAmI                       && Current user name
```

```
SET LIBRARY TO BLNET ADDITIVE        && Core network functions
SET PROCEDURE TO BINDERY             && BINDERY functions

whoAmI = N_WhoAmI()                  && Get current user ID
=N_SCANBINDERY(1,@userlist)          && and a list of all users


*******************************************
* If we are not attached to the network,
* display an error and return
*
*******************************************
IF EMPTY(whoAmI)
   WAIT "Not attached to a network" WINDOW TIMEOUT 60
   RELEASE UserList,whoAmI
   RETURN
ENDIF


*******************************************
* Initialize the variables
*
*******************************************
PRIVATE x,jj,temp
PRIVATE cRegular,cHeader,cFooter,cBold,cFill,cBox,cPath

cRegular = "W/B"
cHeader  = "GR+/GR"
cFooter  = "N/BG"
cBold    = "GR+/B"
cFill    = " "
cBox     = CHR(201)+CHR(205)+CHR(187)+CHR(186)+;
           CHR(188)+CHR(205)+CHR(200)+CHR(186)
cPath    = "I:\EMAIL\"

IF FILE("EMAIL.MEM")
   RESTORE FROM EMAIL ADDITIVE
ENDIF


*******************************************
* Open up the POSTBOX
*
*******************************************
temp = cPath+"POSTBOX"
IF NOT FILE( Temp+".DBF" )
   CREATE TABLE &temp ;
       (FOR_USER   N(12),  ;
        BEEN_READ  C(1),   ;
```

```
         DATE_SENT  D,      ;
         TIME_SENT  C(5),   ;
         FROM_USER  C(15),  ;
         DISCARD    D,      ;
         RECEIPT    L,      ;
         SUBJECT    C(55),  ;
         MESSAGE    M )
   INDEX ON been_read+STR(for_user,12) TAG Prim
   CLOSE DATABASES
ENDIF

USE &temp. SHARE IN Ø ALIAS POSTBOX
SET ORDER TO 1


*******************************************
* Open up the user's MAILBOX
*
*******************************************
temp = cPath+TRIM(SUBSTR(whoAmI,1,8))+"\MAILBOX"
IF NOT FILE( Temp+".DBF" )
   SELECT Ø
   CREATE TABLE &temp ;
       (DATE      D,     ;
        TIME      C(5),  ;
        SENDER    C(15), ;
        SUBJECT   C(55), ;
        READ      L,     ;
        MESSAGE   M )
   INDEX ON DTOS(date)+time TAG PrimMail DESCENDING
   USE
ENDIF

USE &temp. EXCLUSIVE IN Ø ALIAS MY_MAIL
SET ORDER TO 1
```

## MAIN SCREEN DISPLAY

Once the program is initialized, the opening screen is displayed and the main menu is called. The main options are to read mail, to send mail to another user, to erase unwanted mail, to set options, and to pack the user's own mailbox.

```
CLEAR
***************************
* Draw the main screen
*
***************************
SET COLOR TO &cRegular.
@  Ø, Ø, 23, 79 BOX cBox+cFill
```

```
IF SUBSTR(cBox,4,1)==CHR(186)
   @ 2, Ø SAY CHR(204)+REPLICATE(CHR(205),78)+CHR(185)
ELSE
   @ 2, Ø SAY CHR(195)+REPLICATE(CHR(196),78)+CHR(180)
ENDIF
FOR jj = 3 TO 22
   @ jj,11 SAY CHR(179)
NEXT

SET COLOR TO &cHeader.
@ 1, 1 SAY PADR(" Electronic MAIL",78)
@ 1,71 SAY DATE()

SET COLOR TO &cFooter.
@ 24,ØØ SAY SPACE(80)

SET COLOR TO &cRegular.

x = 1

DO WHILE x > Ø
   @ 3,12 CLEAR TO 22,78
   @ 3, 1 CLEAR TO 22,10
   CLEAR PROMPTS
   @ 3,1 PROMPT "Read...    "
   @ 4,1 PROMPT "Send...    "
   @ 5,1 PROMPT "Erase..    "
   @ 6,1 PROMPT "Options.. "
   @ 7,1 PROMPT "Pack/Index"
   MENU TO x
   DO CASE
   CASE x = 1
      DO ReadMail
   CASE x = 2
      DO SendMail
   CASE x = 3
      DO EraseMail
   CASE x = 4
      DO MailOptions
   CASE x = 5
      DO PackFiles
   ENDCASE
ENDDO
CLEAR
CLOSE ALL
RELEASE UserList,whoAmI
RETURN
*****************************************************************
```

# READING YOUR MAIL

The largest portion of the program is the code that reads from the user's MAILBOX. The actual ReadMail function consists mostly of a BROWSE command. There are several key label routines that are used to handle various commands during the mail display.

```
************************************************************
*  Procedure:  ReadMail()
*    Authors:  Joseph D. Booth and Greg Lief
*    Purpose:  Handle the reading of your MAILBOX
*
************************************************************
PROCEDURE ReadMail

PRIVATE running
running = .T.
@ 3,12 CLEAR TO 22,78
@ 3,01 CLEAR TO 22,10
@ 3,01 SAY "Reading "
@ 4,01 SAY "your mail"
@ 5,01 SAY REPLICATE(CHR(196),10)
@ 6,02 SAY  CHR(24)+" Prior"
@ 7,02 SAY  CHR(25)+" Next"
@ 8,01 SAY  CHR(17)+CHR(217)+" Select"
@ 9,02 SAY "  Sort"
@10,02 SAY "  Find"

SET COLOR TO &cBold.
@ 9,04 SAY "S"
@10,04 SAY "F"

SET COLOR TO &cRegular.

DO CHECK4MAIL

SELECT my_Mail
SET COLOR TO &cBold.
DEFINE WINDOW MailDisp FROM 2,11 TO 23,79 DOUBLE TITLE ""

PUSH KEY CLEAR

ON KEY LABEL Ctrl-F    Do FindMail
ON KEY LABEL Ctrl-S    Do SortMail
ON KEY LABEL ENTER     Do DispMail
ON KEY LABEL ESC       Do CloseMail
```

```
IF RECCOUNT() < 1

    WAIT "You have no mail..." WINDOW TIMEOUT 30

ENDIF

DO WHILE running AND RECCOUNT() > 0

    ACTIVATE WINDOW MailDisp
    BROWSE FIELDS date :h='  Date  ', ;
                  time :h=' Time', ;
                  sender :h='  From  '  :12,;
                  subject :h='  Subject ' :36 ;
        NOEDIT  NOAPPEND  IN MailDisp

ENDDO

RELEASE WINDOW MailDisp
SET COLOR TO &cRegular.

POP KEY ALL

RETURN
*******************************************************************
PROCEDURE CloseMail
running = .F.
KEYBOARD CHR(23)
RETURN
*******************************************************************
```

## FINDING MAIL

The FindMail routine allows the user to type in a keyword. It then scans the
Subject field to see if any mail contains the keyword. If the keyword is found,
the mailbox is positioned to the record where the relevant mail was found. If
no mail contains the keyword, an error message is displayed and the mailbox
is positioned back to the current record.

```
*****************************************************
*  Procedure:  FindMail
*    Purpose:  Scan the Subject field in the MAILBOX
*
*****************************************************
PROCEDURE FindMail
PRIVATE cText,x
```

```
PUSH KEY CLEAR

DEFINE WINDOW MailFind FROM 8,32 TO 12,74 DOUBLE  ;
        TITLE "Search text"  SHADOW  COLOR "W+/R"
ACTIVATE WINDOW MailFind

cText = SPACE(25)
@ 1,1 SAY "Text: "
@ 1,8 GET cText PICTURE "@!"
READ

IF LASTKEY() <> 27
   x = RECNO()
   cText = TRIM(UPPER(cText))
   LOCATE ALL FOR cText $ UPPER(my_mail.subject)
   IF NOT FOUND()
      GOTO x
      WAIT "Not found..." WINDOW TIMEOUT 30
   ENDIF
ENDIF

DEACTIVATE WINDOW MailFind
DEACTIVATE WINDOW MailDisp

POP KEY

RETURN
**********************************************************
```

## SORTING MAIL

The SortMail routine allows the user to change the order in which mail from the MAILBOX is displayed on the screen. SortMail merely indexes the file on a new key selected by the user. This causes the display to be sticky, since the index file now contains the new key.

```
**************************************************************
*  Procedure:  SortMail
*    Purpose:  Re-index the mailbox by a different sort key
*
**************************************************************
PROCEDURE SortMail
PRIVATE x
DIMENSION choices(3)
x = 1
```

```
choices(1) = "Date & Time"
choices(2) = "Sender      "
choices(3) = "Subject     "

PUSH KEY CLEAR

@ 8,12 MENU choices,3 TITLE "Sort options" SHADOW
READ MENU TO x
IF x > 0
   DO CASE
   CASE x = 1
      INDEX ON DTOS(date)+time TAG PrimMail DESCENDING
   CASE x = 2
      INDEX ON UPPER(sender)   TAG PrimMail
   CASE x = 3
      INDEX ON UPPER(subject)  TAG PrimMail
   ENDCASE
   GO TOP
ENDIF
DEACTIVATE WINDOW MailDisp

POP KEY

RETURN
****************************************************************
```

## DISPLAY MAIL

The DisplayMail routine allows the user to view the message associated with a
piece of mail. While the message is on the screen, the user has the option to
delete it, to forward it to another user, to enter a reply, or to print the message.
This routine performs the operation the user requests.

```
****************************************************************
*   Procedure:  DisplayMail
*     Purpose:  Display the selected message and give
*               the user various options to execute
*
****************************************************************
PROCEDURE DispMail
PRIVATE x,y,cTo
x = 1

PUSH KEY CLEAR
DEFINE WINDOW ShowMsg FROM 3,12 TO 22,78 DOUBLE TITLE "Messages" SHADOW
ACTIVATE WINDOW ShowMsg
SET COLOR TO &cRegular
```

```
@ 0,1 SAY "FROM:"
@ 1,1 SAY "DATE:"
SET COLOR TO &cBold
@ 0, 7 SAY  my_mail.sender
@ 1, 7 SAY  my_mail.date
@ 1,16 SAY  my_mail.time
@ 3, 0 EDIT my_mail.message SIZE 12,60,0 NOMODIFY
SET COLOR TO &cRegular.


   DEFINE MENU readOptions BAR AT LINE 17  IN WINDOW ShowMsg

   DEFINE PAD  DiscMail    OF readOptions  PROMPT "Discard"
   DEFINE PAD  FwdMail     OF readOptions  PROMPT "Forward"
   DEFINE PAD  ReplyMail   OF readOptions  PROMPT "Reply"
   DEFINE PAD  PrintMail   OF readOptions  PROMPT "Print"


   ON SELECTION MENU readOptions DO ReadChoice WITH PAD()

   ACTIVATE MENU readOptions
   RELEASE MENU readOptions

   DEACTIVATE MENU readOptions

RELEASE WINDOW ShowMsg
DEACTIVATE WINDOW MailDisp

POP KEY

RETURN


*************************************************************************
*  Procedure:  ReadChoice()
*     Purpose:  Process the menu selection from the mail read screen
*
*************************************************************************
PROCEDURE ReadChoice
PARAMETERS mprompt
DO CASE
CASE mprompt = "DISCMAIL"
   DELETE
   PACK
CASE mprompt = "FWDMAIL"
   DO Forward_Mail
CASE mprompt = "REPLYMAIL"
   DO Read_Reply
```

```
   CASE mprompt = "PRINTMAIL"
      DO Print_Mail
   ENDCASE
   RETURN


   *********************************************************************
   *   Procedure:   Forward_Mail()
   *      Purpose:   Send the mail to another user
   *
   *********************************************************************
   PROCEDURE Forward_Mail
   PRIVATE cTo
   PUSH KEY CLEAR
   cTo = SPACE(15)

   DEFINE WINDOW MailFwd FROM 4,42 TO 9,72 DOUBLE ;
           TITLE "Forward to" SHADOW  COLOR "W+/R"

   ACTIVATE WINDOW MailFwd

   CLEAR GETS
   @ 1,1 SAY    "TO: "
   @ 1,5 GET cTo FROM UserList FUNCTION "^ " DEFAULT UserList(1)
   READ
   RELEASE WINDOW MailFwd
   DEACTIVATE WINDOW MailFwd
   IF LASTKEY() <> 27
      SELECT POSTBOX
      APPEND BLANK
      REPLACE postbox.for_user  WITH N_OBJECTID(cTo,1),;
              postbox.been_read WITH "N",;
              postbox.date_sent WITH my_mail.date,;
              postbox.time_sent WITH my_mail.time
      REPLACE postbox.from_user WITH my_mail.sender,;
              postbox.subject   WITH my_mail.subject,;
              postbox.message   WITH my_mail.message
      SELECT my_mail
      DELETE
      PACK
      x = Ø
   ENDIF

   POP KEY
   RETURN


   *********************************************************************
```

```
*  Procedure:  Read_Reply()
*    Purpose:  Reply to the current message
*
*****************************************************************
PROCEDURE Read_Reply
PRIVATE cReply
cReply = SPACE(4096)

DEFINE WINDOW MailReply FROM 10,12 TO 22,78 DOUBLE TITLE "Reply"
ACTIVATE WINDOW MailReply
CLEAR GETS
@ 1,1 EDIT cReply SIZE 10,64
READ

IF LASTKEY() <> 27 AND NOT EMPTY(cReply)
   SELECT POSTBOX
   APPEND BLANK
   REPLACE postbox.for_user  WITH N_OBJECTID(TRIM(my_mail.sender),1),;
           postbox.been_read WITH "N",;
           postbox.date_sent WITH DATE(),;
           postbox.time_sent WITH SUBSTR(TIME(),1,5),;
   REPLACE postbox.from_user WITH whoAmI,;
           postbox.subject   WITH "RE: "+my_mail.subject,;
           postbox.message   WITH cReply
   SELECT my_mail
ENDIF

RELEASE WINDOW MailReply
DEACTIVATE WINDOW MailReply

RETURN
*****************************************************************
*  Procedure:  Print_Mail()
*    Purpose:  Print the current mail
*
*****************************************************************
PROCEDURE Print_Mail
PUBLIC aQlist(1),aQnumbs(1)
y=N_ScanBindery(3,@aQlist)
DIMENSION aQnumbs[y]
FOR x = 1 TO y
   aQnumbs[x] = N_ObjectId(aQlist[x],3)
NEXT

SET PROCEDURE TO NETPRINT
```

```
IF P_Where()         && Select where to print
   IF P_start()      && Able to start printing
      ?? "FROM: "
      ?? my_mail.sender
      ?  "DATE: "
      ?? my_mail.date
      ?  "TIME: "
      ?? my_mail.time
      ?  "SUBJ: "
      ?? my_mail.subject
      SET MEMOWIDTH TO 65
      y      = MEMLINES(my_mail.message)
      _MLINE = 0
      FOR x = 1 TO y
         ? MLINE(my_mail.message,x,_MLINE)
      NEXT
      ? CHR(12)
      =P_end()
   ENDIF
ENDIF
SET PROCEDURE TO BINDERY
RETURN
*********************************************************************
```

## CHECKING FOR MAIL

The Check4Mail routine looks in the POSTBOX file to see if any unread mail
exists for the current user. If mail is found, it is transferred from the POST-
BOX into the user's MAILBOX.

```
*********************************************************************
*  Procedure:  Check4Mail()
*    Purpose:  Check the POSTBOX to see if mail has arrived
*
*********************************************************************
PROCEDURE Check4Mail
PRIVATE yy
yy = N_OBJECTID(whoAmI,1)
SELECT postbox
SEEK "N"+STR(yy,12)
DO WHILE NOT EOF() AND yy = postbox.for_user AND postbox.been_read="N"
   SELECT my_mail
   APPEND BLANK
   REPLACE my_mail.date       WITH postbox.date_sent,;
           my_mail.time       WITH postbox.time_sent,;
           my_mail.sender     WITH postbox.from_user,;
```

```
            my_mail.subject    WITH postbox.subject,;
            my_mail.read       WITH .F.,;
            my_mail.message    WITH postbox.message
   SELECT postbox
   REPLACE postbox.been_read  WITH "Y",;
           postbox.for_user    WITH Ø
   SEEK "N"+STR(yy,12)
ENDDO
RETURN
***********************************************************************
```

## SENDING MAIL

The SendMail procedure is used to place a message into the central POSTBOX for another user to read. It allows the user to select a user ID from a pick list, and then to type in a subject and a message. If a message is recorded, the text is written to the POSTBOX, and the user is notified (using the SEND MESSAGE function) that new mail has been sent.

```
***********************************************************************
*  Procedure:  SendMail()
*    Purpose:  Handle the sending of mail to another user
*
***********************************************************************
PROCEDURE SendMail
PRIVATE cTo,cSubject,cText
DIMENSION aStations(1)

cTo      = SPACE(15)
cSubject = SPACE(55)
cText    = SPACE(4000)

@ 3,12 CLEAR TO 22,78
@ 3,01 CLEAR TO 22,10
@ 3,01 SAY "Sending "
@ 4,01 SAY "new mail "
@ 5,01 SAY REPLICATE(CHR(196),10)
@ 7,12 SAY REPLICATE(CHR(196),66)

SET COLOR TO &cFooter.
@ 24,00 SAY " Press <SPACE> to get list of users "

SET COLOR TO &cRegular.

@ 3,15 SAY   "TO: "
```

```
@ 3,2Ø GET cTo FROM UserList FUNCTION "^ " DEFAULT UserList(1) VALID
WhoIsIt(cTo)
@ 6,15 SAY   "RE: " GET cSubject

@ 8,12 EDIT cText SIZE 15,66
READ

SET COLOR TO &cFooter.
@ 24,ØØ SAY SPACE(8Ø)
SET COLOR TO &cRegular.

IF LASTKEY() <> 27
   SELECT POSTBOX
   APPEND BLANK
   REPLACE postbox.for_user  WITH N_OBJECTID(cTo,1),;
           postbox.been_read WITH "N",;
           postbox.date_sent WITH DATE(),;
           postbox.time_sent WITH SUBSTR(TIME(),1,5)
   REPLACE postbox.from_user WITH whoAmI,;
           postbox.subject   WITH cSubject,;
           postbox.message   WITH cText

   SET PROCEDURE TO messages
   IF N_FindStat(cTo,@aStations) > Ø
     N_SendMsg( "New mail from "+whoAmI,aStations(1) )
   ENDIF
   SET PROCEDURE TO bindery

ENDIF
RETURN
*****************************************************************

*  Procedure:  WhoIsIt()
*     Purpose:  Display the user's full name
*
*****************************************************************
FUNCTION WhoIsIt
PARAMETERS cTO
PRIVATE cName
cName = N_PROPVAL(cTo,1,"IDENTIFICATION",.T.)
@ 3,4Ø CLEAR TO 5,78
@ 4,4Ø SAY cName
RETURN .T.
*****************************************************************
```

# ERASING MAIL

EraseMail is merely a BROWSE screen that allows the user to tag messages to delete. The Spacebar and the Enter key call the procedure that deletes the record (or recalls it if it is already deleted). When the BROWSE is finished, the file is packed. Since the mail file generally stays small, the pack operation does not take much time. If you want to improve performance, you can remove the PACK command and instruct the user to periodically run the PACK operation from the main menu.

```
*****************************************************************
*  Procedure:  EraseMail()
*    Purpose:  Allows the user to delete messages
*                 from the user's own mailbox
*
*****************************************************************
PROCEDURE EraseMail
@ 3,12 CLEAR TO 22,78
@ 3,01 CLEAR TO 22,10
@ 3,01 SAY "Erase    "
@ 4,01 SAY "read mail"
@ 5,01 SAY REPLICATE(CHR(196),10)
@ 6,02 SAY  CHR(17)+CHR(217)+" Erase"

SET COLOR TO &cRegular.

SELECT my_Mail
SET COLOR TO &cBold.

DEFINE WINDOW MailErase FROM 2,11 TO 23,79 DOUBLE TITLE ""
ACTIVATE WINDOW MailErase

PUSH KEY CLEAR

ON KEY LABEL SPACEBAR Do TagMail
ON KEY LABEL ENTER    Do TagMail

BROWSE FIELDS date :h=' Date  ', ;
              time :h=' Time', ;
              sender :h=' From ' :12,;
              subject :h=' Subject ' :36 ;
       NOEDIT  NOAPPEND  IN MailErase
PACK

RELEASE WINDOW MailErase
SET COLOR TO &cRegular.
```

```
POP KEY ALL

RETURN
********************************************************************

* Procedure:  TagMail()
*    Purpose:  Delete or recall mail that the
*              user tags while using the BROWSE screen
*
********************************************************************
PROCEDURE TagMail
IF DELETED()
   RECALL
ELSE
   DELETE
ENDIF
RETURN
********************************************************************
```

# SETTING OPTIONS

Various options, such as the data directory and display colors, can be set using the system. This MailOptions procedure allows the user to change these options. The changes are saved to a memory variable file in the current directory, and the variables are restored from this file whenever the program starts.

```
********************************************************************
*  Procedure:  MailOptions()
*    Purpose:  Allow screen colors and directories
*              to be changed
*
********************************************************************
PROCEDURE MailOptions
DEFINE WINDOW mail_opt FROM 6,20 TO 19,70 ;
       TITLE "Mail Options" DOUBLE SHADOW  COLOR "GR+/R,W+/R,,,GR+/R"
ACTIVATE WINDOW mail_opt

cRegular = PADR(cRegular,20)
cBold    = PADR(cBold,20)
cHeader  = PADR(cHeader,20)
cFooter  = PADR(cFooter,20)
cPath    = PADR(cPath,30)

CLEAR GETS
```

```
@ 1, 1 SAY "Regular...: " GET cRegular
@ 2, 1 SAY "Bold......: " GET cBold
@ 3, 1 SAY "Header....: " GET cHeader
@ 4, 1 SAY "Footer....: " GET cFooter
@ 5, 1 SAY "Fill Char.: ["
@ 5,14 GET cFill PICTURE "!"
@ 5,15 SAY "]"
@ 7, 1 SAY "Box Frame.: "
@ 6,14 GET cBox    PICTURE "╔ ═ ╗‖╝=╚‖ ; ┌ ─ ┐ |⌐—└| ; ╥ ─ ╥‖╜—╨‖ ; ╔ = ╗ |╝=╚|
@ 9, 1 SAY "Data Path.: " GET cPath

READ
IF LASTKEY() <> 27
   cRegular = TRIM(cRegular)
   cBold    = TRIM(cBold)
   cHeader  = TRIM(cHeader)
   cFooter  = TRIM(cFooter)
   cPath    = TRIM(cPath)
   IF RIGHT(cPath,1) <> "\"
      cPath = cPath +"\"
   ENDIF


   SAVE ALL LIKE c* TO EMAIL
ENDIF
RELEASE WINDOW mail_opt
RETURN
*****************************************************************
```

## PACKING THE MAILBOX

Although the deletion function immediately packs the file, you might want to remove the PACK command from the Delete routine to improve performance. In addition, there might be times you need to pack the contents of the MEMO file. PackFiles() takes care of both of these conditions.

```
*****************************************************************
*   Procedure:   PackFiles()
*     Purpose:   This procedure packs and re-indexes the user's
*                mailbox file.
*
*****************************************************************
PROCEDURE PackFiles
SELECT my_Mail
PACK
PACK MEMO
RETURN
```

# Summary

In this chapter, we've presented a usable EMAIL system as an example of network programming. The code in this program makes use of several of the functions from the book. Hopefully, it will whet your appetite for your next network program.

# Appendix A: Sources for Further Information about FoxPro and NetWare

In this book, we have covered many aspects of writing FoxPro applications to run on a Novell network. Following are sources for more information about FoxPro and NetWare.

## Software products

FoxPro is published by Microsoft Corporation, located in Redmond, Washington. For more information about FoxPro and other Microsoft products, you can contact Microsoft at 800-882-2000 in the United States. From other countries, call 206-936-8661.

Besides FoxPro itself, Microsoft also has a distribution kit for DOS and one for Windows. The kits allow you to install your applications royalty-free on computers without FoxPro. Each kit lists for $495.

Microsoft also has a library construction kit that allows you to write C and assembler functions that your FoxPro program can call. The BLNET.PLB and BLNET.FLL programs in this book were created with the library construction kit.

NetWare is published by Novell, Inc., located in Provo, Utah. For more information about NetWare and other Novell products, contact Novell at 800-453-1267 or 801-429-7000.

# Books

There are a number of books available from Ziff-Davis Press that we have found to be helpful with FoxPro and network programming. These include

| Title | Author | ISBN |
|---|---|---|
| *PC Magazine Programming FoxPro 2.5* | Miriam Liskin | 1-56276-164-1 |
| *PC Magazine Guide to Using Windows 3.1* | Gus Venditto | 1-56276-009-2 |
| *PC Magazine Guide to Connectivity, Second Edition* | Frank J. Derfler, Jr. | 1-56276-047-5 |
| *PC Magazine Guide to Using NetWare* | Les Freed and Frank J. Derfler, Jr. | 1-56276-022-X |
| *PC Magazine Guide to Client/Server Databases* | Joe Salemi | 1-56276-070-X |

# Publications

Several magazines are dedicated specifically to FoxPro programming. In addition, NetWare also has various magazines about its use. A few of these are briefly described here.

### DATA BASED ADVISOR

*Data Based Advisor* is a monthly publication that covers a variety of database products available for personal computers.

In addition to regular columns on FoxPro, CA-Clipper, and dBASE, each issue usually includes an in-depth focus on a current topic, such as client servers, porting data from a mainframe, and so forth. The magazine is also a great source for advertisements about many database products and tools.

*Data Based Advisor* is published by Data Based Solutions, Inc., located in San Diego, California. For subscription information, call 800-336-6060 or 619-483-6400.

### FOXPRO ADVISOR

*FoxPro Advisor* is a new magazine, also offered by Data Based Solutions, Inc. (publisher of *Data Based Advisor,* above). This magazine, too, provides coverage of database issues on a personal computer, but focuses entirely on FoxPro. It comes out monthly and is about 50 pages in length. For subscription information, call 800-336-6060 or 619-483-6400.

## FOXTALK

*FoxTalk* is a 24-page magazine of technical information and reviews of products for FoxPro. It is published monthly and does not contain any advertisements. Recent issues have addressed topics such as how to use DDE, and some of FoxPro's international strategy. For more information, contact

> Pinnacle Publishing
> P.O. Box 888
> Kent, WA 98035-0888
> Phone  800-788-1900
>          206-251-1900

## INSIDE NETWARE

*Inside NetWare* is a technical publication of the Cobb Group. It is aimed toward NetWare administrators and supervisors and contains plain-English tips and techniques for solving network problems. Each monthly issue contains about 20 pages. Past issues have covered topics such as managing server and workstation memory, troubleshooting a network, choosing the best cabling, and using NetWare utility programs. For more information, contact

> The Cobb Group, Software Journal Publishers
> 9420 Bunsen Parkway, Suite 3000
> Louisville, Kentucky 40220
> Phone 800-223-8720
>          502-491-1900

## NETWARE CONNECTION

*NetWare Connection* is a technical publication of NetWare Users' International. It contains a mixture of basic NetWare management concepts and solutions to thorny network problems. It also lists questions and answers handled by Novell's technical support telephone lines. Each monthly issue contains about 24 pages. Contact NetWare Users' International at 122 East 1700 South, Provo, Utah 84606, telephone 800-228-4684 and 801-429-7000.

# FOXPRO TRAINING

Microsoft provides FoxPro training at the Microsoft University. Contact Microsoft at 800-227-4679 or 206-828-1507 for more information.

### MICROENDEAVORS, INC.

This company authored the courseware used at Microsoft University to teach FoxPro. They provide two course on FoxPro, one for intermediate users and one for advanced users. Courses are available in Philadelphia, New York, Washington D.C., and Grand Rapids. For more information, call MicroEndeavors at 800-331-9434.

### SYSTEMS DESIGN CORPORATION

This company offers five different courses on FoxPro, from Getting Started with FoxPro to Advanced Programming. They are located in Colorado and offer on-site courses. They also train in R&R Report Writer and do custom FoxPro development. For more information, call Systems Design at 800-848-7742.

### THE INFORMATION MANAGEMENT GROUP

This company offers six different courses, including one for FoxPro end users and one specifically for FoxPro with Windows. Based in Chicago and Los Angeles, they also do custom FoxPro development. For more information, call The Information Management Group at 800-922-2019 or 312-280-1007.

## NetWare training

Novell certifies companies to provide NetWare courses and training. The list of certified trainers changes frequently, so your best bet is to call Novell and ask for trainers in your area.

## Professional developer services

Novell has a program called the Professional Developer's Program (PDP) which gives NetWare-aware application developers streamlined access to NetWare products, development tools, and support services. Through the program you can get discounts on additional copies of NetWare's OS and communications products, with a one-year renewable license.

Joining the PDP is the only way to obtain access to certain Novell Software Development Kits (SDKs). There is a private forum on CompuServe for PDP members. In addition, Novell offers some marketing support through the PDP.

This program is available to professional developers of NetWare-aware software products. Contact Novell's PDP in the United States and Canada at 800-RED-WORD or 800-733-9673. International developers should contact their local Novell office regarding the PDP features in their area. Services vary from country to country.

# Appendix B:
# Using the Disk Accompanying
# This Book

The disk accompanying this book contains the source code to the various routines in the book. In addition, the disk contains the BLNET-.PLB and BLNET.FLL files needed by some of the routines. Finally, the C source code to BLNET is also provided.

## Using the routines

The following routines are included on this disk:

| | |
|---|---|
| Chapter 3 | INITDB.PRG |
| | OPENEM.PRG |
| Chapter 5 | GETAMSG.PRG |
| | PUTAMSG.PRG |
| | DOMSG.PRG |
| | LINK2XLS.PRG |
| Chapter 7 | BLNET.PLB |
| | BLNET.FLL |
| | BLNET.C |
| | XLATE.PRG |
| Chapter 8 | BINDERY.PRG |
| Chapter 9 | NETPRINT.PRG |

Chapter 10    MESSAGES.PRG

Chapter 11    SYSINFO.PRG

Make sure all these routines are accessible; if possible, put them in your Fox-Pro directory. For most applications, you should plan on loading the BLNET library first, using the syntax

```
SET LIBRARY TO blnet ADDITIVE
```

Then you can set the appropriate procedure for the functions you want to perform.

## THE EMAIL SYSTEM

The complete source code to the EMAIL program is included on the disk in the file EMAIL.PRG. In addition, the disk contains an ASCII version of the documentation called EMAIL.TXT. This will allow your users to use the EMAIL program and provide you with the documentation for it.

# INDEX

# X

# Z

# Ziff-Davis Press Survey of Readers

Please help us in our effort to produce the best books on personal computing.
For your assistance, we would be pleased to send you a FREE catalog
featuring the complete line of Ziff-Davis Press books.

## 1. How did you first learn about this book?

Recommended by a friend . . . . . . . . . . . . . . ☐ -1 (5)
Recommended by store personnel . . . . . . . . ☐ -2
Saw in Ziff-Davis Press catalog . . . . . . . . . . . ☐ -3
Received advertisement in the mail . . . . . . . ☐ -4
Saw the book on bookshelf at store . . . . . . . . ☐ -5
Read book review in: _____ ☐ -6
Saw an advertisement in: _____ ☐ -7
Other (Please specify): _____ ☐ -8

## 2. Which THREE of the following factors most influenced your decision to purchase this book? (Please check up to THREE.)

Front or back cover information on book . . .☐ -1 (6)
Logo of magazine affiliated with book . . . . . .☐ -2
Special approach to the content . . . . . . . . . . ☐ -3
Completeness of content . . . . . . . . . . . . . . . .☐ -4
Author's reputation. . . . . . . . . . . . . . . . . . . . ☐ -5
Publisher's reputation . . . . . . . . . . . . . . . . . ☐ -6
Book cover design or layout . . . . . . . . . . . . . ☐ -7
Index or table of contents of book . . . . . . . . ☐ -8
Price of book . . . . . . . . . . . . . . . . . . . . . . . ☐ -9
Special effects, graphics, illustrations . . . . . .☐ -0
Other (Please specify): _____ ☐ -x

## 3. How many computer books have you purchased in the last six months? _____ (7-10)

## 4. On a scale of 1 to 5, where 5 is excellent, 4 is above average, 3 is average, 2 is below average, and 1 is poor, please rate each of the following aspects of this book below. (Please circle your answer.)

| | | | | | | |
|---|---|---|---|---|---|---|
| Depth/completeness of coverage | 5 | 4 | 3 | 2 | 1 | (11) |
| Organization of material | 5 | 4 | 3 | 2 | 1 | (12) |
| Ease of finding topic | 5 | 4 | 3 | 2 | 1 | (13) |
| Special features/time saving tips | 5 | 4 | 3 | 2 | 1 | (14) |
| Appropriate level of writing | 5 | 4 | 3 | 2 | 1 | (15) |
| Usefulness of table of contents | 5 | 4 | 3 | 2 | 1 | (16) |
| Usefulness of index | 5 | 4 | 3 | 2 | 1 | (17) |
| Usefulness of accompanying disk | 5 | 4 | 3 | 2 | 1 | (18) |
| Usefulness of illustrations/graphics | 5 | 4 | 3 | 2 | 1 | (19) |
| Cover design and attractiveness | 5 | 4 | 3 | 2 | 1 | (20) |
| Overall design and layout of book | 5 | 4 | 3 | 2 | 1 | (21) |
| Overall satisfaction with book | 5 | 4 | 3 | 2 | 1 | (22) |

## 5. Which of the following computer publications do you read regularly; that is, 3 out of 4 issues?

Byte . . . . . . . . . . . . . . . . . . . . . . . . . . . . . . . ☐ -1 (23)
Computer Shopper . . . . . . . . . . . . . . . . . . . . . ☐ -2
Corporate Computing . . . . . . . . . . . . . . . . . . ☐ -3
Dr. Dobb's Journal . . . . . . . . . . . . . . . . . . . . ☐ -4
LAN Magazine . . . . . . . . . . . . . . . . . . . . . . . ☐ -5
MacWEEK . . . . . . . . . . . . . . . . . . . . . . . . . . ☐ -6
MacUser . . . . . . . . . . . . . . . . . . . . . . . . . . . . ☐ -7
PC Computing . . . . . . . . . . . . . . . . . . . . . . . ☐ -8
PC Magazine . . . . . . . . . . . . . . . . . . . . . . . . ☐ -9
PC WEEK . . . . . . . . . . . . . . . . . . . . . . . . . . ☐ -0
Windows Sources . . . . . . . . . . . . . . . . . . . . . ☐ -x
Other (Please specify): _____ ☐ -y

**Please turn page.**

6. What is your level of experience with personal computers? With the subject of this book?

|  | With PCs | With subject of book |
|---|---|---|
| Beginner.............. | ☐ -1 (24) | ☐ -1 (25) |
| Intermediate.......... | ☐ -2 | ☐ -2 |
| Advanced............. | ☐ -3 | ☐ -3 |

7. Which of the following best describes your job title?

Officer (CEO/President/VP/owner)........ ☐ -1 (26)
Director/head......................... ☐ -2
Manager/supervisor.................... ☐ -3
Administration/staff.................... ☐ -4
Teacher/educator/trainer............... ☐ -5
Lawyer/doctor/medical professional....... ☐ -6
Engineer/technician.................... ☐ -7
Consultant........................... ☐ -8
Not employed/student/retired........... ☐ -9
Other (Please specify): _____ ☐ -0

8. What is your age?

Under 20............................ ☐ -1 (27)
21-29............................... ☐ -2
30-39............................... ☐ -3
40-49............................... ☐ -4
50-59............................... ☐ -5
60 or over........................... ☐ -6

9. Are you:

Male................................ ☐ -1 (28)
Female.............................. ☐ -2

Thank you for your assistance with this important information! Please write your address below to receive our free catalog.

Name: _____

Address: _____

City/State/Zip: _____

**Fold here to mail.**  1676-04-05

_____

_____

_____

**BUSINESS REPLY MAIL**
FIRST CLASS MAIL    PERMIT NO. 1612    OAKLAND, CA

POSTAGE WILL BE PAID BY ADDRESSEE

**Ziff-Davis Press**
**ZD PRESS** 5903 Christie Avenue
Emeryville, CA 94608-1925
Attn: Marketing

NO POSTAGE
NECESSARY
IF MAILED IN
THE UNITED
STATES

# ■ TO RECEIVE 5¼-INCH DISK(S)

The Ziff-Davis Press software contained on the $3^1/_2$-inch disk included with this book is also available in $5^1/_4$-inch format. If you would like to receive the software in the $5^1/_4$-inch format, please return the $3^1/_2$-inch disk with your name and address to:

**Disk Exchange**
Ziff-Davis Press
5903 Christie Avenue
Emeryville, CA 94608